Why Not?

Why Not?

Lessons on Comedy, Courage, and Chutzpah

MARK SCHIFF

Foreword by *Jerry Seinfeld*

APOLLO
PUBLISHERS

Visit our website at www.apollopublishers.com.

Published in compliance with California's Proposition 65.

Library of Congress Control Number: 2022936517

Print ISBN: 978-1-954641-16-7
Ebook ISBN: 978-1-954641-17-4

Printed in the United States of America.

CONTENTS

....

Every comedian-writer should have a partner who besides being the love of one's life is also a constant supplier of endless new comedy material and a crackerjack editor like my wife, Nancy, is. This book is dedicated to her, as if not for her, my act and this book would be but a dream. And to my kids, who support every crazy idea of mine as long as I keep giving them money and gifts. I love you all. And to all the people who have listened to my jokes and decided they were funny enough not to ask for their money back after my show.

FOREWORD BY JERRY SEINFELD

....

Mark Schiff and I have been joined in comedy our entire adult lives. We met in the hot summer of 1976 in the bar at the Comic Strip comedy club in Manhattan's Upper East Side. Mark was famous for wearing a little knit baby hat as we all sat around waiting to go onstage. We became friends instantly and had millions of 2:00 a.m. breakfasts at all-night diners around the city. Mark introduced me to the greatness of Frank Sinatra, Buster Keaton, and Rodney Dangerfield. We still work together doing dozens of performance dates all over the country every year.

The thing I love about Mark is that his love of comedy is so pure. We still sit in diners talking about how it works or doesn't and who's doing what and how that's working or isn't. This collection of stories by Mark tells of so many amazing events in his life. And it's very true to him. I've known Mark my entire adult life, and I've never seen him go for very long without telling me another absolutely mind-boggling story of something that happened to him years ago—and often something involving some legendary iconic figure like Bob Dylan or Katharine Hepburn.

Mark has been the greatest comedy pal a guy could ever wish for, and I can't imagine taking the journey of comedy life without him. Most of all, he is a great storyteller, and this book really shows off not only his amazing sense of humor but also his warmth, wisdom, and invaluable life perspective, which means everything to me. This book is a great way for you to get to know him too.

INTRODUCTION

....

Thank you for purchasing (I hope) a copy of my new book, *Why Not? Lessons on Comedy, Courage, and Chutzpah*. Please do not let the Yiddish in the title fool you. This book is not just for Jews or, for that matter, the courageous. This book is for everyone who wants to laugh, wants to cry, and wants to lose weight and not gain it back.

How this book came about was that one day many years ago, I received a call from the editor of Los Angeles's *Jewish Journal*. The *Jewish Journal* is a major weekly newspaper that is filled with one article after another mostly by Jews complaining about everything from war to tiddlywinks. All kidding aside, the *Jewish Journal* is a terrific paper and a very important one. The editor asked me if I would write an article for the paper. I had never written one before, but I said, "Why not?" and those two words are why you are holding this book right now. I am sure right before you bought it, you probably thought, Why not? It is not uncommon that two words can change a person's life. When I got married, I said, "I do." Those two words changed my life, my bank account, and what I thought was a necessity for sex. I bet if you tried you could also locate two words that changed your life.

I had so much fun writing that first article. For me it was a whole new creative experience, and the people who read it seemed to really like it. So I decided to write another, and another. After just a few articles, I started hearing from the readers, things like, "When I open the paper, the first thing I do is look to see if you wrote an article this week" and "You're my favorite writer in the paper." Whether or not any of that is true, it is a good feeling to know that people have enjoyed my work.

After a lifetime of writing comedy, traveling the world, and sharing my jokes with strangers in hundreds of towns across the globe, it's nice to have something that I don't have to get on a plane and deliver to you while standing under a row of hot lights. I hope you enjoy the book, and maybe one day someone might ask you to do something that you have never done before. Don't forget the two little words that might also change your life, and ask, Why not?

1
AGE

....

May You Live Till 120

At Marvin's fiftieth wedding anniversary, he toasts, "May my lovely Dora live till 119, and may I live till 120." Someone asks, "How come you to 120 and Dora 119?" Marvin responds, "So I can have at least one year of peace and quiet."

Jews are always wishing other Jews that they should live till 120. That's because Moses lived till 120; but remember, Moses was a mountain climber, so he was probably in better shape than most of us.

The way things are going and the way I'm already stiffening up, I can't imagine being able to lift even a pinky at 120. I have always had trouble telling people my real age. It started young. When I was ten I told them I was twelve. In show business they ask you what age range you think you are. That would be great in real life. "How old are you?" "I'm between thirty-seven and forty-four."

Age has always spooked me. Last year an old friend from high school came to see me. He looked so old, I chased him out of my dressing room.

I remember I once had a date and I lied to her about my age. I told her I was ten years younger than I was. When I told my friend what I had done, he asked me why I lied. I said because I was afraid she would not want to go out with me. He said, "That's ridiculous. You're a good person and she won't care. It's what's inside you that counts." So I told her my real age and she immediately dumped me. I guess she couldn't see inside of me. Because she dumped me, I never got the chance to see inside of her.

Men are famous for leaving their wives for a younger model. And women leave their husbands for the pool maintenance guy. That's why I never got a pool and I live in a "maintenance-free" home.

Just so I can feel younger, the only people I tell my real age to are people much older than I am. A while back, I was with the great comedian Shecky Greene, who was in his midnineties. When I told him how old I was, he looked disappointed. He seemed to be hoping for someone much younger to be sitting next to him.

I'm only now starting to accept my age, because I'm finally starting to accept who I am. When I was younger, aging represented failure. I felt I should be further along for my age, that I should be more successful for my age. About twenty years ago, I told a great writer friend of mine, Hubert Selby Jr., who has since passed, that I thought I should be more successful by now. He said, "I guess I should also."

The truth is, it's always been painful to lie about age. It's been painful not to tell people exactly who I am. Whenever anyone finds out how old I am, it means little to them. In fact, they mostly have nice things to say, like "You look young for your age" or "You're in good shape for your age." Sometimes they can't believe it.

What I now realize is, if I can't accept myself for who and what I am, how can I expect others to accept me? And isn't acceptance a big key to life? Accepting yourself and others. Isn't acceptance one key to a happy marriage and raising kids? When I'm upset or not happy with someone, it's because there is something in them that I am not willing to accept or something in me that I'm not willing to accept. In order for me to change something that I don't like about myself, I have to first accept it in myself.

The one thing I can't change about myself, no matter how hard I try, is my age. I'm stuck with it. Even the great Jack Benny professed to never age past 39. So if you want to know exactly how old I am, as of this writing I'm somewhere between 30 and 120. If you don't accept that, look it up on IMDb.

Oy Vey Iz Mir[1]

I have a friend who told me he takes three pills a day to help him increase his saliva. He told me his doctor said that as you get older, sometimes your saliva dries up. Nice. Something new to worry about as I age—a saliva shortage. Nothing worse for a comedian than to be onstage and a cup short of moist saliva.

When it comes to aging, people have a lot to say about it. For instance: "You're only as old as you feel," "Age is in the mind," and "What's the alternative?" And the funny ones, such as "Don't let aging get you down; it's too hard to get back up" and "Respect old people; they graduated school without Google or Wikipedia."

My most recent birthday was a big one. I prayed I'd still have enough saliva to masticate my lunch that day. Now when I must add my age to an online form, it takes me forty-five minutes to scroll down and find my year. Also, I've been noticing that my skin is slowly drying up, so I now glob on Regenerist antiaging cream every night. All I get out of it are pools of expensive cream stuck in the cracks of my wrinkles, and I'm still aging. I do find exercise and diet help keep my body looking young, but only if you don't see me naked in the steam room. Meditation helps me too and so I meditate twice a day, but I once had to call 911 to unfold me out of the lotus position.

---

1 *Oy vey iz mir* means "Oh woe is me." This is the Jewish national anthem.

My doctor recently gave me a prescription for one Cialis pill so I'm ready when my next birthday comes around. My kids constantly tease me about taking my driver's license away. I tease them about taking them out of my will. What really got me was that my wife and I recently bought two cemetery plots in Simi Valley, California, about forty-five minutes from our home in Los Angeles. If our plots were any farther out of town, we might as well get buried in Norway. The lady who sold us our spots said we had one of the better views. I'm looking forward. Have you ever noticed that the word "fun" is in funeral? Maybe a jazz funeral down in New Orleans is fun, but not the ones I go to. I'm at an age now where every year a few people I know are permanently removed. Some older, some younger. As soon as you're born, you're in the lottery.

What do I do now that I can see the big knockout punch coming? I live my life as if all is going to be well. I just bought a new mattress, and soon I'll probably buy a new car (if my kids let me). I also just bought my first ever handmade suit, and I'm going on trips with my wife before we can't go on them anymore. I'm eating healthier than ever before and exercising more now than when I was twenty-five. I'm trying to stay excited about life. I'm doing it for me, but I'm also doing it for my family. I believe that it would be better for them to have me around. How selfish of me to think that. But what happens if I get very sick and need to be taken care of? You know, when I'm almost out of saliva. Then what?

In the Mishnah[2] one rabbi says, "This world is like a lobby before the *olam ha-ba*.[3] Prepare yourself in the lobby so that you may enter the banquet hall." I hope *olam ha-ba* has vegan options at the banquet.

In Dr. Elisabeth Kübler-Ross's wonderful autobiography *The Wheel of Life,* she told her dying husband that it was his turn to let people help him.

2   The Mishnah is an edited record of the complex body of material known as the "oral Torah." It's where one rabbi tells another rabbi who tells another rabbi what they think they just heard. The oral Torah is the first documented example of people playing the game Telephone.

3   *Olam ha-ba* means "the world to come." Jews believe that olam ha-ba is where we are hoping to be sent after we die. It's Florida without the humidity. Chocolate cake without the calories. Jewish mothers without the screaming.

She told him that his lesson at the end of his life was to stop doing for others and let others do for him. Old age seems to bring many options. If you let yourself be open, the possibilities for growth are still plentiful.

About a minute ago I stopped writing to make a phone call to a woman who booked me to perform at her Yiddish club. No, I don't speak Yiddish. And not everyone there is Jewish or speaks Yiddish or sounds like they need a phlegm removal service. I called her this morning and did not hear back. I figured maybe she was out of saliva. So I called her again. When she got on the phone, she apologized for not calling me back sooner. She said her husband's heart had stopped that morning, but the paramedics got there in time and luckily jump-started it back up. As my mother used to say, "Oy vey iz mir."

The Incredible Shrinking Man

Potential: A latent excellence or ability that may or may not be developed.

You know, Mark, you're a smart boy and have great potential. If you keep fooling around, you'll never get anywhere. Now write on the blackboard "I have great potential" one hundred times.
—Mrs. G, my fifth-grade teacher

In 2021 I was fifty years out of high school. In the last ten years, I've shrunk an inch, my toenails are starting to grow in different directions, and my ear and nose hairs grow faster than Jeff Bezos's bank account. Everywhere I go I'm now called "sir." Getting older is like being a captain in the army—"No, sir," "Yes, sir," "Right away, sir." The first stranger who calls me "Pops," I am going to choke.

The days of people telling me I have great potential are long over. According to the potential focus groups, when you hit a certain age, you've potentially outlived all your potential. When I walk down the street with any of my three sons, I see the way women smile at them. I'm practically invisible to the opposite sex. By the way, I use the word "practically" just so I don't feel like a complete dishrag.

Most people under thirty-five, except friends and family, want absolutely nothing to do with me. If I'm at a urinal, men don't stand behind me because they figure I'll be awhile. Sometimes when I pee it sounds eerily similar to a faucet dripping. I'm keenly aware of people my age starting to trip and slip in the shower. Hips and knees are being replaced as fast as teeth on a pro hockey team. When I drive at night, the lights from the other cars coming at me seem so bright. I say good evening and do a tight five.

One day my wife gave me the "no more climbing ladders" speech. If I need to change a ceiling bulb, I now have to hire an electrician at seventy dollars an hour or get a kid on stilts.

I also go to more doctors now than I ever did before and they are starting to find things wrong with me, but I'm chasing it as best as I can. As I shared earlier, I exercise more now than ever and also eat better and have more confidence in my body than I used to. Unless I suddenly drop dead, which at my age is quite possible, I believe I have a relatively good shot at a decent old age.

When I look back at my life, I have to admit I'm guilty of not appreciating all the good health and wonderful things that I was given as a young person. I was so blessed. Thank you, God. I had it all and didn't know it. I was your textbook "lack of gratitude, do what I want when I want" young person, and a few times I almost paid the ultimate price for my stupidity. I was wasting my potential.

Growing up, I remember older folks saying, "Young people just don't appreciate what they have." Truth is, I'm not sure young people *can* appreciate what they have. I think when you get older, you can appreciate things you still have because you took care of those things back then, or didn't take care of them but lucked out. Like your teeth. If you took care of your teeth when you were young, then when you are older, you can say, "Boy, I'm grateful I took care of my teeth back then." Maybe potential is given in stages. Maybe as a young person I didn't have the potential to be more grateful in that area. Maybe I wasn't ready for that yet.

Even now I'm sure I could be a lot more grateful. But I disagree that I don't have potential. For most of us, potential is in our mind. It has little to do with our age. Don't dwell on what you used to be able to do; instead, do all you can today. As you get older, you may lose some of your drive, but you still have potential. Every day that I sit down and write, I get better at writing. Every day that I exercise, I get stronger. I remember speaking with a great rabbi who was way up there in years. He had been studying the Talmud[4] for hours and hours a day for most of his life. He said, "What bothers me most is that with all the studying I've done, I feel like I've only dipped the tip of my pinky into the well. I'll just have to be satisfied I've done the best I could do." No one fulfills all of his or her potential. There will always be the unfinished. Do the best you can and know that's all any of us can do.

---

4   The Talmud is a collection of writings that covers the full gamut of Jewish laws and traditions and was compiled and edited between the third and sixth centuries. Since there were no lawyers or accountants between the third and sixth centuries, these laws have been updated many times to add the necessary loopholes to give their clients enough wiggle room to stay out of jail.

The Show Must Go On

You get word before the show has started
That your favorite uncle died at dawn—
Top of that, your pa and ma have parted,
You're brokenhearted but you go on.
—Irving Berlin, "There's No Business Like Show Business"

On December 10, 2019, there was a shoot-out at a kosher grocery store in Jersey City, New Jersey. It was a terrorist attack that left six dead: four innocent people and two terrorists. The shooters' next target was a Jewish school with fifty children but, thank God, they didn't make it.

Twenty-one miles from there, on December 14, I did a show at Congregation Agudath Israel in Caldwell, New Jersey. Three hundred and fifty people showed up for the night of laughter, knowing damn well it could have easily been them in the blink of an eye. I ended the show with "I hope we all had a good time tonight. Thank you very much. But we need to remember what happened four days ago, twenty-one miles from here. There are some people that are not able to laugh tonight. Thank you very much, and good night."

On 9/11 I was the comic hired to perform aboard a cruise ship that was docked for the day in Juneau, Alaska. The day before a performance, my cabin phone rang and my friend Dave said to turn on the TV. It was then that I learned that the Twin Towers had been hit by planes. Some hours later, the captain made an announcement: "May I have your attention, please. This is an important announcement." You could have heard a pin drop. "I am sorry to announce this, but America is at war." Click.

About an hour later, I saw the cruise director. I asked, "What do you want to do about my show tomorrow?" He responded that we should still have the show.

"Really?" I asked. "You think they'll be up for it?"

"We will see," he responded. So we did the show and it was fine. I closed with "Let's keep the people in America in our prayers."

When I went to Israel with Jerry Seinfeld several years ago, it was during the daily stabbings that were taking place in the streets. Nevertheless, seventeen thousand people came to the show. We had bodyguards around the stage to stop a potential lunatic from climbing up onstage and stabbing us. And the show went on.

Twenty minutes into a show I was doing in Arizona, someone dropped dead during my set. They took a forty-minute break to take him out, and then I finished. The show went on.

I was booked to do a show for almost a thousand people just a few days after my father died. That was a hard one because I talked about him in my act. At times it was like the audience was making a giant shiva[5] call to me.

Outside of the performer not being able to get to a show, the show must go on. Isn't that also true of Shabbas[6]? Outside of life and death, no matter what, Shabbas must go on. My mother died on a Friday afternoon in Florida. I was home in Los Angeles. Everything was on hold until Saturday night when Shabbas was over. On Shabbas, I went to shul[7] and had my meals with friends and family. Then after Shabbas, I called the Chevra Kadisha.[8]

Sometimes the only thing you can do is do what you're supposed to do. The bottom line is life goes on. I've been blessed to have known a few

---

5 Shiva is the traditional seven-day period of mourning observed by Jews immediately following the funeral of a parent, sibling, child, or spouse. It is when we get to eat the favorite foods of the deceased without the actual deceased hogging any of it.

6 Shabbas is the Jewish Sabbath. Observed from sundown on Friday until sundown on Saturday, it commemorates God's rest on the seventh day in the book of Genesis. Orthodox Jews do not drive cars or watch TV during these twenty-five hours. Unless of course the World Series or the Super Bowl is on TV, and then they are hoping God marks on a big curve.

7 *Shul* is a Yiddish word for "synagogue." An example of shul is where Jewish people go to worship and also talk sports and business. The word temple is used by conservative and reform Jews. The temple is where people go to play bingo and have board meetings about raising dues. There was a temple that was so reform, it was closed on Jewish holidays.

8 Chevra Kadisha, literally "Sacred Society," is the volunteer group that performs the final rites for the Jewish deceased. This is especially true for the Jewish husband who lost all his rights during his time alive.

Holocaust survivors who have told me as much. These are people who lost everything and everyone and had to start over, sometimes more than once. What choice is there but to carry on and live a good life? After you've been beaten to a pulp, isn't the ultimate revenge doing well? Isn't it the best thing a Jew can do, to have a few children to counter what Hitler tried to do? Life goes on.

My friend George Stanley lost his wife, Sally, of sixty-three years. At the shiva, he asked me to get up and do fifteen minutes in honor of Sally, who loved my comedy. George actually said to me, "The show must go on."

I know there are some pains that seem intolerable, but if you look hard enough you'll find someone somewhere somehow has gotten through. The important thing is that life goes on. Isn't "choose life" the same as "the show must go on"?

2
COMMUNITY

....

Craving Community

I've gone from having no community to being in the stand-up comedy community and a member of the LA Jewish community. I'm a lucky man.

When I was growing up, I had no community. My family didn't belong to a synagogue. My mother would say, "All they want is money." And I rarely, if ever, visited other family members. My mother would say, "Whatever you ask them for, it's always no," so we didn't visit. I was a Boy Scout for a short time, which I enjoyed until I got pink bellied and kicked out for stealing a flashlight I didn't steal. I didn't have many friends because they thought I was nuts. And since I was an only child, evenings were pretty much Mom, Dad, and me. They went to sleep early, and I wasn't allowed to call anyone after nine because I was told that after nine you only use the phone if someone died. All I had was my fourteen-inch black-and-white TV and a cocker spaniel who mostly liked to hide under the bed.

My first real taste of community was when I became a comedian. I would see the same people every night at the clubs, and we shared a common bond in comedy. Night after night at the comedy club bar just starting out were Jerry Seinfeld, Paul Reiser, Gilbert Gottfried, George Wallace,

Rita Rudner, Sandra Bernhard, singer Pat Benatar, and many others. Many of my comedian friends had felt the same loneliness I'd felt growing up. It was an amazing time being with a group of people who on a daily basis were trying to get better at something that few other people had any interest in doing. By 1984 I was living in Los Angeles. Then one day I saw a poster advertising a Torah class and went. Not because I wanted to learn Torah, but because I was lonesome and thought maybe there'd be girls there.

When the student is ready, the teacher will appear—and that's exactly what happened. I met Rabbi Nachum Braverman and his wife, Emuna. I was a live wire, and they helped ground me. They introduced me to what I'd always lacked and always craved but hadn't realized: a community. They invited me for Shabbas dinners and lunches and told me to come back anytime. I'm a literalist and took them up on it. I would show up, mostly on Saturdays, uninvited for Shabbas lunch. They never blinked. (If I'd tried that with my aunts and uncles, they'd probably have yelled at me or had me arrested or committed.) I also kept taking classes from the rabbi and his wife, which were held at their house, and continually met new people who seemed genuinely nice there. Many of these new friends soon started getting married and having kids, so I started getting invited to weddings and brises,[9] in that order. I didn't really recognize it at the time, but I was building my community. It was a great feeling.

In 1990 I got married myself. My wife, Nancy, did have a community growing up, so she quickly understood when I suggested we live in the Pico-Robertson neighborhood of Los Angeles because of its strong Jewish community. We started having kids and—bingo—we became fully entrenched in the community. Over the last twenty-five years, I have been to more weddings, bar mitzvahs, brises, and funerals than you could imagine. It has been nothing short of amazing. The joy and happiness that this has brought to me and my family are amazing.

---

9 A bris is the rite or ceremony of male circumcision, usually performed on the eighth day of life. This is one that most Jews still observe. It would have been nice if instead of God saying "Snip the tip," he'd said on the eighth day, "Cut his fingernails and let's be done with it."

My wife and I are members of the Young Israel of Century City (YICC) shul. Recently, the building that the synagogue had called home for the last twenty-five years was put under renovation, so we had to have Shabbas services at Hillel Day School on Saturday mornings. A few weeks back, I walked into Hillel and went up three flights of stairs to the basketball court where the service was being held. As soon as I walked in, I saw about one hundred people I recognized and immediately felt a sense of warmth and security. I realized it wasn't the old YICC building we had been in that gave me that feeling but rather the people who filled the place. I grabbed a tallit[10] and a siddur[11] and sat down to pray. I closed my eyes, took a breath, and said, "Thank you, God, for this community."

When I was in high school and on the verge of flunking out (which I deserved), a teacher said to me, "At some point in your life, you will have to decide what is important to you." She was 100 percent right. Three of those things were getting married, having kids, and building a community. I am grateful for those decisions every day. If you need a community, come to the Pico-Robertson neighborhood of Los Angeles and I'll introduce you around. If you need a kid, I'll even lend you one of mine for a while.

I Don't Have to Go, Now I Get to Go

As a child I was told that I had to go to shul to pray, and, like a lot of other kids, I didn't find it fun or interesting. For a lot of people, because of that experience as a child, that's where it all ended. When I was seven I asked Sarah Jacobson for a kiss and she turned me down. Thank God at thirty-seven when I asked my future wife for a kiss she said yes. Imagine

---

10 A tallit is a Jewish prayer shawl. As per the Bible's instructions, the rectangular tallit has fringes attached to each of its four corners. Non-Jews are forever telling Jews that they have strings hanging out and to tuck them in.

11 A siddur is a Jewish prayer book for everyday use, which most Jews never use for any day use.

making a future decision when you're a kid and riding that out for the rest of your life. But that's what people do.

For me now, going to shul covers so many things. It's serious, fun, and interesting. Now when I go, not only do I get to pray but I also get to watch other people pray. Praying is one of the few very private events that people do publicly. Watching someone commune with God is amazing. I also get to see people not praying but, rather, sitting very relaxed, reading a newspaper like they're at a bus stop. In some ways that's more amazing than watching them pray. I'm guilty of that one.

At shul I also get to see people celebrating or mourning milestones in their lives: bar mitzvahs, upcoming marriages, anniversaries, the passing of loved ones. I get to see people hugging each other in very loving ways. I get to hear the rabbi or the guest speaker give a talk that they hope will change our lives for the better. I get to ask people how they are doing after an operation or how their new baby is or how they're holding up after a major loss. I also get to laugh at new jokes, and I get to tell jokes that people have never heard before. I get to have a bite to eat with friends, and I get to watch people put food in their pockets to take home for later. I get to watch boys and girls giving their bar and bat mitzvah speeches and talking about how much they love their families. I get to watch the proud faces of crying parents and grandparents, aunts, uncles, brothers, and sisters as these kids move on to the next stage of their lives. And I get to watch six-year-olds lead part of the service. I get to find out about worthy causes to donate to. I get to take a nap when the rabbi is speaking. I get to watch people wheel disabled loved ones into the building, and I get to watch them leave to bring them back home four hours later.

What moves me the most is the tremendous loving care I see people give their older friends and relatives when their lives have taken a turn for the worse. I get to watch someone help put a tallit on a father-in-law, Popo, and turn the pages of his prayer book while pointing him to where we are. That one makes me cry every time. I'm also moved by seeing people who are sick praying for miracles and people who are well praying for the same. I see people thanking God nonstop for what they have. And because of my shul community, I get to go to people's homes for meals and say hello to their elderly parents who now live with them following the loss of a spouse. I get to see people opening their hearts.

There are a million things I get to see by just showing up at shul, and I believe I have become a better person by going and seeing all these things. If someone tells you religion does more harm than good, take him or her to shul on a Saturday and point out all the good that is taking place. Let the person see goodness and hope up close, as I so often get to.

It's in You, So Share You

I was an only child and a lonesome kid. Rarely was I hugged, and rarely did I hear the words "I love you." As a kid I didn't know that I wasn't the only one in the world feeling lonely. I wish I'd known that there was a wealth of needy kids just like me. Not knowing there are others like you makes you feel more alone. For me sometimes the feeling of lonesomeness turns to agitation. When I'm agitated is when I might act out. As a kid, when I would act out, my family would label me a "wild man." I probably was—and that wild man label followed me all the way into my early thirties.

I went to Yeshiva from first through third grade, and when I would upset one of my rabbis, he would smack me on the palm with an oak ruler or hit me on the back of the head with an open hand. I probably deserved to be punished, as I was not an easy kid, but was smacking or hitting a child with a ruler the appropriate response? Later, my fifth-grade public school teacher called me an idiot in front of the whole class. I craved people thinking I was smart, but there went that dream. After that I became known as

"Hey, idiot" by a few of the kids. I was told people had no idea how to reach me. Truth is that *I* had no idea how to reach me. Even my parents would say, "Mark, we have no idea how to reach you." I felt I had no idea how to reach them either. I was told that I frustrated people.

Almost everything they said about me I also felt about myself. I frustrated myself. I had no idea about almost anything. I was what was commonly known as "a lost soul." The world's mantra for me was "What is wrong with you?" I became angry. My mantra back was "Screw 'em all." Then I'd shrug my shoulders and walk away, holding back the tears. People said they wanted to help me, but I was told not to trust anyone. My friend Marva told me that when I was nine, her father had asked me how I was and I had responded that I felt like I was locked in a broom closet and could not get out. Not bad imagery for nine.

I remember these feelings like I had them yesterday. They still chill me. I could be wrong about some of my memories, but one thing I know for sure is that the feelings of isolation and despair were real.

Looking back, I could cry thinking about how sensitive I was, how raw. As raw as the slab of ginger that comes with your sushi. Some nights it was just the lonesome little kid in bed watching a blurred cloud as it passed over the moon as I looked out my bedroom window. I remember wishing I could reach down my throat and pull all the pain out of me.

The thing about sadness and emptiness is that it cuts deep, some might say right down to the bone. I say it's deeper, right down to the soul. What part of a person is more sensitive and open than the soul? Is the soul not our headquarters, our command center? Is the soul not God's pilot light? The soul does try to speak to you, but if you don't get quiet enough, you may never hear what you are supposed to, or if you do manage to separate the sound from the noise, you may misinterpret what it is saying. I know I did. I heard things that were not said and saw things that were not there. Simply put, I was like every kid: I just wanted to be happy and to make my mother and father happy. That was an impossible task.

Happiness is an inside job. I wanted to stop my parents from arguing, but the yelling never seemed to stop for long. Like ocean waves or a great waterfall, it just kept coming. I looked miserable, because I was miserable. I told the doctors that I couldn't sleep, and they told my mother that I was all knotted up in my stomach. In my early teens, doctors gave me the drug Sinequan, an antidepressant. I took it for a while, but it did not go well with my self-prescribed drugs. People said things like, "I am not happy around you." For anyone, but especially a young person, the thought that one makes the world an unhappy place is a lot to handle. Many times I thought I'd had enough. I thought that I would show them. But it won't show them. It is rare when anything shows them. I am lucky to be alive.

With no known options, hardly any schooling, no discernible talent, and a modicum of hope, somehow, some way, I was quiet enough to hear the voice. The good voice that said, "Mark, you need to become a comedian." With it, the hook was lowered. I bit into it and have never broken loose.

When I was twelve, I told my parents I wanted to be a comedian and they stared at me. Up to that point, my last big decision was when I was three, and that was "No more diapers." After my decision to become a comedian, I made the choice to homeschool myself on how to become a comedian. The more I learned about it, the more I knew I was onto something. Before finding comedy, I was interested in nothing. After finding comedy, I began to heal myself. Laughter, I thought, just might be the key.

My prayer, going as far back as I can remember, has been to make people happy. It's not because I am a good person; it's because I am attuned to other people's pain. With comedy came my chance to create light and laughter. I loved what my parents looked like when they laughed. I wanted to lighten people's loads, even if briefly and by just a little. By following that whisper, I have also found some degree of happiness.

The truth is that I was never alone. All I had to do was look and I would see my comedian mentors all over TV trying to teach me: Milton Berle, Don Rickles, Joan Rivers, Lenny Bruce, George Carlin, Robert Klein, Alan

King, and Phyllis Diller. When I was working and it was clicking and the people were laughing, like them, I was also forgetting my troubles.

There are many ways to climb out of hopelessness, sadness, and despair. My way was my way. I was lucky and heard the call. Everyone must find the special key that fits their lock. We all have our own truth. A lemon tree doesn't look at another lemon tree and think, *He's doing it right. I'm a loser and my lemons are worthless.* They just give all they can and don't overthink it. If you too are suffering, take it from one troubled kid to another: Find your special gift, give all you can, and then share it with the world. Don't judge it, just do it. The world is waiting for you. The world needs you. Only you can deliver you. The world will love you for it. And isn't that what you always wanted anyway?

Amazing, Amazing

Our goal should be to live life in radical amazement . . . get up in the morning and look at the world in a way that takes nothing for granted. Everything is phenomenal, everything is incredible, never treat life casually. To be spiritual is to be amazed. —Abraham Joshua Heschel

Really, I get both soup and a salad with the dinner? Amazing. —Mark Schiff

It is rare when a day goes by that something does not amaze me. I am amazed when people treat me nicely, but not so amazed when they are nasty. I am amazed by how fast I can lose my temper. It is something I must work on every day. When I was a kid, a car ride amazed me—still does. A simple thirty-mile round-trip visit to a friend can cause me to utter something like, "Ninety years ago, this trip would have taken three days."

When I was a kid, I had a friend who rang for an elevator, and when he stepped inside what he thought was the cabin, he fell eight floors to his demise. That was horrible yet amazing.

Next to my office building, a new apartment complex was just completed. For almost a year I watched the workers as they sat idly on the curb, ripping chunks off their Slim Jims and eating hero sandwiches while washing it all down with liquid from large thermos bottles. To my amazement, the building is now complete. Walking around inside are high-rent paying smoothie drinking people in their Fruit of the Loom undies. Amazing.

Folks, I remember more than once having had a glass of cold water that was so good it practically brought me to tears. It was that crazy amazing.

Most people cannot just sit in a chair and amaze themselves, unless of course they are a Jenner or Kardashian.

Even certain deaths are amazing. If you fall off an eleven-thousand-foot mountain, there must be a split second on your way down when you think, *This is amazing.* When someone dies quickly, you always hear "Amazing. I just saw him yesterday."

What also amazes many people are other people's bad habits. For instance, they might say things like "I am amazed that every time I see you, you are stuffing your face," or they might say, "I am amazed by how long a person can sit on a couch and do absolutely nothing." Likewise, I constantly amazed my parents, and they would tell me so by saying, "We are amazed by how little you listen to anything we have to say to you."

When you start dating a new person you like, it is not unusual to be amazed by each other. "She's amazing." "He is the most amazing guy I have ever met." But that window, when everything the other person does is amazing, does not last long. The fact that we have something called infatuation is amazing.

What really amazes me is that other people are not interested in things that amaze me. For instance, I will watch a movie and freak out and try to share it with the family. My family's response is generally tepid. They mock the movie: "Wow, Dad found another great one. Bet it's a black-and-white." If they do end up watching something I suggest, then nine times out of ten, they have a group kumbaya amazement festival, poking fun at me. They are all beyond amazed that not only did I like the movie, but I loved it. When this happens, it could easily be a year or two before any of them trusts another one of my suggestions. But screw 'em—I know good movies.

Trying to pass your amazement on to others is dangerous. There is a good chance it will lower their opinion of you unless, of course, you are über-wealthy. Then your amazement will be tolerated and applauded until the reading of your last will and testament.

I am sorry that not everyone is as easily amazed as I am. Being amazed is a beautiful thing. It's a gift. It makes life exciting. Being amazed is a giant life bonus. Being amazed un-blahs life. Being amazed just happens. That is why it is amazing. Because you have no control. Life just gives it to you. Being amazed is as exciting as riding sidesaddle without holding on.

Tonight I will probably be in the bedroom with my wife where we will, amazingly, be watching our umpteenth show about Queen Elizabeth and her pain-in-the-neck family. I have easily logged over one hundred hours of screen time watching the royals walking around Africa kissing little black babies or shaking hands with chubby women in print housedresses with whom they have nothing in common. Hands down, I have watched more videos of the queen's family than my own.

One night while watching these royals as they were exiting their eighteenth-century horse-drawn carriages, wearing jewelry so expensive its cost could buy the Dodgers and all of Beverly Hills, I wondered if the queen wears her crown when she sits on the loo. I thought that would be amazing. I personally have dropped my phone in the toilet and fished it out myself. If she dropped her crown in, I wondered if she too would fish it out herself. That could easily be a Netflix six-episode limited series called *Fishing for the Tiara*.

So here we are, my wife in bed and me next to her in my vibrating, heated, and reclining faux leather chair, wearing my Häagen-Dazs print boxers and black socks, eating rinsed blueberries, and sipping decaf Earl Grey out of a faded "Father of the Year" mug. Believe me when I say I am an amazing sight to a select few. Here we are after more than thirty years of marriage. I sit totally and utterly amazed that this is my life. Because when I turn to my left, I see I have a partner to go through it with. We are the king and queen of a 1,705-square-foot, one hundred-year-old house that is more of a bungalow. And I have never wanted to exchange my life for anybody else's.

Shimon ben Zoma, a sage of the first and second centuries CE, famously said, "Who is rich? The one who appreciates what he has." I appreciate what I have, and that to me is utterly amazing. When my cousin asked his mother for Oreos instead of Hydrox, my aunt famously said, "Who is rich? Everyone but us."

Gooood Shabbas

Comedian David Brenner said, "So I'm in New York and I say to someone, 'Have a nice day.' He looks at me and says, 'No thanks. I've got other plans.'"

On Shabbas I'll often walk with a friend, also named David, to and from shul, and I notice that he says hello to almost everyone who walks by him. In a booming friendly voice, he gives them a "Good Shabbas. Good Shabbas. Good Shabbas." Whether the person is Jewish or non-Jewish, he greets each with a smile and a hello. He even draws out the word "good" and makes it into Gooood Shabbas. It's a beautiful thing to see. But then, I also notice that a good percentage of the people do not return his wish. I guess they have other plans, or perhaps they are thinking about something else and it just goes by them (let's not be judgmental here).

I know there are many reasons why people may not return his kind gesture, but probably few of them are good ones. If someone says hello to me, I need to respond. In *Ethics of the Fathers*, the scholar Shammai advises to "receive everyone with a cheerful face." Our sages explain that "The only way to steal from a pauper who owns nothing is to rob him of his dignity by refusing to return his greeting." My mother, in *Ethics of the Moms*, says, "When someone says hello, you say hello back." Even my dog, who was not known for his manners, would respond with a helicopter-type, hearty tail wag when someone said hi to him.

Despite rarely receiving a response, David keeps on Good Shabbas'ing everyone, and it never seems to bother him when he gets little or nothing in return. He just continues with his smiling salutes and then returns to whatever conversation we are having. Don't you hate people like that? People whom nothing seems to bother. I myself have always been big on saying hello and holding doors for anyone. I'm an equal opportunity door holder. My parents taught me to hold doors and help blind people across the street. The difference between David and me is that when people don't return his kind gesture, he is fine. When they don't return mine with a thank-you or a nod or some acknowledgement, I get terribly upset. Sometimes I even mumble something underneath my breath about how rude they are. I might even blurt out a sarcastic "Thank you."

So why do I do this? Why do I wish people nice things or hold doors for them if I know a lot of the time, I'm going to get nothing back and I'm going to get angry? Why do I set myself up like that? I don't really have time in this chapter to figure that out, nor do I want to see a therapist for fifteen years and trace the root of why it hurts when people let me down or don't live up to my expectations. A friend once told me that "expectations are resentments under construction." The more you expect people to react a certain way, the more disappointed you will be.

The much simpler cure for me is to keep opening doors, keep wishing people a good everything, and get over my petty annoyances, and hopefully one day I'll grow up and get to the point where I don't care what their reactions are, where it's a bonus if they say "Thank you." It's their loss if they say nothing, not mine. My job is to be kind, and that means getting hurt sometimes.

I read that Rabbi Israel Meir Kagan, better known as the Chofetz Chaim (Desirer of Life), let someone stay overnight at his house and in the morning realized the guest had robbed him. He told his wife that the next time someone wants to stay with them, she shouldn't let him use the experience as an excuse to say no. I feel the same way. I'm not going to let other people dictate what I do, especially if it's the right thing to do. But do me a favor: if I ever open a door for you or help you across the street or say "Good Shabbas" to you, at least nod your head or, even better, give me a little smile back. It might make my day.

I Love My Neighborhood

I've almost always lived in mostly Jewish neighborhoods. To be exact, religious Jewish neighborhoods, walk-to-shul and kosher butcher-shop Jewish neighborhoods. I live there not because I am incredibly religious but because I like living among Jews.

I like seeing Jews walking the streets. I like seeing pictures of rabbis in store windows. I like seeing new shuls popping up, and I like peeking in to see people praying. I like seeing women in supermarkets wearing sheitels,[12] which I can spot a mile away. And I like living where it's not a rarity to see men in kippahs[13] wearing tallitot.[14] I also like seeing people who seem to

---

12 *Sheitel* is the Yiddish word for a wig worn by some Orthodox Jewish married women in order to conform with the requirement of Jewish law to cover their hair. This practice is part of the modesty-related dress standard called *tzniut*. An Orthodox single woman does not wear a wig. Instead she wears a sign around her neck with her phone number and email address on it.

13 A kippah, also called a *koppel*, or yarmulke, is a brimless cap, usually made of cloth, traditionally worn by Jewish males to fulfill the customary requirement that the head be covered. As opposed to their penis, where the head of it is never covered.

14 Tallitot, or tallisim (plural for tallit), are the prayer shawls mostly worn by men. Wearing a tallit during prayer establishes a special connection to the One Above. We're talking about God, not their wives.

fear God. I like seeing Jews in outdoor cafés. I like waiting in line behind Jewish husbands in bagel shops while they are on the phone checking with their wives as to what kind of bagels to bring home. I like hearing the words *tatala*[15] and *nisht*.[16] I like names like Shlomo, Chava, and Moshe.

I really like my neighborhood because you still see families of five or more. I like seeing five young girls all in identical homemade dresses. It reminds me of the von Trapp kids from *The Sound of Music*. I like seeing a two-year-old with tzitzit[17] hanging out. If you are in my neighborhood and it is four minutes before Shabbat, be careful crossing the street because an old beat-up station wagon with bald tires driven by a man with a long beard and kippah that's almost hanging off his left ear might come screeching around the corner at sixty miles an hour to get home before the clock ticks Shabbat.

On any given day, my neighborhood almost feels like I'm in the Holy Land. It's a wonderful feeling. Plus, look at all the airfare I save if I can get the feeling while staying put. I don't mind the flight to Israel though. I like flying on planes with four hundred other Jews except when they wake me to pray.

Truth be told, the older I get, the more I like Jews. You might say I love Jews. Not all Jews, but an awful lot of them. I say most because how can I like Ben and Jerry? Nobody likes all of anything. Do you like every item in a bakery? I don't.

When my kids were little, we lived in San Antonio, Texas, for two years. We lived in a very gentile neighborhood. Our Christmas manger was two doctors and three lawyers. But the people in our area were kind to us. When we were walking to shul, donning our Shabbat best, our neighbors

---

15 *Tatala* means "little papa." The word is usually used by Jewish grandparents right before they slip the kid a five spot. "Come here, *tatala*. *Zaide* (Grandfather) has something for you."

16 *Nisht* means "NOT" and can be attached to many other words. Here are three of them: *Nishtkefelecht*: No big deal! *Nishtgedeiget*: Don't worry. *Nishtyetstithhobakopf vetaug*: Not tonight; I have a headache.

17 Tzitzit are specially knotted ritual fringes, or tassels, worn in antiquity by Israelites and today by observant Jews. The knots remind the man of the knots in his stomach from constant worry about things he has no business worrying about.

would greet us with a big hello and even stop mowing their lawns to wish us a good Shabbat. Shul was a five-minute walk if we crossed a creek. Some months the creek water rose to over two feet. We wore high rubber boots to protect our shoes and clothes and to protect us from rattler bites. It's not easy getting a Jewish woman to walk through rattlesnake-infested water. Texas was great and the people amazing, but it was not a Jewish neighborhood. For me, something was missing.

With the recent uptick of anti-Semitism, I love my neighborhood and the Jewish people even more. I love living where people are not afraid of openly showing that they are Jewish. I love seeing people I know doing mitzvahs, and I especially love hearing from people about random acts of kindness that were bestowed upon them.[18] When I walk my neighborhood, I feel a rush of gratitude that I don't feel in other neighborhoods. In truth, I love seeing devotees of all religions. If they respect me, I certainly will respect them. But Jews get who I am at my core. To me, that is a very comforting feeling in a very unsettling world.

So here we are, living in the Pico-Robertson area of Los Angeles, a neighborhood where you pay lots of money for a tiny house so you can be near other Jews. But where else except a Jewish neighborhood can you walk to the corner and get a freshly baked kosher rye or homemade shakshuka? Or on a Friday afternoon get a phone call from my neighbor Aaron asking if I want to walk with him to shul? Where? If I'm not going to move to Israel, this is the next best thing. Shalom.

---

18 The simple meaning of the word *mitzvah* is "command." It appears in various forms about three hundred times in the five books of Moses. That's about the same number of times a Jewish mother tells her child not to run with scissors in his hands.

3
DIETING

....

Excuse-Aholism

OK, it's been twelve years now. I'm starting to think I'm not
bloated. —Unknown

My name is Mark and I am a recovering excuse-aholic. One day at a
time, I try not to make any excuses for anything. It's not easy being
an excuse-aholic, even though it's not my fault that I am one. That might be
an excuse—I'll have to check with my sponsor.

Growing up as an only child, once my dog died I had nobody to blame
except myself for not doing my homework. If something was broken, my
parents knew who did it.

Excuse-aholics are liars. Previously, if someone asked if I'd exercised, I
might have told them that I needed to fix my treadmill, even if I didn't have
a treadmill. I had to blame anything or anyone but myself. When I gave up
cake and cookies and then ate some at a party, I'd tell myself that that was
all they had to eat. I'd even make excuses to myself: "Why should I lose
weight? I'll only gain it back." My favorite excuse was "I'll start tomorrow."
But tomorrow hardly ever comes.

If I was late picking you up for something we were going to, I might even have tried to get you to join in with my excuse. Let's tell them, "We were helping my neighbor find his dog." The worst is when they tell you that you used the dog excuse the week before.

Excuse-aholics are always on the run. When I would see people coming toward me whom I had lied to, I might cross the street. If the phone rang and I owed you money, I didn't pick up. It's an incredibly lonely existence, and the really sad part is that I got to the point where I started believing my own excuses. My friends and family, however, were onto me. They would say things like, "I've never heard so many excuses. You have an excuse for everything." Before I even started talking, people would cut me off with "What's it this time?" People even brought sickness and death into it. "I'm sick to death of your excuses." They were fed up.

The biggest problem with excuses is that you have to remember them. Truth, on the other hand, you never have to remember. Many nights I would fall into bed, exhausted from a day of excusing. It is a horrible way to live. One day a friend tough-loved me and told me he was done with me unless I called Excuses Anonymous (EA) and got help. It took me three months to call. I kept telling myself I was too busy. Truth was that I was in fear. If I had to give up my excuses, I'd have to become accountable. That meant finding out exactly who I am. I didn't know if I had it in me. When I finally did call, they told me about a meeting the next day. And I went. I had hit rock bottom. I was sick and tired of the way I was living. I was all cashed out of making excuses.

Today, all around me, I see people who have the luxury of making excuses for themselves. Not me. I've lost my right. I've used up my share. If a cop pulls me over and I've done something wrong, I now have to own it and thank him for the $500 ticket. Even after being in EA for a good while, if I'm not careful at any moment I could reactivate my excusing.

I can't say it's been easy, because it hasn't. They tell me it's progress, not perfection. I try not to make up any excuses for anything. I'm not perfect, but I'm better. I never want to go back to the life I was living. Never.

I was once writing some jokes for someone and they'd been due the week before. As an excuse for the lateness, I'd said I'd had to have my wisdom teeth taken out. In my mind it was a half excuse. I really had them taken out, but it was fifty years prior. Who was I kidding? It was an excuse, a bank safe full of BS. End of story. Slowly but surely, I'm catching on. But I still need a lot of help. And that's not BS.

Jews, Non-Jews, and Weight Loss

My first wake-up call to how heavy I was took place when I was walking on Cashio Street in Los Angeles and I dropped something on the ground. When I bent down to get it, let's just say, it wasn't easy to get back up. I was almost two hundred pounds with a big puffy face, and I was really starting to feel old. A day or two later, as I was being introduced to go onstage, Dom Irrera, a comedian friend, said to me, "Look how fat you are." Soon after that, I was walking with Jerry Seinfeld when he pointed to an old guy with a walker crossing a street and said, "We don't want to end up like that." Few people are as dedicated to exercising as Jerry.

With all this, the message came across loud and clear: lose weight and get healthy. So the next day I decided to crawl out of my fat suit and do something about it. It took a year, but I lost fifty pounds and have kept forty-six of them off for over ten years. Losing the weight was not hard—it was exciting—but keeping it off has been murder. I have been an overeater and food addict my whole life, still am and always will be. I remember I was three months old being breastfed and my mother screamed at me, "Enough already. Don't you ever stop eating?" My problem is I'm never full. I could eat a fifteen-course dinner and then on the way home stop for hot buttered caramel popcorn. I have an emptiness inside me that is extremely demanding and never satisfied.

In order to lose the weight and keep it off, I had to do just one little thing, and that was to change just about everything. Diet to me means not eating things I used to enjoy ever again, and doing this one day at a time. I don't eat pizza, pasta, or bread (except challah[19] on Shabbas, and even that I may have to give up). My dessert is fruit, no more cakes or cookies. To the best of my ability, I've given up all sugar. My diet is now plant-based. No meat, dairy, or eggs. Nothing that had a mother or a face. That means I basically eat exactly the same as a rabbit, but because I wash the dirt off my vegetables mine have slightly less flavor.

If possible and I am still able to chew, I would like meat for my last meal. I'd like a hot pastrami on rye with mustard and coleslaw, and a Dr. Brown's Black Cherry soda. At that point, who cares about cholesterol, diabetes, or saving the planet? I even talked to my rabbi to see if he could somehow get rid of holidays like Passover,[20] Sukkoth,[21] and Shavuot,[22] as they are killers for a person like me. All you do is eat and then take a break to do some praying before you eat some more.

As I was losing the weight, a funny thing happened. I noticed that my losing weight bothered my Jewish friends more than my non-Jewish friends. Jews get very worried when you lose weight. They all think they are doctors and diagnosticians. They say things like, "Are you OK?" "Why did you lose

19 Challah is yeast-leavened egg bread, usually braided, and traditionally eaten by Jews on the Sabbath, holidays, and other ceremonial occasions. If a challah is permitted to get stale for three days or more, it can also be used to make French toast or to play touch football.

20 Passover (*Pesach*) is the springtime holiday observed by Jewish people celebrating when God took the Jewish people out of Egypt. It lasts for eight days (seven days in Israel), during which no bread or anything that contains grain that has been fermented or has any flavor is to be consumed. God giveth and He taketh.

21 Sukkoth is a weeklong Jewish holiday that comes five days after Yom Kippur. Sukkoth celebrates the gathering of the harvest and commemorates the miraculous protection God provided for the children of Israel when they left Egypt. We celebrate Sukkoth by dwelling in a foliage-covered booth (known as a "sukkah"). And like with Passover, we try as much as possible to avoid working.

22 *Shavuot* means "weeks," and it refers to the anniversary of the giving of the Torah at Sinai. On this holiday, Jews eat mostly dairy products for a few days in a row. The holiday celebrates Jewish cardiologists and open-heart surgery.

the weight?" "Did you want to lose the weight?" On the other hand, when my non-Jewish friends would see me, I'd hear, "You look great!" "You're like Benjamin Button," and "How'd you do it? Bet you feel terrific!" and "Want to go to the rodeo?"

A few of my Jewish friends called my wife to try to pry out of her how long I had to live. Sometimes they would walk up to me in the street and scream, "Enough already! Stop it! Don't lose any more weight!" The crème de la crème was when I was in the neighborhood supermarket and a woman I know looked at me, turned white, and started running away. I quickly caught up with her and asked if she was all right. She was trembling right there in the middle of the store. She had heard I was extremely sick and that I had died. She said she'd always liked me and was incredibly sad to get the news of my death. I thanked her for her kind words, told her I was all right, and went back to get some grapes. About an hour later, I thought if she liked me so much, how come she didn't come to my funeral, send a card, or make a small donation in memory of me? Phooey on her.

A few months later I was visiting my eighty-five-year-old aunt, and she offered me a piece of cake. I said, "I don't eat cake."

She said, "Life is not worth living without cake." I guess if I were married to my Uncle Louie, like she was, I might feel the same.

One rabbi who wanted to lose weight called and asked me to meet him and tell him how he could also lose weight. I said, "Where do you want to meet to talk?" He said Schwartz's Bakery.

Keeping the weight off is a daily fight. It's by far the hardest thing I've ever done. Every day I am on the battlefield trying to stay alive. To my Jewish friends, I know you mean well. And when I do die one day while eating a bowl of broccoli, you can all have your laugh. What I've come to understand is that I hardly ever miss all the foods that I thought I could not live without. As I've gotten older, I've realized that almost everything in life is overrated anyway. Keeping weight off is a full-time job. My paycheck is getting my health back and wearing my kids' clothes. Now go for a walk.

My Downfall Is Bread

Rosh Hashanah,[23] Sukkoth, Shemini Atzereth,[24] and Simhath Torah[25] are wonderful holidays but hell on wheels for an overeater. You go from feast to fast, then back to feast. I eat enough during these holidays to last me the rest of the year. When they are over, I have to go to the tailor just to let my underwear and socks out. Yes, feet can also get fat.

I have been blessed to have kept off almost fifty pounds for years. It is easily the hardest thing I've ever done. The fat man inside me is relentless. He is a liar, a cheat, and a con man, and he will do anything to get me ballooned back up. He thinks it's funny when I can't button my pants. He loves me fat, out of shape, and sick. I know this because I must deal with him daily.

Yesterday I swore off peanuts and today I've already had three fistfuls. I later grabbed a Lärabar and said to myself, "Eat it slowly." It was gone in two bites. For me, two bites is a snail's pace. Then I went back for a second one. I'm hopeless. When I go to supermarkets, I might lob some "no-no items" into my cart and with the help of God (which I really mean) toss them before I get to the register, but not until I push the items around the store while talking to them. "You're not going home with me. You're not. I'm the boss." Thank God people think I'm on the phone and don't know

---

23 Rosh Hashanah, literally meaning "head [of] the year," marks the Jewish new year. The Jewish new year is very different from the secular new year. During the secular one, a million people gather in New York's Times Square, get drunk, watch the ball drop, and then kiss each other. The Jewish new year is celebrated with a big family dinner that ends in a fight until someone storms off and you do not see them for another year. One ends in good cheer, the other in good riddance.

24 Shemini Atzereth is the holiday that follows immediately after the seventh day of Sukkoth. Literally, Shemini Atzereth means "the eighth [day] of assembly." Only nine Jewish people know what this holiday is all about, and only four of those nine celebrate it.

25 Simhath Torah is a Jewish holiday that celebrates and marks the conclusion of the annual cycle of public Torah readings and the beginning of a new cycle when we start reading the Torah from the beginning. The first line is "In the beginning God created heaven and earth." If you don't buy that premise, you might as well stop reading.

I'm having a conversation with a bag of SkinnyPop.

A lot of people ask me how they can lose weight. I give them my phone number and tell them to call me. Ninety-nine percent of the time they never call. Last week at shul, a guy told me he was diabetic but that bread was his weakness. He knows what his downfall is and can't stop.

One rabbi told me he wanted to pay someone to be all over him about his eating habits. That used to be called a mother. Now it's a highly paid food coach.

There are no permanent fixes. If you want to keep weight off, get ready for the fight of your life—or join the Hare Krishnas. I've never seen a chubby Hare Krishna. Heart attacks, stents, open-heart surgery, erectile dysfunction, diabetes, and strokes: most of the time, these do not lead to people changing. Fear wears off. People tell me they want to change but usually stipulate that they don't want to do anything too drastic. When did having a surgeon cut you open down the middle stop being drastic? (I just got up for more nuts and ate them. I'm such a lost soul.)

Why I've kept off the weight is because it's not about the weight; it's about health. I'm trying to get healthy, not skinny. Skinny is the gift of getting healthy. Getting healthy is for people who want to get healthy, not for people who need to get healthy. You must want it, and want it badly. Most people who need things never do anything about them. It's the people who want to do it who are driven to do it. They're the ones who succeed. Those people understand that if they don't change, they will die. They are the ones who make the changes. I've been to funerals of people who died of lung cancer or a heart attack and as soon as the service was over, you could see some of their friends and family lighting up on the way back to their cars. One of the top three deathbed regrets is not taking better care of one's health.

I know beyond a shadow of a doubt that if I go back to my old habits, what will happen is no mystery: I'll be history. I made a deal with myself that when the time comes and I must give my body back to my creator, I want to return it, to the best of my ability, the way it was given to me. That means in good shape. I want to know that when the day comes—and it will—that I did all I could to prevent it. If not, that voice inside me will have a field day berating me on my deathbed. *Please, God, no more nuts today!*

Eat, Pray, Eat

We Americans love our holidays and special occasions. Many non-Jews have told me that they have thought about becoming Jewish just because we have so many more holidays. If you're an American and an observant Jew, there is a good chance you work only five days a year (and if one of those days falls on a Friday, you get to go home early).

Life is wonderful, and the marking of special events is important. But string them all together and we've become a nation of overweight, sickly, wobbly people. If you keep Shabbas, then that means fifty-two Friday-night dinners, fifty-two Saturday lunches, and fifty-two *seudah shlishit*[26] every year. Considering the amount of food at each of these meals, that is about 156 Thanksgiving-size meals. Thank God for the five fast days to get us back to even. You can't party 150-plus days a year and expect your undies not to ride up on you.

I've listed some of those special days you need to be careful of if you're trying to stay healthy and lose weight. If you have food and festivities to celebrate some of these events, it's not enough to just pass on dessert. If you want to stay healthy, you'll probably have to pass on most or all of what is served. Sounds draconian, but it's not.

I live it as best as I can and don't feel cheated one plank length. I try to eat at these events the same way I eat on February 19 or any other unspecial

---

26 *Seudah shlishit* is the third meal of Shabbas. It is eaten in the late afternoon on Shabbas before sunset. This meal is the last meal of the twelve-thousand-calorie Shabbas. You have this holy meal about an hour before the family goes out for banana splits.

day. There are no days off and no cheat days. There is only "Not today." I'm not saying that my children's birthdays or my wedding anniversary are not important, just that I try not to associate them with the building of a triple chin. Keeping off weight means I have no red-letter days. If I go to an event, I either bring my own food, eat something before going, or try to be extra careful with what I put on my plate. Like the sober alcoholic, if you don't take that first bite, there will be no fiftieth bite. Even with years of practice, many times I crumble like a warm piece of coffee cake, but the important thing is to always get back up.

At first, the people throwing these soirees may be slightly put off by what they perceive as rigidness. Be nice, don't ever preach, explain that you appreciate what they have prepared, and then offer them a bite of your celery. If you stick with your plan, they will eventually see that you're serious and respect you for your commitment. One day they may even ask you for help. Best of all, you will respect you.

Here is a semi-list of land mine events. Add your own that I left off. See how many of these you celebrate; then add up the total days and divide the number by 365.

New Year's Day, New Year's Eve, Memorial Day, Independence Day, Labor Day, Thanksgiving and the day after, Presidents' Day, Independence Day, Shabbas (fifty-two times a year), Passover, Shavuot, Sukkoth, Hanukkah,[27] Purim,[28] Mother's Day, Father's Day, birthdays, anniversaries, funerals, shivas, raises, settlements, graduations, restoring of health, close calls, Super Bowls, World Series, Olympics, hockey games, basketball games, golf matches, your kids' sporting events, tennis matches, a new job, after an orgy (although you might want to eat before so you have strength),

---

27 Hanukkah is a Jewish festival commemorating the rededication of the Second Temple in Jerusalem at the time of the Maccabean revolt against the Seleucid Empire. It is also known as the Festival of Lights. Hanukkah lasts for eight days. Many non-Jewish people believe that Hanukkah is a Jewish form of Christmas. To make the non-Jewish people feel bad, the Jewish people hand out presents for all eight days. Even though some of the presents are only two-cent pieces of chocolate.

28 Purim is a Jewish holiday that commemorates the saving of the Jewish people from Haman, an Achaemenid Persian Empire official who was planning to kill all the Jews.

quitting a job, retirement, hitting the lottery, births, finishing radiation or chemo, circumcision (I never quite understood how this makes people hungry), paying off your house, buying a new house, engagement party, wedding, new relationship, renewing old friendships, your in-laws leaving town, waking up from a coma, coming-home party, beating-a-rap party, getting-out-of-jail party, going-to-jail party, going-away party, coming-out party, visiting kids in other cities, losing-weight party, divorce, freed from being kidnapped or held hostage, new dog, pool party, just-for-the-hell-of-it party, picnics, most dinners at home, Sunday-night family dinner out, before bedtime snack.

I get hungry just reading that list. I'm sure you can add another dozen to it. You get the point. Go anywhere you want, but make sure you're mentally fit to endure sensory overload. Like kryptonite is to Superman, food can buckle your knees. Good luck.

You're Too Thin

You tell me the truth, or go to your room. —My mother

I told her the truth, and she still sent me to my room. —Mark Schiff

Once you've lost a significant amount of weight, some people will compliment you and others will start saying disturbing things to you. The latter group think they are being helpful, and maybe they mean to be helpful, but they're not. They will come at you like pelicans dive-bombing for fish. I call some of them the "You're too thin brigade."

In the beginning of your weight loss journey, you're fragile. You need to stay strong, and most of all you need encouragement. Don't—and I repeat, don't—let these people drive you bonkers. Don't listen when they say "You're too thin—you've lost enough weight. Stop it already; it's not healthy. You need to put some meat back on your bones—you're starting to look sickly." Granted, there are people who lose too much weight and do make themselves sick. Those people need medical and psychological help. But that's not what I am talking about. I'm talking about people who just want to get down to the weight that's right and healthy for their body. There are no fat animals in nature. No fat squirrels. No fat deer. There can be naturally fat people, but you are probably not one of them. We can make ourselves fat, and we can make ourselves flat.

Also, where was the "You're too thin brigade" when I was overweight, sickly, and dying? I do mean dying. My blood pressure—the number one killer—was sky high. My cholesterol was high. Not a word when I was splitting my clothes at the seam or when I wore ties with pictures of cake on them. The brigade's excuse was they didn't say anything because they didn't want to hurt my feelings. Thank you, but worrying about hurt feelings could very easily spell the end of a person. How many people wish they'd said what they'd wanted to say, only to one day find it was too late? People need to hear the truth, and they need to hear it in a kind and loving manner. If you can't say it in a kind and loving manner, maybe say it anyway. If that doesn't work, you might have to punch them in the head, but get their attention. After that, let it go.

That's what happened to me. I had a real aha moment when someone didn't worry about my feelings. It was that moment with my old pal Dom Irrera at the Laugh Factory, when as I was walking to the stage, he whispered in my ear, "Schiff, you are so fat. Look how fat you are." Not a second later, I heard, "Please put your hands together for Mark Schiff." I turned and looked at Dom, then raced up onstage. My shirt was hanging out. No matter how many times I would tuck it in, it would untuck on its own. I could not button my shirt at the neck, and my face was Pillsbury Doughboy puffy. My belt was pinned on the first belt hole. I didn't feel good. I didn't look good. Little did Dom know that he'd just changed my life by telling me the truth. For some reason, his words went deep into my innermost self and shook me at my core. I've not been the same since. I can still hear and feel him standing behind me. I've told Dom more than once that I owe him for helping with my losing the weight. His push startled me.

By the way, Dom himself has packed it on. Hey, Dom, I love you, but lose the chins. I say that in a kind and loving manner.

When the truth hits you in the face, grab on to it and start walking on the new road that was paved just for you. Remember, there is no question that doesn't have an answer. Your job, if that's what you want, is to never quit looking for that answer.

4
FAMILY

....

Here Comes the Judge

Do not judge your fellow, until you have reached his or her place.
—Hillel, *Ethics of the Fathers*

Everyone hates to be judged, yet most of us do it.

My cousin Sarah died five days short of her thirty-fourth birthday. She left behind a twelve-year-old son, the father of the boy, and her divorced mother and father. She had a brother who'd killed himself a few years earlier and another brother with heart issues. Also, a close family member who is a pill addict. Sarah's life was not an easy one.

When Sarah was around nine years old, my wife and I offered to have her mother, who is my first cousin, and Sarah fly out from Long Island, all expenses paid, to sunny California to stay with us for a week. "Just come and have a good time," we said. The plan was for Sarah to go to Disneyland and see a taping of a TV show. The works. When Sarah and her mom exited the plane, I noticed that Sarah was holding a small bag over her face. It was an airline barf bag. Her mother said that Sarah was sick the entire flight.

Heading to our house, she sat with the bag over her face in the back of the car. When we got home, I showed Sarah to her room, where she immediately went to sleep. A few hours later, we woke her for dinner. Still carrying her barf bag and a little doll, Sarah said she wanted to go home. The rest of the night she sat watching TV and holding the same bag and the doll.

The next morning Sarah's mom told me Sarah didn't want to do anything except go back to the airport and go home. After trying to talk her out of leaving, we all agreed it would be best if they headed home. A part of me was glad to be rid of them. And as soon as Sarah heard I booked them a return flight for that evening, she perked up and had her first meal. She seemed like a completely different person. That's when my judgments of Sarah really began.

After sending them home, all I could think was how ungrateful she was, what a little brat. I made those judgments without knowing anything about what her life was like. I was convinced she was just a spoiled, ungrateful kid.

Over the next few years, except for sending her a birthday card with fifteen dollars in it, I don't remember much communication. When Sarah got older and Facebook became a big deal, I would read some of her very dark and depressing posts. She seemed like an incredibly sad person. Once again I judged, and I decided to stop following her on Facebook.

A few years later, her brother came out to Los Angeles and stayed with us for a few days. I helped get him into rehab at the Salvation Army. A few months later, he blew his brains out with a shotgun in a motel room. I called Sarah, sent her my condolences, and didn't talk with her much after that. Then I found out that she, my Jewish cousin, had found Jesus and was attending church regularly. Her Facebook posts were filled with crosses and Jesus quotations. More judgments on my part. I thought this girl must be so lost even though I knew truly little about her. I thought if only she'd stayed Jewish, blah, blah, blah. More judgments.

Then, a couple of years ago, I heard Sarah was sick with cancer. At this point I had almost zero communication with her, but I did have a trunkful of judgments and stories I'd made up about her in my head. I thought I knew everything.

I happened to be heading to New York, so I thought, *Why not call her and go visit? Isn't it a mitzvah to visit sick people?* I called and told her that I would like to visit. She was thrilled. She said, "I'd love to see you!" It had been at least twenty years since I'd last seen Sarah, and so I rented a car and drove out to Long Island.

Sarah was living in a tough neighborhood known for its MS-13 gang members. After my first visit, something happened to me. Most of my judgments seem to fall completely away. After visiting with her, I realized how sweet and wonderful this young lady was. She was a beautiful person with a great smile and a heart of gold. Her friends loved her. Her religion was giving her strength. She had a huge, poetic heart. She even had a motto: "Save the world."

I realized how wrong I had been about her. How so much of what I thought about her was based on misinformation. I'd made it all up. We visited a bunch more times, spoke on the phone, and exchanged email and Facebook messages. She was always so kind and so loving, and so fragile. Never, ever did she guilt me out with "Where have you been for the last twenty years?" or "Sure, now that I'm sick you drop by." She was simply happy to see her cousin, and I felt the same.

As Sarah's cancer progressed, she never complained. It just made her sad that she would soon have to leave her son, her friends, and her family. She said she knew she was in God's arms and would be protected. Even though she told me she didn't exactly know what that meant, it still gave her great comfort.

Little by little, as her pain increased, communication became less and less frequent. When she could talk, she apologized for not calling back sooner. I can honestly say that I felt nothing but love for Sarah since reconnecting with her. Without knowing it, she taught me that I needed to be much less judgmental, that what you think you know about someone is not the whole picture. Sarah was deep.

Then one day I got a call from Sarah's mom. She told me that according to Sarah's doctor, Sarah had six weeks to live. I immediately made a plane reservation to go to New York the following week. I figured I'd see Sarah one more time. I figured wrong, and Sarah died a few days later. After she died, I asked a cousin of mine about the funeral. He said there would be a wake and then a funeral the next day. I asked if Sarah would be buried. Then I decided to shut my mouth before I started judging all over again because her burial wasn't the way I would do it. Or the way the Jewish people would do it.

Sarah was buried on the day of her thirty-fourth birthday. I love you, Sarah. Please forgive me for judging you.

I Used to Have a Life

I remember when my three boys were all around ten years old, I was watching as they argued over the remote control. One of them yelled, "Hey, give me that, you little rat!" I remember thinking at the time that if this was any indication of how they would conduct themselves in their future business dealings or marriages, my kids would never get jobs and my wife and I would probably be forced to run a young-age home for unqualified children. I also realized that, more than likely, the next time I was going to be alone with my wife would probably be on my deathbed when she said to the kids, "Just give us a few minutes." However, even then I imagined either a ball bouncing off my heart monitor and hitting me in the head or my wife telling me she just realized she had to drive one of the kids to a friend's house for a swim lesson but she promised to see me in the next world.

I love my family, but who has this kind of time? As a comedian, I used to laugh at people who had to get up before the crack of noon. As a father,

I rose so early each day I could probably have applied for a grant from the Board of Farmers. I hated homework when I went to school, and I hate it twice as much now. The great thing about having kids is you get a chance to fail twice in life. Once when you're a kid, and the other when your offspring hand in homework assignments you helped them with the night before. I loved the look I'd get when I would tell my kids, "I don't understand the assignment."

What had I gotten myself into? I used to have such an exciting life. I had my own apartment in the middle of Manhattan. I had more girlfriends than most rock stars. I had pockets stuffed with cash for whatever I wanted. But as a parent I had one kid who wouldn't get out of bed without me using a crowbar, another son I imagined holding on to his blankie and sucking his thumb when he was standing under the chuppah,[29] and a third who had already figured out most of my tricks by the time he was in the fourth grade. And to top it all off, I had a wife who'd convinced me that her sleep was more important than my connubial needs. I used to have a life. Really, I did.

You may be asking: Mark, wasn't your life much fuller, richer, and ultimately closer to the way God wants you to live? That might be true, but the problem was that I was much too tired to enjoy most of it. And the other problem—a much deeper one—was that no one wanted to hear me complain. There was not one person in my home who was the least bit interested in how tired or stressed I felt. Oh, sure, my wife made believe she cared. "Honey, I'm sorry you are so tired, but could you do me a favor and mop the roof and rebuild the garage before you come to bed?"

There were those who told me that my old life was nothing but a selfish, self-centered, think-only-about-myself, feel-good, narcissistic existence. They were 100 percent right about that. Oh, to have the energy to relive those days just once more! To be able to sit in my New York apartment alone with the stereo blasting, a six-pack of beer, and a body

---

29 The chuppah is a tapestry attached to the tops of four poles. The word *chuppah* means "covering or protection" and is intended as a roof or covering for the bride and groom at their wedding. You know what they say—"No chuppah, no *shtupa*."

so thin I could sit and eat all the peanuts and Entenmann's Sour Cream Loaf Cake I wanted. To have two tickets to a Broadway show and a date with Miss Sweden, whose extent of the English language was "Yah, yah. Sure, sure" and whose only care was that I was happy and smiling at all times. Then again, with my luck, Miss Sweden would probably want to have kids with me.

What Is the Typical Jewish Mother?

I've heard people say, "My mother is the typical Jewish mother." I have an Italian friend who says his mother is the typical Italian mother. All groups have their typical everything. But what does this mean? There is the joke "What's the difference between a pit bull and a Jewish mother? The pit bull eventually lets go."

In my family now, my wife is not the typical Jewish mother. She doesn't hang on and nudge the kids to death like the stereotype goes. That's why they tend to confide in her more than they do me. I'm much more the typical Jewish mother than she is. I'm much more of a nudge than she is. That's because my mother was much more a typical Jewish mother than my wife's mother was. My mother must have asked me ten thousand times when I was going out if I was going to wear a sweater. And she always told me to take gloves. One time she actually said to me, "I hope you're smart enough to button up if it gets cold." My mother had a great fear that the temperature might drop fifty degrees at any given moment and a new ice age would be upon us.

She was also worried about me not being able to find lunch when I went out for the day. You would have thought I lived in the Sahara, with the nearest restaurant four thousand miles away. I grew up in New York

City, where the trains and buses ran 24-7. If I was hungry and didn't have enough for a meal, I could always go down to the subway and grab a large rat while waiting for the D train. She would tell me that my father and she would come and get me any time of the day or night if I couldn't get home. She always worried that I didn't have enough money to get home. "Do you have enough money to take the bus?" The bus was twenty-five cents. My mother was also a face reader. She would say, "Why the long face?" Something John Kerry's mother probably said to John all the time. "Why the long face, John?"

My mom also said she was dying at least once a week and would tell me, "One day I won't be here anymore." She was right about that, in the end. She's been gone more than twenty years. I miss her a lot. I went through a period where everything she did annoyed me. I guess I was the typical Jewish son.

As far as I can remember, all my aunts were also typical deviated-septum-nasal-blocked, extremely worried, fearful women. They were always scared that it was the day the big horror was coming down on them. None of my family were in the Holocaust; none suffered inhumane tragedies. They were just old-fashioned poor Jews from the Bronx who learned young that nail-biting and extreme worry were their destiny. If there were a game show called *Extreme Worry*, my family could have cleaned up. You'd have middle-aged Jewish women and men competing with each other about who has it the worst and who has the most heartache from their families, and, of course, who has had more operations and diseases. The bonus round could be "Guess how many stents Grandpa has in his chest?"

I was in therapy for years complaining about my overbearing mother and my weak father. I spent thousands to talk about how I got shafted and how I was misunderstood. It was never suggested by any of my therapists that I try to understand what my folks might have been going through. My mother would say to me, "Our life is not a picnic," but as a teenager I couldn't have cared less.

"You? What about me?" I'd shoot back. It was all about me. All I could do back then was wonder why these people had to annoy me so much.

What I did learn from all the therapy was that I like to complain a lot. Where I faulted my therapists was that they never gave me a solution. We never talked about forgiveness. They did a lot of head shaking and agreeing with me. I'm not saying all therapists are like this, but mine were. Here I am again, complaining.

Then one day I lucked out. If you live long enough, it's possible to change. Out of nowhere, I was gripped with something called empathy. It came on like a bad flu. All of a sudden I thought, *Gee, my parents probably didn't have it all that easy. It must have been hard on them.* Then I thought, *Maybe I wasn't such an easy kid to deal with.* When I look back at it, I admit I gave my parents a lot to worry about. Soon after this realization, I had another thought. *It must have been so hard on my parents when I moved from New York to Los Angeles.* I was an only child. My parents, not being big world travelers, must have felt a little like those parents in the old country when their kids left the Polish town of Grodziec to get on the boat to go to America. Somewhere deep down they probably thought it might be the last time they would ever see me.

And so, with that thought, the love my parents had for me came flowing through. The dam had broken. I finally realized, in my fifties, how much my parents really cared for me and how much they really loved me. I also think having my own kids made it easier on me to feel what my parents must have gone through. Hopefully, my kids won't have to wait until they're in their fifties to realize how much we love them, and it is more than they could imagine. But I still think Los Angeles gets cold at night and they should wear a sweater. I know I do.

The Miserable Side of Dining Out

Dining out has always cost a lot more money than eating at home, but these days it could cost a small fortune. I can make myself a dinner at home for about two or three dollars. At a restaurant, it might cost thirty dollars or more. I was in a vegan restaurant once and ordered a buckwheat shake and cage-free melon. When I got the recycled paper check, I wanted to start eating meat again. For me to take my family out to dinner at an upscale restaurant, I must either start a GoFundMe page or call my broker to sell some stock. I'm waiting for the day that they tell me that the meal is over my credit card limit.

With all the money I've spent in restaurants, I could have put an Olympic-size pool in my backyard. That's if I had a backyard. But as I live in Pico-Robertson, what I have is a few blades of grass and cement. I once timed a fly going from one end of my yard to the other. Two seconds, and he wasn't even out of breath.

Going to restaurants has gotten so complicated. You used to walk in and they gave you water, but in California in 2015 it became against the law to give diners a glass of water without them asking for it. And now if you ask for a plastic straw, you're labeled a porpoise killer. I don't remember anyone ever dying in a restaurant from drinking tap water, but I'm sure there have been plenty of heart attacks when the bill came. Today if you order tap water, they make you feel like you're drinking straight out of the human-remains-filled Ganges River in India. "Tap water? I hope you're not planning on having more children. May I suggest some bottled water?" It's eight dollars for a bottle of water, ten dollars if you want bubbles. It's cheaper to get a kid with a straw to blow bubbles into your water. And you can't take the water bottle home with you if you don't finish it. "I'll take a to-go cup for my water." It sounds so cheap.

Some of these upscale joints have a different person just for drinks. "Hi, I'm Ed. I'll be taking your drink order." My wife might order a glass of wine. Most places used to have a house wine. Now if you order the house wine, they treat you like you're some wino derelict who doesn't care if you destroy your liver. "Oh, the house wine? I'll go out back into the alley and grab the bottle from the homeless guy in his tent. You drink it straight out of the bottle in a paper bag. If I see a cigarette butt on the ground, I'll also grab that for you. Then I'll put you on the liver transplant list."

Whatever you do, don't ever ask them what wine they suggest. That's like asking a dog to suggest a nice steak. Once the waiter says to you, "We have a lovely . . ." the word "lovely" means expensive. How about if they are just honest with us? "We have a very, very expensive Cabernet Sauvignon, which you can get by the glass." This is a lie. You never get a full glass of wine. The restaurants sell it by the thimble. Maybe a third of a glass if you're lucky. They pour it like they're pouring liquid gold. This will ensure you'll need another three ounces in the next minute and a half.

Now, I don't know about your family, but when mine knows I'm paying for dinner, suddenly everyone acts like they have just gotten out of an Iranian prison and off a twelve-year hunger strike. They want soups and salads and appetizers. They are walking around the restaurant looking to see what other people are having that they can order. Going out with my family is like going out with a family of chimpanzees. They sit there with the menu in their hands, jumping up and down, making sounds. Bring on the bananas. Then when the appetizers come, if I try to take one, they look at me like I've lost my mind. I once had to beg them for a lettuce wrap. I get nauseous listening to them order ("I'll have two of these and three of those") while I'm sitting there adding up the bill in my head. By the time the waiter is ready for my order, I've lost my appetite. Worst of all, when we get outside, they want me to pay for valet parking. I give up.

All You Need Is Love? Maybe

Love is all you need, love is all you need, oh yeah, love is all you need.
—The Beatles, "All You Need Is Love"

Every relationship is unique unto itself. For seventeen years I watched my parents deal with each other, often through threats and shouting matches. I could never figure out how and why they stayed together, but they did. Not only did they survive some horrendous battles that I had a front-row seat for, but they ended up in love and happy with each other.

Eventually I realized that my parents loved me, but only through hard work did I realize I loved them. But "eventually" doesn't come for everybody. I was a lucky one. Some say love should be easy. For many, it is not. Do I wish they could have done better? For sure. Will there always be painful memories? Perhaps. When I was ten years old, it was on them. They had control of my reins. At my age today, it is on me.

I moved out at seventeen. If I could have, I would have left at four. With the amount of screaming that could be heard from our apartment, it is utterly amazing the cops were not at our house every other day. Even more amazing is that I am here to tell you about it. Know this, my friend: when my mother and father were alive, I never would have written and sent this out to you. If my parents had read this, it might have wounded them worse than they already were. But with them both gone and hardly any anger left in my heart, I felt it was time to tell a small part of my story. Reaching a place of acceptance for a person's flaws does not mean forgetting what was done. But even without forgetting, forgiving is very possible. Nobody could forgive them for what happened to me except me. I chose to take that step. I chose to have a good life. Happiness is a choice.

My childhood was a mess. Frightening and out of control. My mother was prone to extreme highs and lows. In the fifties and sixties, it was called high-strung. When in good spirits, she was sweet and loving, the best mother I could imagine. But when the shoe dropped and the timer ran out and darkness befell her, all hell would break loose. She could go from "I have some nice cake for dessert" to "This is no life for me."

We always lived in one-bedroom apartments that doubled as a mini–insane asylum. It was Mom, Dad, me, and for a while our cocker spaniel, Sandy. I loved that dog. I called her my sister. Without the dog, I might have felt totally unloved. I remember on more than one sad occasion holding the dog close to me and saying, "You love me, don't you?" Then pulling her even closer and crying bitterly into her warm skin.

When I was around six, I remember being told something about my mother being pregnant. I had no idea what it meant. She lost the baby somewhere in the seventh month. Having my own children now, I realize how extremely hard that loss must have been for my parents. Back then if you asked me my thoughts, I might have said, "Lucky kid." Because of complications, my mom almost lost her life. I remember my father seemed so worried that she might die.

At ten I sold illegal fireworks. At twelve I started smoking and stealing cigarettes from my parents. At fourteen I started drinking and drugging. I was also a liar. Remember how I told you about joining Excuses Anonymous? Well, here's where the roots of the lying started. Lying seemed to flow as easily from me as water from a garden hose. My first big lie was probably telling my mother that I loved her. It was painful to say "Mom, I love you." Buying her a Mother's Day card was almost impossible. None of the Mother's Day card sentiments fit the way I felt. I needed something like "Dear Mom, Happy Mother's Day. I hope you fall off a cliff." I was angry. I really should have given her a get-well card. What helped me continue on was that I knew I was a troubled soul. A lot of people are tied into knots and do not know it. Knowledge is power, and the fact that I knew I was troubled is a big part of what saved my life. But growing up, I had no one to tell it to.

I felt a virtual prisoner in my own body. At times, my body seemed to vibrate and hum. I feared most people, places, and things. My hands shook and I had a bad stomach. I failed practically every school subject. Worst of all, I lived in fear I might be murdered. By whom, you ask? Not by a stranger, but by my mother. Why would I think she wanted to kill me? Because she said so. She told me and my father over and over that she was going to kill us both. She threatened my life with everything from throwing me out a window to stabbing me. More than once during one of her frequent fits, she claimed that it was a good thing she did not own a gun, and she was right. People prone to depression should not own guns. Forget knives—some of them should not even own forks.

My father was of little help. He was a dear man but useless when it came to protecting me. Akin to providing food and shelter, protecting a child ranks at the very top. Sometimes it comes before food and shelter. What good is food and shelter if you are dead? But he feared her. She could be a runaway train, and he had no idea how to stop her.

It was not unusual for my father and me to be finishing dinner while my mother was grabbing dishes from the kitchen cabinets and throwing them against the wall. She destroyed so many sets, yet I never remember her buying or unpacking new ones. One evening while my mother was banging pots and pans off the walls, my father told me not to worry, that soon she would cool down. There was never a cooldown though. Only a burnout. Eventually she would collapse into a migraine and lie in bed for a day or two. I would keep bringing her fresh, cold washcloths for her head and asking how she was. She was mostly silent during these periods. Poor lady.

When my mother was off and running, my father had the capacity to continue to eat his meal until her rage became too painful for him to endure. Many times it was so bad that he would get his coat and start to walk out. A few times when she heard me asking him to take me with him, all hell would break loose. She would tell him that he'd better say goodbye now because if he did walk out, she would kill me and herself and that when he returned, he would find us both dead on the floor in a pool of blood. At ten years old, I stood with my hands folded in front of me, watching and listening to all of this. Drinking it all in. This was my relationship class. The well that holds pain seemed almost bottomless. But it was not. One day it would overflow. He would beg her to stop, as he put it, "all this craziness."

My father had enormous powers to block out her words. Many nights as he put on his pajamas, she would threaten to slit his throat after he fell asleep. Even with that threat hanging over his head, he could sit in bed sharing a pint of butter pecan ice cream with the dog while he watched TV. When finished, he would put the bowl in the sink for her to wash, then climb into bed, face the wall, and conk out, perhaps secretly praying this was the night he would be put out of his misery.

When my father would attempt to leave, my mother would block the door. He would grab her, pulling her from in front of the door, always trying not to cause her pain. I was a pawn. She would look at my father and say, "You're not sticking me with him." Sometimes upping the ante, she would rip off her blouse and occasionally pull hair out of her head or even bite herself and leave teeth marks in her bloody skin. All four and a half feet of me would stand watching it all. These were my parents. They were my mentors.

I now know that she was sick, he was sick, and I became a sick child. But I did not know that then. How could I? This was the only life I knew. Once he was out the door, she would follow him into the apartment-complex hallway. The halls were dimly lit, and there were at least six other apartments on our floor. As he headed down the stairs, at the tip-top of her lungs, she would start screaming obscenities: "You'll find us both fucking dead when you get back." "Go run off to your fuckface whore." "If you leave, I promise you I will kill him and myself." All I could hear as my dad barreled down the steps was the sound of his feet slapping against the slabs of marble. And as each step became less audible it left me feeling more alone and scared.

Our apartment door was made of heavy metal. When Mom came back in and slammed the door with all her might, everything in the house reverberated, including me. I watched as she locked the door then latched the chain, mumbling that she was never letting him back in again. Alone now, just the two of us, not knowing if my life that had barely begun was about to end, I stood waiting to see what was going to happen.

The most frightening was when she would go into the kitchen, pull out a large, serrated carving knife, walk over to me, point the tip of the knife to her heart, look straight into my eyes, and then tell me to push the knife through. She told me she had nothing to live for. I'd say, "You have me!"

"No, I don't," she would say. "Please kill me."

I begged her to stop. She told me she knew I wanted her dead, that it would be best for all of us if she were gone. I cried my eyes out, saying it wasn't what I wanted. "Yes, it is," she would say. Did she really mean for me to kill her? I will never know. The truth is that she was partly right. I thought about stabbing her many times. How could I not after what she continually put me through? It would be abnormal not to think that. It all seemed so endless. When you are a little kid, you think this will go on forever. Truth is, if you do not get help, it just might.

She never did try to kill herself, or us. It was words from a woman who God knows why or what was wrong with her but at certain times would go almost stark raving mad. My mother was ill, but nobody ever said it. Maybe these days there is a pill for that. Back then, there was next to nothing.

My parents were married for thirty-nine years. I think my father understood early on that if he left her, she may not have survived, that she was too fragile and scared to be on her own. In a strange way, it worked out for them. But if my mother had gotten the help that is available to people today, she would have had a better, happier life. It's not that she didn't love us. It's that much of the time she thought we didn't love her. She was so often living in her head and in fear. She was both prisoner and warden. I have no doubts about how much she cared for my father and me. I'm sad when I think of what she missed out on and what might have been. So much opportunity for her having happiness was lost.

The last few years of their marriage, they seemed very much in love. Perhaps to some degree, the anger had burned away. I would see them holding hands during evening walks that I took with them when I was in New York. They cared about each other. They needed each other. They protected each other. When we would go out to dinner, I could see and feel the love they had for each other. It was something that I had never been able to see before. Thank God they had it then, even if it was for a short amount of time. When my father died of cancer, my mother slipped into a depression that lasted for almost the entire ten years she lived after his death.

Years later and with help, having my own family helped me to see my parents more as the wounded souls they were and not just the crazy people I thought they were. Forgiving my father was easier than forgiving my mother. After my father died, my wife and I helped support Mom as best we could. I did my best to be a good son. I have been able to feel deep sadness for what I know she missed out on in life.

I Saw Ma

My father was not one to tell strange and bizarre stories. When my dad and I would come home from a day of fishing in Sheepshead Bay, for example, he never told my mother about the "big one that got away." Even when I was small, I don't remember him ever reading to me or telling me a bedtime tale. Truth is, it never bothered me. Not everyone is great at tucking kids in goodnight. If I got my kiss on the forehead or the lips, that was enough to make me feel protected.

My father was a truck driver. He drove mostly in Manhattan and New Jersey. A few summers when I was off from school, he used to let me ride up top with him. Sitting ten feet up off the ground was the best. He was a genius at squeezing the truck past double-parked cars in the middle of Manhattan in what looked like an impossible situation. He would yell, "Mark, pull in the mirror! Stick your head out the window and let me know if I'm getting too close."

With my head sticking out like a German shepherd, I loved yelling back, "You're good, Dad."

"Now pull your head in and sit back."

His major talent was going to and coming from work. On Friday nights, he would hand over his paycheck to my mom and spend most of the weekend trying to catch up on sleep so he could begin again on Monday morning.

Working in Manhattan, he must have seen things. Everyone sees things, but for some reason he chose to never speak of those things. He was a straight-shooting, blue-collar, Marlboro-smoking, black-coffee-drinking working stiff, and except when he was laid up in the hospital or dying of cancer, I never knew him to miss a day of work. That's what fathers do, I guess. They don't miss work. They die trying to stay alive.

He also did not drink or do drugs, and I believe he was straight with my mother and did not fool around. The one time he did get into trouble was when he was caught carrying an unlicensed pistol. As far as I know, he only used it to practice at a gun range. The police took it and fined him. I'm sure he told his share of lies, just like everyone, but as far as I remember, I never caught him in one. Most of our conversations were short—mostly him asking me how I was and me not telling him.

Then one day, at his normal time of 7:00 p.m., he walked through the front door. After an hour and a half on the Long Island Expressway, he usually headed straight for the bathroom, where he would wash away ten hours of work filth with his bar of Lava soap. As usual, he looked tired, but this tired was different. This tired seemed to have aged him since morning. It was accompanied by the absence of any color in his face. Looking drawn and pale, he removed his bomber jacket and sat down at the dining room table. The nine-bulb chandelier hanging over the table made him look that much more pallid. Just by looking at him, my mother and I could tell something seemed wrong. He seemed scared. Something had happened. He looked bone-shaken.

Elbows on the table and his face in his hands, he started to cry, and I mean *cry*. The only other time I ever saw my father cry was when his mother died. (My grandmother Grace was somewhere in her sixties when her soul skipped town. Her entire life was spent in small, rusted-tap-water rented Bronx apartments, where most of these buildings already seemed old when they were new.)

My mother sat across the table from my dad. She tapped her fingers five times before she spoke. I stood with my hands clasped in front of me, too afraid to sit. I just looked at him in silence. My mother said, "Julie, what happened?" He just sat shaking his head from right to left as if he was trying to shake whatever happened out of his mind. Then he blurted it out.

"I saw her."

"Saw who?" my mother asked.

"I saw my mother today."

"What do you mean, you saw your mother?"

"I saw her walking as I was driving my truck. I saw her walk into Alexander's on Queens Boulevard." At one time, Alexander's was a moderately priced department store in New York. We shopped there a lot.

"What do you mean, you saw your mother walk into Alexander's? How is that possible?" she asked.

He said, "I don't know. I was driving my truck and I saw her walk in. I pulled the truck over, jumped out, and ran into the store after her. There she was, a few feet in front of me. I've never done anything like this in my life. I grabbed her arm. She stopped walking. I looked her right in the face.

It was her. It was her. I said, 'Ma?' She just looked at me. 'Ma?' I then asked, 'Are you my mother?'

"She pulled away and then spoke. She said, 'I must go now.' She turned and walked toward the entrance to the store where I came in. I couldn't move. It was as if my feet were planted into cement. I just stared at her walking out. Before leaving, she turned, looked at me, half smiled, then turned back and left. She seemed sad. She walked back out onto the street using the revolving door. I was now free to move. I ran out after her. I could not have been more than two seconds behind her. When I got outside and looked around, she was gone. The street was completely empty of people. Except for my truck and some cars driving by, there was nothing."

My father then looked at my mother and said, "I saw my mother." He looked at me and said the same thing. "I saw her. It was her. I know it." He then rested his head onto his folded arms, not unlike what kindergarteners do when they take a nap. He took a big sigh, and then another.

Monday morning, as usual he went to work, and this was never mentioned again. His way was to not bring up anything painful. He kept his emotions close to the vest. But the next week, he placed a framed photo of his mother on the windowsill.

My father's been gone for many years now. Maybe one day I'll be lucky enough to see him again, if even for a few seconds.

Traveling with My Father

When I found out my dad was dying of cancer, I spent a lot of time in New York with him and my mom instead of Los Angeles, where I was living at the time. Road comics have no office, so New York became the base I booked myself out of.

My dad loved my act. He thought I was the funniest person in the world. I guess you are the funniest person in the world if someone thinks you are. My parents came to see me dozens of times before my father died in 1988. He would come and see me wherever I was doing a show, and he always got dressed up. I would say, "Dad, you don't have to wear a sport coat. I'm at the Comic Strip, not the Copa."

"I don't care if I'm going out on a Saturday night with your mother. I'm not going to look like a slob."

He asked me to do certain bits about my mother. He loved it when I talked about how they'd been married so long that she'd sucked the brain out of his head.

"She loves when you talk about her. Do me a favor. Do that thing about her cleaning the house." My dad really loved my mom. He was just so proud of her, and with me being an only child, we were his life.

I remember that my dad had just gotten out of hospice and they sent him back home to die. The night he came home, I had a show to do. I said, "Dad, maybe I should stay home instead."

He wouldn't hear of it. "You go and be funny." I did.

About three days later, I had this gig about two hours away in upstate New York. That afternoon we were all sitting at the dining room table when my dad said in the weakest of voices, "Can I come with you tonight? I'd really like to see your show." I knew what he was saying: I really want to see your act one more time before I die.

I asked my mom what she thought. "If you think you can handle him, then fine."

My dad was very weak, but he could go a short distance if you helped him. I said, "Yeah, I can do it."

That night as we were leaving, my mom said, "You boys have a nice time tonight. I've got things to do here at home. Call me when you get there." So off we headed to my gig. It was a cold winter night, and a light snow fell for most of the drive. We didn't talk much on the way up. As I remember, my dad slept most of the way anyway. I kept looking at him as he slept in the car. I cried most of the way up, but that was OK. I was with my dad.

When we got to the hotel parking lot, we noticed that it was empty except for three or four cars. "Hey, Marko," my dad said, "can I drive around the lot?"

My dad loved to drive. He was the one who'd taught me to drive just a few years earlier in the empty parking lots of New York on Sunday mornings. He'd done every single bit of the driving for the thirty-nine years he was married to my mother. She never drove once. Now he was asking me to let him drive. "Sure, Dad."

I got him around to the driver's seat, and for two minutes he drove very slowly around the lot. "That's great," he said.

I helped him park, and we checked into the hotel and went to our room. It was still early, so I helped him unbutton his pants and we got the bathroom done, and then he took a nap. I then called my mother, told her we were safe, and she started crying. "Take good care of him. I love him."

I said, "I love him too, and I also love you."

At about 8:00 p.m. we went over to the club, which was attached to the hotel. Before we went in, my dad said, "Thank you for taking me."

"You're welcome," I said. "Thank you for being a great father." Then he asked me to do the routine about my mother that he always liked. I did them all for him.

A few weeks later, he died. About a year later, my mother came to see me work. On the way to the club, she asked me to do the routines about my father. I kissed her on the head and said sure. I also did the ones about her because I knew he would have wanted to hear them.

The Orphan

My wife and I were on a walk one day when I mentioned to her that if my father were still alive it would be his ninety-fourth birthday and that when he died many people fell out of touch with my mother. I then said I remembered learning that the Torah says, "You shall not cause any pain to a widow or orphan" (Exodus 22:21). It's taught that their pain and loneliness are great, so you're asked not to forget about them.

My wife said, "I don't know any orphans."

"Yes you do. Me."

She then said, "Oh. I suppose I am one too."

Though my parents have been gone for decades, that reminder that I am an orphan hit me like a sledgehammer. I felt lonely and, in a profound way, deeply missed my parents. Loss is a big part of life. Ages nine to ninety, everyone experiences it. I remember when my friend's father died, I asked, "Are you OK?"

He said, "I'm built for this." He was, but not everyone is.

Hours after our conversation, the feeling of emptiness and lonesomeness still lingered. The thought that I am an orphan is not a new thought. I've had it many times. But with this new awakening, I could almost feel their presence as if they were speaking to me. I almost felt enveloped by them. I could feel how they also miss me. I could feel how badly they would love to put their arms around me and kiss me and how I would love to do the same back.

If I could have a wish, it might be to see my parents and hug them like I never hugged them before. I owe that to them. To tell them how much I love them and how grateful I am they are my parents. To let them know how sorry I am for the pains and worries I caused and how scared I must have made them when they would try to reach out to me and I was not available, physically or emotionally. How quick they were to forgive and just wish me well. That is not something to take lightly. You don't get many of those people in one lifetime. How sad they must have been when I was depressed and could not be pulled out of my doldrums. Underneath all the pain—me not understanding them, them not understanding me, the out-of-control arguments—was a deep love they had for me.

As I got older, little by little I realized how much I loved them. As parents to three boys, my wife and I spent many nights talking about our kids and how we wished we could fix their problems. If my parents had had the choice, they never would have orphaned me. They would have been happy to stay put and spend time and eventually rock my grandchildren to sleep. But that is not how life plays out. People come and go. One day the last pitch is thrown, and then you walk off the mound. How and when life starts and ends are not up to us. Every tear is a broken heart. You learn the meaning of powerlessness when someone you love is sliding away.

My job is to love, respect, and care for people when they are here. The last few years of my parents' lives, I did better than the previous ones. I once heard a woman who was giving a talk on sobriety say that the more she tried to stop her mother from the ultimate slide, the more that struggle was killing them both. But how long people live is God's business, not mine. With my father, there came a day when I just surrendered him over. I remember one rainy afternoon not being able to distinguish my tears from the raindrops while walking the noisy New York streets of Greenwich Village. I said to myself, "God, he is yours." Then I asked him to show me what it was he wanted from me.

I didn't know the answer then, but I know it now. It's simple. God wants me to be happy simply because it's what my parents wanted for me. It's what their parents wanted for them and it's what we want for our kids. As my mother used to say, "Who can argue with that?"

5
FRIENDS

....

The Importance of Friends

My parents didn't have many friends. So when my father died, my mother had almost no one to talk to. I would call her and say, "Who did you talk to today?" Her answer most of the time was, "No one."

Mom lived by herself in Florida, and I lived in Los Angeles. When a person you love is thousands of miles away and in pain, the phone does little to alleviate it. Each time I hung up with her, I felt stunned. Two of her sisters lived near her, but after a lifetime of arguing there was little communication between them. I tried to get her to join a senior club or a temple. She always had an excuse. Her only visitors were the bugs trying to get in through her screen windows. Her shades were drawn, and a musty humid Florida damp permeated her apartment. Most afternoons she would sit in her rocker watching talk shows. I can't imagine how lonesome her evenings must have been.

One morning, we got a call that they found her dead on the floor of her apartment. She had been like that for a day or so. Was her cause of death natural? She had been depressed for years. The coroners said it was a heart attack. I choose to believe them. The other possibility, that she did it to herself, is too painful to conjure.

In her younger days, Mom had a real warm, outgoing side to her. She loved movies, theater, reading, and music. She was also a terrific knitter. When I was a kid, some Sundays, if she needed yarn, we would all go down to the Lower East Side of Manhattan around Essex and Delancey to get it. Then at home I would hold a skein of yarn between my hands while she rolled it into a ball so she could later do her knitting. I loved doing that with her, and for her. She made the best sweaters. Putting one on, I could feel the love that went into it. Some fifty-plus years later, I still occasionally wear a few of the sweaters.

But all that seemed to fade after my father's death. I saw the way my mom's life was and how it ended, and I realized how important it is to have friends and to fight off loneliness. We are born alone, and we die alone. In our hour of greatest agony, we're also alone. How especially important it is to have someone to talk to and spend time with.

I have a great family and many friends, but there are days I feel all alone. I know I'm not, but that doesn't stop me from feeling that way. Don't ever forget that *feelings aren't facts*. New Yorkers will tell you it's easy to feel alone in a crowd of ten thousand.

I accept the fact that loneliness is part of the human condition. Everyone feels it sometime or another. When you get a doctor's report that you didn't expect. When someone close to you dies. When you have a fight with your child and they refuse to talk to you. When your spouse threatens to walk out. When you wake up at two in the morning and think that you'll never find someone to share your life with. When you have to put your dog down.

The consensus is that having friends is good for your health and helps fight loneliness, so here are a few things I do. I belong to a synagogue and I go regularly. People know me, say hello, and seem genuinely glad that I'm there. That helps. For the last fifteen years, my wife and I have also belonged to a Shabbas potluck group that meets at a different house once a month. That helps. I meet with men friends at least twice a week. That helps. I have a job that I love doing and friends who respect what I do. That helps. And I call someone almost every day to see how he or she is doing. By checking in on someone else, you get a chance to stop thinking about yourself and your problems, even if it's for only five minutes.

If you have friends, be grateful you have someone to talk to and laugh with. If you don't, get some. It's not that hard. You know that person you've been telling for years that you need to get together and have lunch with? Get together with them. There are plenty of people waiting for you to call them or knock at their door. You're never too old to make friends.

Get a Couple

My wife and I spend time with many other couples and mostly find it rewarding. It's not always easy for a married couple to find another couple where both husbands and wives all get along. We're lucky to have many such friends.

There are a million reasons why people do or don't like each other. But let me tell you about this one couple, June and Yosy Schames, and why I think we all get along. First of all, we all enjoy hanging out and doing things together. We never feel like they are squeezing us in, like we are on the "we owe them dinner" list. In a way, it's very reminiscent of friends when you were a kid. It's not complicated like many adult relationships can get.

We've traveled with them to Israel, Canada, Europe, Alaska, and Mexico and look forward to our next trip. One of their great qualities is they say yes to practically everything. If we are on a trip and we say, "Let's meet in the lobby at 9:00 a.m.," they're in the lobby at five to nine.

Last year, June suggested we see a show called *Shen Yun*. It was $160 a ticket and was so bad, we left halfway through. A few weeks later, I suggested we see a play called *Happy Days*, which was worse than *Shen Yun*. Guess what? We are still going to plays together and still laughing about it.

As is true in a lot of Jewish marriages, the husband, Yosy, makes no decisions about what show he's going to and when. I used to ask him first if they wanted to join us. His answer was always, "Call my wife." The day before we are going out I'll say to him, "See you tomorrow at the play." Like a three-year-old, he'll say, "Oh, good. I'm going to a play. I didn't know that."

Here are a few other reasons I think this relationship works. The women enjoy talking to each other and doing things together with and without us husbands. Many nights they talk on the phone, which means that's thirty minutes when I won't say something stupid and cause a fight. Also, Yosy and I are proof that two men can get together and not use the s-word. We never, ever talk sports. We never sit down and watch a game. What we like doing is telling each other jokes, and many times we discuss deep subjects. We both love learning things. We never talk about women other than our wives and rarely gossip, and we enjoy discussing family and children.

June and Yosy, like my wife and I, are passionate about Judaism. With Yosy, he likes to teach, and I like to learn. When we go on a trip together, we always bring a Sefer (holy book) to learn with and discuss. The wives are also included in that (which I know thrills them to no end, but we married good sports).

But most of all, we like to laugh and make each other laugh. That really helps. We have had some incredible belly laughs where we thought we might have to call a medic if we kept howling much longer. We were driving in Italy a few years ago when we got to a tollbooth and for some reason we were laughing so hard the guy in the booth thought we were laughing at him. He would not lift the tollbooth arm and let us through until we stopped laughing. That caused us to laugh even more. We sat there for almost five full minutes laughing while the tollbooth man looked the other way. Every time someone said "Stop laughing," we started laughing even harder.

Maybe most importantly, we like being with good people, which they are. Twice a week, for years, June and Yosy have opened their home to whoever wants to come and learn Torah. They also supply dinner for anyone who comes. For years they've delivered food with their children for Tomchei Shabbos, an organization that gives free food to people who may not have food for Shabbas. June and Yosy also opened their hearts by moving Yosy's elderly mother into their home. Years later she moved to her daughter Henny and son-in-law's home. Everyone in the family treated her with the utmost respect and love until she died.

And of course with June and Yosy there's trust. You have to know that if push comes to shove, your friends are there for you.

When you find a couple like this, hang on to them. They are rare. I hope you find that couple for yourself, or you can borrow ours, but not for too long.

Abu Mustafa Calls Me His Brother

These days, we all know how difficult it is for a Republican and a Democrat to be friends. But how about a Palestinian Muslim and a Beverlywood practicing Jew? Oy gevalt.

One morning, while I was saying my prayers, my phone rang. I saw the call was from my friend Abu Mustafa, or Maz. Maz is a good guy and a Palestinian Muslim who practices his faith. When Maz calls me his brother, he hits his heart with his hand.

I once heard a radio talk show host talk about something he called "black and white dinners." He was touching on how, on a personal level, many black people and white people don't have friends of the other race, and the talk show host had the idea that if you get together for dinner and get to know one person from a group you normally don't socialize with, then you can't stereotype the whole group. Before I met Maz, it wasn't that I thought all Palestinian Muslims were bad, I just didn't know any. So, for now, Maz is my one.

First thing you should know is that Maz and I never talk about Israel, conflict, occupation, or war. Maz has his strong beliefs, and I have mine. I'm sure there is much we don't agree on. Plus, he's 6'4" and I'm 5'9", so we both verbally agreed not to venture into that area. Are we ostriches with our heads in the sand? I think not. Like in marriage, you learn there are some red flag areas where you just don't go.

Maz and I met through a mutual friend, and we found we had a few important things in common. For instance, Maz and I have both written plays, Maz and I are both on a spiritual journey, and Maz and I have both married a Jewish woman (and both lived to talk about it). I believe (and hope Maz agrees) that we have a mutual respect for each other. Maz knew I was a Jew long before I knew he was a Palestinian. Then one day I found out and I thought, *This is interesting. I have a Palestinian Muslim friend.* Because I didn't prejudge him but instead got to know him first, we got closer.

One of my friends, on many occasions, has made terrorist jokes about Maz in front of Maz. He says things like, "If Maz sells you a car, get a mirror on a long stick and check underneath before you pull off the car lot." As it happens, I bought my Toyota Prius from Maz, and it was the most pleasant car-buying experience of my life.

Maz seems to handle these terrorist jokes better than I do. I did do a joke about Maz at my birthday roast. I said, "In Maz's honor, I asked the manager of the restaurant to remove the 'Occupied' sign from the bath-room door." The joke killed. I admit I did this joke at my roast, but I'm not a fan of doing terrorist jokes at Maz's expense. I don't think it helps my relationship to keep bringing up suicide bombers. Just like I wouldn't like it if Maz did cheap-Jew, big-nose, and Israeli-bulldozer jokes.

When my sons Jacob and Eli had their bar mitzvahs, I invited Maz to my shul for the event. Maz came and wore a kippah. When Maz was in a play that he wrote and one that he starred in, I attended both. We also did a Showtime Special together called *Bridging the Gap*. It was about how humor brings together Jews and Muslims, two groups that ordinarily would not mix.

It's not uncommon for Maz to wish me nice things on Jewish holidays and for me to wish him an easy Ramadan fast. It's the only Muslim holiday I know. But whatever happens to be going on in the Jewish-Palestinian world, we don't talk about it.

So, can you really be friends with someone whom you so disagree with on ideology? The answer is yes. Maz has shown up for the Jewish people in ways some of my Jewish friends have not. We had a sick friend, a Jewish man named Jack Lavitch, who spent his last years in a nursing home and hospital. Maz was there for him. When I'm going through things, Maz has been there for me to talk to. Maz is a good man. Maz calls me his brother. We need more Mazes in the world.

And so, my brother, assalamu alaikum,[30] and to you and your family, shalom aleichem.[31]

The Big Snub

As I was leaving the theater once, Byron, a fellow comedian, approached me. He's the type of guy who never rubs people the right way. You'll see why.

Mistake number one: I asked him how he was. Without even a hello, he asked me if I remembered when he and a mutual acquaintance, a guy

---

30 *Assalamu alaikum* is a greeting in Arabic that means "Peace be upon you." It is a term uttered very often when a Jew is building a new home in Antarctica.

31 *Shalom aleichem* means "Peace unto you." There will be no justice and no peace if you go back to a deli and try to return a pound of belly lox because it's too salty. Then, instead of peace be with you, you're told, "You can drop dead."

named James, came backstage to say hello in Las Vegas. I mumbled, "Sure do." Then he told me that James said I really hurt his feelings. I asked, "What did I do?" And he said, "James said you snubbed him."

"Snubbed how?"

"I don't know," Byron said. "He felt snubbed by you."

That James would have felt this way seemed strange to me because, of the two of them, if I had to pick one to snub, it would have easily been Byron. I said, "Give me James's number so I can apologize."

Byron said, "Forget it. It was no big deal."

I pushed back. I said, "To me, it is important. If I snubbed him, I owe him an apology." He then squinched his face so he looked slightly like a shar-pei and with his fat fingers AirDropped me James's info. We bumped knuckles and went off into the frosted night.

Driving home, I tried to replay backstage Las Vegas. No matter how hard I tried to recall the snubbing, I came up as flat as a can of Coke left open for two days.

The next day I called James. Righting a wrong excites me. Before Las Vegas, I had not seen James in over twenty years. Even back then, we weren't close. We knew each other from the comedy clubs. I got his voice mail and left my number. Two days later we spoke.

"Hey, James."

"Hey, Mark. What's up?"

Before getting to it, I asked him where he was living. He said in Las Vegas with his second wife. I wondered if it had been wife number five if he would have mentioned that number. I told him I'd bumped into Byron and then said, "I snubbed you, so I'm calling to apologize for the snub."

He said, "Byron said you snubbed me?"

"Yeah, and I'm sorry."

And here's why people hate Byron. James then said, "Absolutely not. You did not snub me."

"Are you sure?"

"One hundred percent. No snub." Stupid me, but I asked why Byron would say that. James chuckled. "Byron's a pot stirrer. He loves upsetting people."

I said, "In all my years, I'd never before been accused of being a snubber."

Now is where I should have ended the conversation. That was mistake number two. Instead, I asked, "So how are you?"

With a deep breath, he said, "Not so good."

"What's up?" I asked. Mistake number three.

"You sure you want to know?" James asked.

"Yes, of course," I responded.

And we are now on mistake number four. For the next thirty minutes, I heard about his rectal polyps, mini-strokes, blood loss, heart stents, and sex problems with wife number two. Around four minutes into this conversation I already knew I wanted off the phone. But I was trapped like a rat. How could I tell him I wanted off? How could I graciously remove myself from this call? If I told him I wanted to hang up, he might think I was snubbing him, and since I swore on a stack of Bibles that I was not a snubber and never had been a snubber, I was stuck. Snubbing him now was completely out of the question.

He'd been talking for thirty minutes, and I was slipping into a coma. Then when he said he was coming to Los Angeles and would love to get lunch and stay with me for a day or two, my head almost exploded. I was so done with this guy. Part of me now wished I were a professional snubber. Then I could have brushed and snubbed in a flick of the wrist. He now owned me. I was like a chess piece for him to move anywhere he wanted. That rat Byron ruined my life. I should have snubbed him outside the theater.

How about this? Now I hate myself for not being a snubber. I thought, *My only way out now is if James miraculously dies.* Even then, I'd feel obligated to go to the funeral or chance being labeled the ultimate snubber.

Don't Ever Quit on Yourself

So much of my life has been a series of things dropping out of the sky, after which, somehow, the right person picked it up and handed it to me. People have been kind to me when they did not have to.

This was one of those times. One night, after I got offstage at a local comedy club in Los Angeles, a young guy in his midtwenties with a nice, happy face approached me. His name was Donovan Cook. Donovan told me he was a huge fan of my comedy and that he was in the process of creating an animated cartoon series for Hanna-Barbera. Hanna-Barbera was composed of pioneers of TV animation, responsible for some of the longest lasting and most beloved cartoon characters of all time. I personally enjoyed their shows so much that I could often be found lying on my stomach on the living room floor, watching for hours at a time. Donovan said he thought that my voice was perfect for one of the two leads in a show they were developing. I thanked him and then asked the name of the show. He said, "*2 Stupid Dogs*."

The show *2 Stupid Dogs* was about two unnamed dogs—neither of whom, as the title states, is highly intelligent—and their everyday misadventures. These dogs loved each other and would do anything for each other, especially if there was food involved. Donovan said they were called Big Dog and Little Dog and he had me in mind for Little Dog.

I said, "Great. When can I audition?" Nobody just hands anyone a starring role without first hearing him or her read. Even big stars must audition. It would be stupid to assume otherwise.

But after all, this was *2 Stupid Dogs*. Even though I don't really do voices in my act and had never done a voice-over in my life, Donovan said no audition was necessary. "It's yours if you want it." If it's meant to be, there is no stopping it. This was meant to be.

How long does it take you to snap your fingers? That's how fast I had an animated show. Voice-over people work their whole lives hoping for a break like this.

A few weeks later, I was given a call time to meet at a recording studio in North Hollywood. Up until that day, I had never been in a soundproof studio; this was my maiden voyage into a recording studio. The plan was to tape the first episode. Donovan introduced me to Big Dog, who was being played by Brad Garrett. Not too long after *2 Stupid Dogs* aired, Brad would costar in *Everybody Loves Raymond* as Ray Romano's brother.

The first day, Brad, a few other actors, and I were waiting to start. Some people were sitting on high stools, while others were standing. Each actor had a music stand to place his or her script on and a microphone placed about an inch from the person's face. A few feet above our soundproof studio floor was a soundproof booth with a giant glass window. Behind the glass were Donovan, sound people, writers, and maybe an exec or two. In my shaking hand I held the script. I'd highlighted all my lines in yellow. The yellow matched the streak down my back.

Out of the speakers from the booth, Donovan welcomed us. He wished us luck and thanked us for being part of this wonderful new project. This was a big deal for Donovan. It was not easy to sell a show, and it was important to him; he had worked hard to get this off the ground. He called to us that there were two minutes until we would start.

All the other actors were chatting away while I was sweating. They seemed to know each other. Most of them, if not all of them, were professional voice-over people. They were pros and champing at the bit to get going. I, however, knew nothing about how to do any of it. I didn't know how to create the dog's voice and, once I did, how to keep doing the same voice over and over. I was way out of my league. All I knew was that I had the script and, in less than a minute, I would have to invent something out of thin air. But what? How? I thought, *You're in trouble now*.

Donovan said, "OK, good luck, everyone. Let's go." Above the recording studio door, a red light came on. When the red light was on, nobody came in or went out of the studio. When it was on, we were taping. I don't remember who had the first lines, but what I do remember is that after I read a few of my lines, taping came to a screeching halt.

From the booth, Donovan said, "Mark, by yourself, would you please take those lines again?" I quickly read the lines into the microphone.

"Please wait until the red light is back on," he said.

About five minutes later, Donovan announced we should relax for a few minutes. I saw through the glass that they were all talking about something. I knew that something wasn't right, and it was probably me. While we were waiting, one of the voice-over actors said, "Mark, have you ever done this before?"

The room became dead quiet, and all were waiting to hear my answer. "No, never."

Then someone else said, "How did you get this job?"

"Donovan likes my voice."

I don't know who, but one of them made a gagging sound (like if you stuck your finger too far down your throat). Donovan was then back on the speaker, "OK, everyone. Let's pick up from where we left off."

The red light was back on taping, and taping resumed. Three minutes later, taping was again halted. Through the speaker, Donovan asked me to meet him in the hall. I said to the group, "I'll be right back." As I went out the door, I heard a chuckle. I'm sure they were thinking what I was thinking: we will never see this guy again.

In the hall, Donavan said, "I know you're nervous. That's OK. But I know you can do this. Relax and be patient. This will be fine. I love your voice and you're a funny guy. Don't worry."

After he gave me one of the kindest, most reassuring talks, I took a deep breath, let it out, and thought, *He's nuts. I'm quitting. I can't take this.*

The rest of that day went even worse. Every word out of my mouth was horrible. I could see the actors looking at me like I had not taken a bath in a month. And I know they were thinking that, because of me, this was going to fail and they would all be out of work. Every time I looked at the booth, everyone in it looked like he or she had just been diagnosed with a rare, incurable disease.

Generally, when these things are going well, everyone in the recording booth seems to be laughing or at least looking happy. Not that day. I was completely thrown and mortified. My head throbbed so badly I thought I was having an aneurysm.

The second I walked into my apartment that night, I phoned my friend and mentor Hubert Selby Jr., who was from the dregs of Brooklyn. He was also known as Cubby, or Cubbynanda. Cubby was a terrific novelist whose books were made into great movies. I told him about my disastrous day and then said, "Cubby, I'm going to quit. I can't take it."

He reached up to heaven for just the right words and replied, "Don't quit. Let them fire you. Don't fire yourself. You're not the boss. They must see something in you that you can't see in yourself."

I was not happy about what he said, but I said OK, since I had called him for advice.

It was painful and sad to me how quickly I felt scared, hurt, and humiliated. Wounded children wound quickly as adults. I was one of those. One wrong word would unleash an ancient hurt. Rejection to me felt like the end of the world.

The next day we were all back at our microphones. After I launched a few lines, Donovan was back on the speaker. "Calm down, Mark. You'll get it. Just try to relax. You're doing great."

I heard someone expel a snort-laugh. By this time, none of the other actors were speaking to me. They just stared in disbelief that I still had this job. I was even more amazed than them. I wondered if this was one of those secret psychological tests to see how much a person could take before cracking.

When I went home that night, I called Cubby again.

"I'm quitting. It's horrible. They all hate me."

"You are not to fire yourself. What's the worst that can happen?"

"They fire me."

"Then what?

"Nothing. I'm fired."

"Do you have a life to go back to?"

"Yes."

"Your problem is you think about yourself too much. Nobody cares if you get fired." He then laughed, which, to be honest, hurt a little.

"I have another reading tomorrow."

"Just show up."

I didn't sleep at all that night. I was back in the torture chamber at 10:00 a.m.

The next week a few of the readings went slightly better. I did not quit, and to my surprise and everyone else's, they didn't fire me. Somehow, little by little, I started developing a voice for Little Dog. I also learned how to get to that voice when I needed to. After about twenty pep talks from Donovan, amazingly, I turned a corner. I got the hang of it. Slowly, I started to feel like I knew what I was doing. Unbelievably, people eventually started to tell me that they loved what I was doing.

One session, they hired the amazing Carol Channing, who said I was a perfect Little Dog. After the show started airing, kids who watched it told me it was one of their favorite cartoons ever. We did two seasons, from 1993 to 1995. I ended up being proud of my work on it. Donovan also seemed happy.

Over the years I had some more small shots at voice work. Every voice I did was reminiscent of Little Dog. I was stuck in that one voice and could not change out of it. Eventually, they stopped calling.

Cubby was 100 percent right to tell me not to fire myself. Let other people make that decision. I'm quick to think I can't do something. My friend Donovan gave me a chance. He stuck by me. He believed in me when I did not believe in myself.

Donovan and Cubby are partly responsible for this book getting done. When I started writing it, I didn't think I could do it. I remembered back to when Donovan told me I could do something I didn't think I could do. And Cubby told me not to fire myself. If there's a lesson in that, it's to find people who believe in you.

6
FUNNY

....

Consult Your Doctor

Don't get me wrong. I really like my iPhone, iPad, Apple Watch, Dell laptop, smart TV, and Alexa. I'm connected, baby! I recently took an EKG from my Apple Watch, downloaded it to my iPhone, and then emailed it to my cardiologist. After viewing it and consulting with me, he took a photo of my bill, downloaded it, and emailed that to me. I almost had a heart attack.

While my wife and I were watching Netflix at the airport waiting to board our flight, I got updates on my watch that our flight was on time and our bags were loaded. Thirty seconds later, United Airlines let me know that they had a hummus plate on board for me. We were in boarding group number four, and when we tried (by accident) to board with group three, the machine that reads the barcode started dinging and we were busted. We were sneered at as we crawled to the back of the line, covering our faces like mobsters after a drug bust.

When my son was in Cuba, we connected using FaceTime. When I was a kid, you had to stand next to a real person for face time. When I was growing up, if you needed to send a short message in a hurry, you had Western

Union. Now with texting, I've probably sent half a million short messages. When I was growing up, we knew almost nothing about the world. Now I can find out about an earthquake in Bangladesh while standing at a urinal in Finland.

But am I better off with this global connection, or was I somehow better off before? Maybe both? My mother used to say, "What you don't know won't hurt you." There's wisdom in that. Is it good for my health that I find out first thing in the morning that four hundred people died in a ferry accident in China, or two hundred young children were kidnapped and tortured by Boko Haram while I was fast asleep on my Sleep Number bed?

I now know a lot more about the world and the people in it, and less about my own family and myself. I used to spend more time with myself and other people. Now I'm spending more time with devices. These devices don't care a hoot about us human beings. Devices don't care about bettering the world. Nor are they supposed to. But the amount of time spent with these things is insane.

Good friends or family will tell you things because they care about you. When's the last time your iPhone said, "You look tired" or "Go to sleep; I don't want you to get sick" or "You should call your mother and apologize for yelling at her" or "Dinner's on me tonight." People tell you things because they sincerely care about you. Machines tell you what they are programmed to tell you.

Go to any restaurant and you'll see people staring at their phones instead of the people they are with. Even sitting alone for a few minutes doing nothing has become a thing of the past. The other night I was out to dinner with my wife and when she left the table, I thought, *I'm not pulling out my phone. I'm just going to sit and think and look around like I used to.* About thirty seconds later, I thought, *This is hard.* Then I thought this would be a great idea for an article. I would write about how hard it is nowadays to just sit and do nothing. So I went to my Apple Watch and left myself a message. I then checked my email, went to Yahoo!, and saw that the stock market had dropped six hundred points and that a whale had washed up dead on the shore in Northern California. When my wife came back to the table she said, "Sorry it took me so long. There was a line. What have you been doing?" I told her something my watch or phone would never tell her. I told her, "Waiting to tell you I missed you." And I meant it.

The War on Culture

Not far from where I live, we have the ballet, museum exhibits, and the opera. These are all lovely cultural pastimes, even though I haven't taken much advantage of them in recent years. If I heard that the ballet had gone out of business, to honor it I would stop everything for one minute and stand on my tippy toes. But if you offered me tickets to either the ballet or pro-wrestling. I'd rather see someone try to get out of an ankle lock or vertical suplex or my favorites, a Frankensteiner and hurricanrana.

You see, my own assessment of myself is that I have very little "culture DNA" in my bones. The few ballets that I've been to, I never left thinking about the great artistry of the danseuse or the danseur. I was never awed by the plié or pirouette or, for that matter, the fouetté. What did amaze me was when the danseur would put his hand onto the wishbone section of the danseuse (an actual wrestling move called the "gripper") and then lift her up over his head and spin her around. Who lifts people like that? I can't imagine my grandfather ever lifting my grandmother like that. "Sadie, come a here. I vant to try sometin' on ya."

I believe most museums are nothing more than big storage lockers for old paintings. Send in Marie Kondo. Ninety-five percent of the paintings I see in a museum I walk by so fast you'd think my shoes were on fire. Put me in front of a Monet, da Vinci, or Rembrandt and I'm done in less than forty-five seconds. Rembrandt's *The Night Watch* is 11'11" long and 14'4"wide. Except in north Beverly Hills, who has walls that size? I grew up in a one-bedroom apartment. We didn't have room for an extra spoon.

A while back, my wife and I went to MoMA in New York City. I saw a few paintings I felt I could actually do myself. One was a white canvas with a black line drawn through the middle of it. I asked someone, "Why is this great art?"

They said, "Because he did it first."

I said, "No, he didn't. I did that same painting when I was six." My masterpiece is not hanging at MoMA because my mother said it was garbage and threw it out. She also threw out my collection of Elvis photos and baseball cards. I could have been a millionaire today.

In 2019 a well-known artist sold a banana duct-taped to a wall for more than $100,000. If it didn't sell, at least he could have eaten his masterpiece. Imagine if every artist worked in fruit, there would be no more starving artists.

That brings us to the opera. Not just opera. It's called "the opera." We have "the opera" and "the ballet." Have you ever noticed that there is no "the wrestling" or "the bowling"? To me, the opera is just chubby people screaming, mostly in Italian. I honestly believe that all the bravos and cheering at the end are from people totally relieved that it's finally over. A few years ago, someone took me to *La Bohème* at the Hollywood Bowl. It was two hours and thirty-six minutes long. *La Bohème* changed my life. I slept through the entire first act. Then I woke for intermission, had a pretzel, and slept the entire second act. Now every night I play Donizetti or Puccini for the best sleep I've ever had.

Entertainment-wise for me, nothing compares to the zoo or roller derby or sumo wrestling. A few years back, my friend Jonas and I went to a sumo competition. Five-hundred-pound men in diapers trying to push the other guy out of a circle. *Bravo!* A truly unforgettable evening. And how about roller derby? Women on roller skates elbowing and punching each other in the face. *Brava!* So much fun. When you're at the zoo and you see an orangutan or gorilla swinging from a rope and banging its chest or a snake eating a rat, tell me that's not great entertainment. Show me a children's play that produces as much laughter and gaiety as when kids see an elephant pee or a horse poop.

You're probably thinking: this guy needs "culturalizing." He's a beast. Hey, shoot me because I know what I like. Tonight I have a choice of watching the documentary *RBG* or a two-hour *Hoarders* special. Guess what I'm watching?

What's All the Complaining About?

A waiter comes over to a table of old Jewish women and says, "Excuse me, ladies. Is anything all right?"

Jews have a history of complaining. They complained to Moses about not having bread, meat, or water. But complaining isn't always a bad thing. If we complain to our politicians, that's sometimes a good thing. Complaining to your neighbors about late-night noise or nonstop dog barking is also all right. If you knock on your neighbors' door ready to kill them because they don't mow their lawn, that's not all right. If you're calm and explain the situation, most people will understand.

It seems that these days people complain about things that just aren't that important. The chimney sweep scene in *Mary Poppins*. Plastic straws. Airplanes ruining the world. As my mother used to say, "People have too much time on their hands," or "They have nothing better to do than complain."

Because America is a great country and most of our needs like food, water, and shelter are taken care of, we tend to look for things to complain about. You'll never hear someone in Sudan grumble about something green growing out of an onion.

I come from a long line of complainers. There was constant complaining about other family members, food, and, of course, the weather. I even had an uncle complain about the day someone died: "He picked the worst day to drop dead. He couldn't wait till Tuesday?"

There's an old saying, "Be careful what you pray for, because you might get it." Jews pray for rain, but when it rains they complain. "Every time I go on vacation, it never fails to rain." "Of course it's raining. I just washed the car." In addition, people talk about rain as if animals were falling from the sky: "It's raining cats and dogs."

People worry and get others worried. "Driving home from work I couldn't see a thing. It's amazing I wasn't killed," or "I'm not going to venture out in this." They even try to convince others not to go out. "Stay home today. What's so important that you have to go out in this kind of weather?"

People tell you the obvious. "If you go out, I guarantee you you'll get soaked." They bring illness into it: "Are you looking to get pneumonia?" When it rains hard, they make it sound like they were part of a targeted assassination: "Oh my gosh, I didn't think I'd make it from the car to the house." And of course they drag God himself into it: "A few more days of this, we might as well build an ark."

When it doesn't rain, that also upsets them. "I wish it would rain so I could shut the sprinklers off." After only one day of rain: "Enough, already. When's it going to stop?" And heat too drives Jews crazy: "It better cool off soon. My AC bill is a fortune." And then they talk like they've spent time in hell. "Have you been outside? It's hotter than hell out there." They throw in cooking references: "You could fry an egg on the sidewalk." They bring nonkosher animals into it: "I was sweating like a pig."

Wind also gets Jews crazy: "I'm afraid a tree is going to come down on the house," or "If we lose power, everything in the refrigerator is going to spoil." Even going to the beach becomes nonstop terror for Jewish people:

"Put on a lot of sunscreen. Otherwise, fifty years from now you'll regret it." And let's not forget sand: "This time, try not bringing half the beach home with you," or "Thanks to you kicking the sand around, I have an extra crunchy tuna sandwich."

You get the point. It's endless what a person can complain and worry about. I had an aunt who spent most of her life trying to figure out where the draft was coming from. She'd walk around with her hands up, feeling the air.

Complaining, worrying, and living in fear may not ruin your life, but it certainly will make your life less pleasant. I work very hard at trying not to complain about people, places, and things. It's not easy, but I am improving at it—except, of course, when it comes to complaining about my wife. After all, I must have *some* fun.

The Most Jewish Comedian Ever

It's no longer a question of staying healthy. It's a question of finding a sickness you like. —Jackie Mason

I am blessed to have spent time with Jackie Mason. He made me laugh as much as, and at times more than, any other comedian I ever saw. For me he was one of the top five comics who ever lived.

Mason was so Jewish that other Jews told him not to be so Jewish. That would be like telling an alligator not to look like luggage. And like the alligator, Jackie had tough skin. You need to be tough to be a stand-up comedian.

Mason was fearless. He said what he believed and did not shy away from other people's opinions. Everything about him was funny. The way he walked, talked, and dressed. The sounds he made to accentuate a comedy idea were priceless. This man, with dyed hair and in a crinkled suit, would have people doubled over in the aisles. If you ever had the honor of seeing him at a Broadway theater, you noticed that not just the Jews were laughing, everyone was convulsing with laughter.

One of his greatest assets as a performer was that he made you feel like he was personally speaking to you. "Hey, mister, I'm talking to you." What Mason could do to an audience with just words and his Yiddishy, phlegm-filled New York Jewish accent was genius.

I met Mason in the 1990s. I once told him I had some material for him, so we met at a diner on Wilshire Boulevard. I did the material for him in the best Jackie Mason impression I could muster. He did not like any of it, but that was OK, because I had an hour alone with Mason.

Way back before becoming a comedian, Mason was a rabbi, and word has it, he used to cause his congregation to double over. People were afraid they would drop the Torah because they were laughing so hard. When we met, Mason knew that I was becoming more religious. He used to say to me, "Mark, I used to be a rabbi and became a comedian. You are a comedian, and you want to be a rabbi." He said that to me more than a few times. I came to expect it and always loved it.

Another time, after seeing Mason's show with my wife, we took him out for dinner. The only place open was a diner called Ships on La Cienega Boulevard in Los Angeles. Ships was famous for having toasters on every table. So if you ordered toast, they would bring you the bread and you would toast it yourself. Jackie could not get over the fact that in a restaurant he had to do his own cooking. He started going from table to table asking people what they thought of the fact that they had come to a restaurant and had to make their own toast. He got people laughing at every table he visited. "Hey, mister, how come you have to make your own toast? When people come to your house for dinner, do you make them cook at your house?"

During that meal, we reminded Mason that Rosh Hashanah was

coming up and that if he was in Los Angeles, he could come to us for dinner. He quickly turned us down and explained that he never goes to people's homes to eat because he can't leave whenever he wants to. He feels trapped at people's houses. In a restaurant, he said, he can come and go as he pleases.

A few years later, my wife and I, and another couple with a female friend of theirs, all went to see Mason perform in Westwood. After the show, we went backstage to say hello. After again telling me I was becoming a rabbi, Mason zeroed in on the attractive single woman who was with us. He got her phone number and called her a few times. He was about seventy-plus years old at the time. When he found out she was in her fifties, he said she was too old for him and never called her again. She laughs about it to this day.

A few weeks before Mason died, my wife and I and some friends took a ten-day road trip from Niagara Falls to Massachusetts and on to Newport, Rhode Island. Through the very goyish backroads of these states, we listened to Mason's Broadway show *The World According to Me!* As we passed cows, ducks, and American flags, we were all laughing our heads off. We weren't laughing because we are Jewish or because Mason was Jewish. We were laughing because he was so spot on and so flipping funny.

I wish Mason had gotten a chance to see me work. I would have loved to hear what he thought and maybe even gotten a few pointers. But I was never so lucky.

Mason's death hit me on many levels. The fact that he is no longer here to entertain us and speak for us. The fact that we will not have more of his fabulous comedy pouring out of him.

It's true that Mason was a comedian, but he also never stopped being a rabbi. He was an important person who was so unabashedly unafraid to be Jewish in the face of the whole world. Every word out of his mouth screamed, "I'm a Jew." We lost a real spokesman. A goodwill ambassador for the Jewish world.

If there is a heaven, Mason is performing for his biggest and best crowds ever. I can hear him now: "Hey, mister, with the beard, you look just like Moses. Oh, you are Moses. Hey, Moses, forty years in the desert is a long time for Jewish women. You should have taken them to Miami to a nice, air-conditioned hotel and room service. Jewish wives don't like hot sand; they like coffee and cake. What a *shmendrick*."[32]

The Punchless Punch Line

Let's say I'm an architect and my latest creation is finished and in public view. Then some people walk by and hate it. Even worse, they say they are offended by it. Should I never work again? Should I be publicly vilified? According to some, the answer is yes.

I am a stand-up comedian. I deliver punch lines. They call them punch lines because they are supposed to pack a punch. As you know, a punch can hurt. But today, that is not acceptable to many people, often the young and well educated.

For more than forty years, I've performed in some of the nicest the-aters, including in front of Chagall's tapestries in the Knesset, the home of Israel's parliament. I even performed one night at the foot of the bed of a dying man. I am a road-dog clean comic. Early on, I did do some cursing and talked more explicitly about things, but I found I didn't like doing that, and the audience agreed.

When onstage and off, I try not to offend or demean any person or group. I try—I don't always succeed. And except for one occasion, I have never ever asked another comic to stop saying anything, even though I have been repulsed by many things I've heard.

32 A *shmendrick* is more lovable, more forgivable, than a schmuck. But a human being can be both a *shmendrick* and a schmuck. That makes you a *schlemiel*.

Back in the 1980s, in Cleveland, a comedian performing before me went into a full-on racist act. One "N-joke" after another. And if that wasn't bad enough, much of the audience was clapping and laughing. For the first time in my life, I was ashamed to share the same stage as another comic and embarrassed for my profession letting this guy earn a living. Many times, stupid breeds stupid. The next day I complained to the club owner, and he fired me.

The audience has always been in control of what a comic keeps in or throws out of his or her act. The audience controls the act simply by the laughs they give or don't. The audience is our barometer. These days, it's not only about them laughing or not laughing. It's about power and control. When people think you've offended them, they want you to stop. If you don't, they've decided it's because you're a bad person and need to be publicly punished.

People now get right in your face, and it's shocking to us longtimers. They act as if you're trying to inject them with rodenticides. In gentler times, it was enough to walk out of a show. Now they must get you.

Thirty years ago, I used the word "retarded" in a set, as in "That was a retarded thing to do." After my show, a woman politely approached me and asked if I could find a different word to use. She said her son had Down syndrome and that word hurt. I understood and took it to heart. I never used that word again. True comedy is a wake-up call, a realizing, at times even a reckoning. It's a different way to view something. It's a shot of clarity. For sure, it's not a hammer banging down on your big toe. Unless, of course, you deserve it.

Those gentler days are long gone. We now are living in an age when groups tell you what you can and can't say. And if you don't stop, you must be banished. The punishments by these know-it-alls are severe. Everything from getting you fired to marching outside your show or home to shaming you on the internet to making death threats. These people are what I call "Self-Proclaimed Parents of the Universe." These were the tattletales and the bullies when I was growing up. These mental wet brains, or deadbeat boneheads, who have never even written a joke or created anything life-affirming cause more pain than almost any word I or anyone I know might utter. They are the fly you can't get out of your house.

This is new behavior. Until recently the audience had one job and one job only: to come and laugh (or not). As comedians, we are laughter merchants. Most of us just want to make you happy, and in turn that makes us happy. Next time, if you don't like what you hear, instead of cutting the brake lines on our cars, do the world a favor: stay home and knit some earmuffs.

Heeere's Mark Schiff

My friend David told me that when I was a kid I said I wanted to be a comedian on *The Tonight Show Starring Johnny Carson*. Well, be careful what you wish for. When I was eighteen, I attempted my first live performance as a stand-up comic and my first step toward getting on *The Tonight Show*. I performed almost all non-original material, mostly old jokes from a book. I bombed so miserably that I quit until I was twenty-three. Then, somehow, I got the nerve to get back up onstage. And since my triumphant return, I've never looked back. It took a good five years of doing stand-up seven nights a week until I began to grab hold of this thing. Building the act one word at a time, I worked hard and eventually was told I was pretty good at it.

Twice a year, the talent booker Jim McCauley would come to New York to look for new comedians for *The Tonight Show*. If you were lucky enough to grab an audition, it was possible you would get a shot on the coveted show. I was one of the lucky few chosen for McCauley to see. The year was 1981. I was now eleven years into stand-up. The audition took place at the Comic Strip in New York in front of a live audience. These aren't like acting or singing auditions that you do in an office somewhere. This is the real deal. It was at night, in front of strangers who had been drinking and were hoping to grab a few laughs for their hard-earned money. It was a very uncontrolled situation where anything could happen. One of the waiters could drop a tray during your set, and that could be the end of your career.

There were about ten of us lined up for McCauley. One after another, the MC brought us up to do our five minutes, the length of time a comic was given on the show.

McCauley sat by himself somewhere in the back, in the dark, watching and taking notes. That's a good thing, because you didn't want to see him looking at you or, God forbid, ignoring you. The only thing worse than getting no laughs is being ignored.

I remember my five minutes went gangbusters. The audience was laughing at everything. I could do no wrong. I was Moses parting the sea. I don't ever remember doing this well in another fiver. The hard part about five minutes is that it's barely enough time to warm the audience up, so you'd better grab them by the throat the second you hit the boards. An audition could be the difference between becoming a working comic or keeping your day job.

When I said "Thank you, goodnight" and started to walk off the stage, I received a standing ovation. I waved at the audience like a returning astronaut stepping from the capsule. Then I went out to the bar to wait. That was what you did when you were done. You sat at the bar or in a booth and waited for Jim to come out and hopefully give you the thumbs-up and offer you a spot. Back in the eighties, getting on *The Tonight Show* legitimized you. It was the gold seal that you had talent. It made the industry and your own family sit up and take notice.

About a half hour later, Jim came out from the showroom and talked to a few of the comics. I was not one of them. If you didn't get picked, he usually did not want to get into a conversation about why you didn't get the show. I don't blame him; it could get heated.

Naturally, I felt my case was different. I wanted—no, I *needed*—to know why he didn't pick me. As I watched him leave the club, I felt a surge of anger rise from within. That should have been a sign not to follow him out. Two of my biggest character defects are anger and the feeling of abandonment, and rejection brings them both right to the surface. That night, my defects, like molten lava, were bubbling over.

I went outside, and he was about twenty feet away. I yelled, "Hey Jim," and he immediately stopped and turned to face me.

Politely, he said, "Hi, Mark. Nice set tonight."

I walked up to him.

"Thanks, Jim. Thanks for coming. Did you see I got a standing O?"

"I did."

"So, what do you think?"

"It was a good shot. Very funny. But it's not right for our show."

"I got a standing O," I repeated.

"I know what Johnny likes, and you're not his type. Sorry."

Pushing harder, I said, "I killed them. You saw I got a standing O."

"Maybe some other time."

He then turned on his heels and started to move away. I was now in full abandonment mode and bitterly angry that I was rejected. After all, I got a standing O. What more does a person want? I now turned him into a bad person.

Again, I called Jim. This time, when he turned, I shouted "Fuck you" at him two times. My second "Fuck you" was even more intense than the first one. Staring straight into my eyes, he sternly said, "You will never do the show. *Never*."

He turned and walked off into the night. There I stood on Second Avenue, alone, dejected, seemingly all hope for my future down the sewer. I was still too angry and in shock to realize I was the cause of it all. Like my mother used to say to me, "You never take no for an answer." I stood and watched as vacant taxi cabs flew down Second Avenue, realizing that even if I got in one, I now had nowhere to go. I walked back into the club, sat at the bar, and started drinking.

Three years later I moved to California. My drinking had progressed by then. I don't remember moving or how I got out there. Blackouts will do that to a person. In New York I took cabs and subways and walked. In California you have to drive. After falling asleep at the wheel more than a few times and going off the road twice while driving back at midnight from San Diego, I got help, got sober, and have remained that way for almost four decades. It can be done. Now, I still have anger and abandonment issues, but less so. Some things never go away. On some level, I'm always working on it.

Back then, McCauley was a semi-regular at the local LA comedy clubs, always looking for new acts for the show. I wanted to be one of those people so desperately but realized if it never was to be, I had to accept it. A few times a month, he would come into the clubs and we would say a quick hi to each other. But that was as far as the conversation went. There was never a mention of my dreadful acting out.

It had been seven years since my explosion, and I had performed hundreds of times since that day, playing every club in every town across the country, as well as in Canada, Europe, even Israel. This one week, I was headlining the Punch Line in San Francisco. It was fifteen minutes before showtime when I saw McCauley walk into the club. I walked over.

"Hi, Jim. Good to see you."

"You too, Mark."

"What brings you in?"

"I'm here to see your opening act."

He seemed to be in a good mood and upbeat. He asked, "Do you mind if I also stay and watch you? I have nothing else to do tonight."

"Of course." I found out what he was drinking and got him one. Was he reopening the vault that I had locked myself out of? I didn't even want to think about it.

I went up and did about an hour. If I remember right, it was a pretty good show. Blinded by the bright stage lights, I was wondering my whole time onstage if he was still there and, if so, what he was thinking.

When I got off, I looked and saw him sitting with my opening act in the back of the club. I swallowed hard, tapped my foot on the floor twice for luck, and went over.

He did the talking. He said, "That was a good set. Very funny stuff. I haven't seen you in a while. You're good. If you want to, I'd like to have you on with Johnny."

After hearing the words "have you on with Johnny," I remember my ears clogging, like when you're in an elevator and it drops too fast.

I looked at him and said, "Fuck you, Jim. Kiss my ass."

Just kidding—I didn't say that. I'm crazy, but not *that* crazy. I said, "I'd love to do it. Thank you." I shook his hand. It was soft, almost like a ball of pizza dough. He told me to call him at his office on Monday. I called, and two weeks later, I was standing behind the blue-gray curtain, waiting for Johnny's introduction. Thank God for diapers.

I did my five-plus and knocked it out of the park. As I was walking back to the curtain, Johnny flashed me the OK sign, what every comic hoped for. It meant that he liked what you did. Back on the other side of the curtain, Jim McCauley, with a big smile on his face, said, "Terrific spot. Get ready with another one, because we'd like to have you back soon."

I ended up doing six spots with Johnny. After my third appearance, Johnny called me over to the couch. I was now on the panel. Being called over to the panel was and remains one of the highlights of my life. At that time, there was nothing bigger for a comedian than sitting inches away from that famous face, the master of talk shows (I believe he still holds that title some thirty years later). He was so kind and so generous to me. When I first sat down, they broke for commercials. I could not believe it when I heard him say, "We will be right back with Mark Schiff." Mr. Carson then leaned over to me, complimented me on my material, and even offered a few suggestions to make things better. I was freaking out. Johnny Carson saw me as (might I be so bold as to say) sort of a peer.

After the show, Johnny invited me to come back soon.

I never did apologize to Jim for my outburst that night in New York. I was scared to. He never brought it up either. I figured I should just leave well enough alone.

One night around 1990, I saw Jim walk into the Improv in Los Angeles. He said hello to me and then asked me if I wanted to go fishing with him on his boat. I never did go with him. Why? I was afraid I might say something stupid and lose the show. Who wants to hang out with the boss? Perhaps his offering to take me out was his way of saying "I forgive you." I hope so.

Jim did exactly what he was supposed to do. He picked the acts that he felt were right for his boss. He was also right about not picking me that night in New York. I was not Johnny's type, and I also wasn't ready. It was amazing to me that he did not let his personal feelings get in the way of some dopey kid who screamed at him like a crazy person out in public. It's even more amazing that he took a shot on me after that. Jim not only opened the door for me to the show, I believe he also opened his heart.

Before Johnny's death, he put out a set of DVDs called *The Ultimate Collection*. One of the disks is his favorite comedians from his thirty-year run. He included my first spot on that disk. All this from a dopey kid deciding one day to step onstage and take a shot at the big time.

7
HELPING OTHERS

Coronavirus and Sumo Wrestling

Because of the coronavirus, it will take twenty years for spin the bottle, sumo wrestling, and bobbing for apples to make their way back into society. I'll tell you how bad this coronavirus thing is: a rabbi told me that *mashiach*[33] was planning to come next month, but he has canceled his plans for now.

Not too long ago, I was kissing and hugging and shaking hands with everyone. I was taking bites off of other people's forks and sipping from their coffee cups. I was opening and closing bathroom doors in city parks. I was putting my feet on hotel toilet seats to clip my nails. I was riding exercise bikes and soaking in health club Jacuzzis.

Those days are gone. That person is long gone. If you watched the news, you'd know the whole world was turning into one big prison. We were told to stay a few feet away from one another when interacting. If someone sneezed or coughed near us and no soap was available, we were

---

33 *Mashiach* is the Hebrew word for "messiah." The word *messiah* in English means "a savior or a hoped-for deliverer." It is believed that when the messiah comes, he will bring the dead back to life and return them to their souls. My uncle Louie died owing over $3 million to mobsters. He is not anxiously looking forward to coming back anytime soon.

to run through the nearest car wash and pay extra for a coat of hot wax. We were being asked not to touch almost anything or anyone without first wiping them or it down. If this kept up and if I dared to go to a restaurant, the cutlery for my meal might have come in those sterile bags the dentist tears open, full of instruments used to poke your gums.

In just a few months, I turned into a major hoarder. Purell was going for fifty dollars a bottle. I had forty bottles of sanitizer in my safe-deposit box. I had one hundred rolls of toilet paper and sixty-three hundred Lysol wipes in my closet. I was ready for whatever comes. And no, you couldn't have any. I turned mean and selfish. Shortages, fear, and disease will do that to you. I am not a germaphobe. Never have been. Up until March 2020, I would've licked the handrail on an escalator for a laugh. But things have changed. People I know are scared.

Truth is, we didn't know if COVID-19 would be gone soon or would be here for a while. As of this writing, we still don't know what damage it will do. Our rabbi said that only God knows when this will end. I believe that. But God doesn't work on our schedule. Sometimes he takes a long, long time. I'm not insensitive to the fact that people have died, and many are getting sick, but so far it's not the black plague. Let's hope it stays that way.

But people were afraid. Some of them had families; some didn't. We were told that people of a certain age (my age) or who have certain illnesses were more vulnerable. I have a friend who was seventy and recovering from leukemia. The man was beside himself. People were being quarantined: some in their homes, some on ships, some in hotels. Some were not sick but so afraid that they created their own personal quarantine hell. They had created an internal bogeyman. They became obsessed with coronavirus.

A friend of mine used this time to increase his mitzvah portfolio. As much as he could, he used that part of himself that was created in God's image. He lived "Love your neighbor as yourself," which is the universal golden rule. The Talmud defines it as a "great principle" of Judaism. I watched him seek out those who were suffering from this. If not in person, then through email, phone, or an old-fashioned, hand-delivered get-well card. He taught me that sometimes, if you look hard enough, you'll see the person suffering the most could be the person in the same bed as you.

How close are the words "COVID" and "*kavod*"? As far as COVID-19, do what you can, but don't let it ruin your life. For *kavod*[34] honor your parents and God and be grateful that they brought you into the world. Even a world with COVID-19. Live in gratitude, not in fear. Because these are days you won't get back. You can't bank days. You only get so many. So live your life. Be of service. Tell the people you love that you love them. And like your mother always said, "Wash your hands, and stop playing with your face." Hey, wait until you see COVID-27. That's going to be a doozy.

Willingness

I have a friend who is at least 150 pounds overweight. I have talked to him, suggested books that have helped me. He has read some of them and even bought some exercise equipment. He has gone to doctors, psychiatrists, tried all sorts of different programs, even tried meds. I've taught him as best as I could about how I took my weight off and kept it off.

My friend has already lost two friends who were grossly overweight. Gone forever, and they were young. I told him and his wife that he may well cut his life short if he continues the path that he is on. I told him that since I got into shape I've been able to run, play ball, hike, and bike ride with my kids. I told him I couldn't do these before. He shakes his head and agrees with everything I say, but it hasn't been enough to convince him.

It is not because he is stupid or uninformed, or because he doesn't care. It's because he does not yet have a major ingredient. He doesn't have the

---

34 *Kavod* is the Hebrew word for "honor and respect." Honor and respect are huge in Judaism. The fifth
   commandment is "Honor thy father and mother" or they might leave you out of the will.

willingness to change. One of the keys to making almost any change in your life, big or small, is your willingness to make that change. Even the smallest amount of willingness can make a huge difference. A small change can open a big door. The problem is that without this willingness, no matter how much you want to change or need to change—and even if you do make some changes—without willingness they probably won't stick.

At eighteen, I was smoking, coughing, and wheezing. It took decades until I stopped. I was overweight with high blood pressure. I was killing myself, and I knew it. One night I had pain in my chest. At the time I was driving over the Triborough Bridge in New York, and when I got to the tollbooth, I said to the man, "Please throw my cigarettes away. I'm quitting smoking." He smiled, took them from me, tossed them in the garbage, and wished me luck. Not five minutes later, I got off at the first exit and bought another pack. I'm lucky to be alive today. I had a great intention but no willingness to stick with it. I wanted to do the right thing, but I was short on conviction.

When I finally did stop smoking, I was standing with two friends. I said, "That's it. I quit." I pulled five packs from my trench coat pockets and never smoked cigarettes again. I was so sick of stopping and starting and lying to myself that I finally became able and willing.

Willingness is one thing that I believe nobody can give to you. You cannot pass willingness on to someone. It's not DNA transferable. Somehow, a person must get it for himself or herself. The way it sometimes works for me is that one day I don't have it and the next day I do. On more than one occasion, I literally have had a psychic change. I go to sleep and awake a different person. But know this: You never own willingness. It's a gift you need to renew every day. It's not a vaccine. Willingness can wear off very quickly. Another way, I've found, is to pray for it. I ask God to please give me the willingness to do what I need to do. Then I act as if I have it until I do have it.

Either way, almost any change demands you take a long, hard look at yourself. And many times, that's painful. Looking at where I'm lacking is really rough stuff. I remember once asking God for the willingness to complete some writing that I was avoiding. Every day before I began to write, I asked for enough willingness for that day. I worked at the writing as hard as I could manage, and before I knew it, I was finished with the project.

I know there are some things that I may never want to give up. I don't ask for the willingness to change those things. It's my loss. If you are struggling with anything at all, take a good look at yourself and ask God for the willingness to change. Then act as if you have it, and you just might be incredibly surprised at what happens.

A Great Phone Call

The afternoon before *erev*[35] Rosh Hashanah 5782, I got a phone call from my fifth-grade buddy David Dibo. David is one of those guys who every time we talk, it's fun. I kicked off the conversation by telling him that one of the kids from our old class died. At our age, these things happen more and more. It's almost always better to be the one spreading the news than the one it's being spread about.

When we were twelve years old, David and I were leaving my apartment building when I teased him by singing, "David loves Marva, David loves Marva." Marva was a girl in our fifth-grade class. David shot back that he did not love Marva. I sang it again, but this time louder. Since David was twelve, his only recourse was to chase me, yelling, "Take it back." Running after me at full speed, he ran smack into the two-inch-thick glass entrance door to the building. He was immediately knocked semi-unconscious.

Now mumbling like a wino coming off a forty-year wine habit and with

35 The day before a Jewish holiday or the Jewish Sabbath is called *erev*. People who were religious Jews but have left the religion and now celebrate Christmas might call the day before Christmas *erev* Christmas.

blood pouring out of his nose, he let me walk him home, where I handed him over to his mom. Freaking out at the sight of the blood, she asked him, "What happened?"

David mumbled back to his mom, "Who are you? Where am I?" We soon found out that besides a busted nose, David also had amnesia. (This was especially bad for me, since he was one of the kids I used to cheat off on school tests.) After a week or so, David, thank God, was back to normal (and days later my test grades had miraculously improved).

A few years later he was voted most popular boy in high school, even with a bent nose. We both still talk to Marva.

So fifty-three years later, after a few minutes of catch-up, David tells me that some years back I shared that when he and the other kids would choose sides to play ball, it was painful for me that I was almost always chosen last or not at all. When you are a kid, that is a big deal. When kids were choosing sides, I was what you call "What about him?" After everyone else was picked, they would look at me and say, "What about him?" or "Who wants him?" Many times I would be completely left out and walk home kicking the dirt, sometimes crying and always feeling angry and very alone. To be quite honest, to some degree I deserved some of this treatment, but that's another story.

David continued, "You know, Mark, I just want to say I am sorry if I was one of the kids who hurt you. Because if I did, I really didn't mean to." Wow. When he said those things to me, even though the rejection had happened fifty-three years earlier, I felt an almost immediate release of pain I had been carrying around ever since. I felt lighter and happier, and it brought a big smile to my face. Jokingly, I fired back, "Thank you, David. I have waited fifty years to hear that." We both laughed.

The power of a simple "I am sorry," even five decades later, can have tornado-power impact uprooting ancient wounds. I have told the story of being left out many times to many people, but until David's call I only had a sad ending to the story. It always ended with how much it hurt to be left out and forgotten. It always ended with "Poor me."

I also realized, for the first time, we were all just kids groping around in the dark hallways that housed our feelings and emotions. Thank you, David, for the call, and thank you, God, for giving us the power of *teshuva*[36] and the ability for us to accept a heartfelt apology when it's handed to us.

Recently I was tossing a baseball around with some neighborhood twelve- and fourteen-year-olds when they then decided to play football instead. I asked if I could play, and they said no. I look forward to that call in fifty years.

A Valued Customer

When I was growing up, every business answered their phone. Not so anymore. Some businesses don't seem to even have a phone. Eventually even the suicide hotline might start putting people on hold. "Please hold. We have two jumpers in front of you."

One time my internet went down, so I called AT&T. A recording told me that there were no outages in my area and I should go to the internet for more information. But I didn't have internet to go to. For the next forty minutes, before I got to speak to a real (albeit script-reading) live person, I was bombarded with different recordings. Over and over I heard that I'm a valued customer and how much they appreciate my business. The valued customer thing hit a nerve in me because at certain times "low self-esteem" could be my middle name. Telling me I have value deeply touched my heart.

One recording asked if I would take a brief survey at the end of the call and tell them about my experience with AT&T. Does a call to AT&T really

---

36 *Teshuva* means "to repent." We recognize our own wrongdoing and then turn around and face the one we have wronged. It is regretting our sin and showing remorse. Unless the person you wronged is an idiot and deserved it. But who am I to judge?

qualify as an experience? What about AT&T helping me out with my own survey? I would love to hear from them what they really think of me. They could let me know if I've been rude or overly aggressive with their honored team members. They could tell me if they are upset with me because of my two late payments. I opted out of their survey. I was then told they were recording my call for quality control. I have seen enough people dragged away in handcuffs on *60 Minutes* and TV shows about lawyers to see how phone recordings come back to haunt even the best of us. Then they said their prompts have recently changed and I should listen carefully to the new menu.

Next I heard, "Due to an overwhelming number of calls, this call will take longer than usual to answer" but that someone would be with me as soon as possible. No one would be right with me. They knew it and I knew it. It's a lie. Think of your own family. Has anyone that has ever told you he or she would be right with you been right with you? Never.

When they finally do pick up, the worst is when you hear "Please hold." That additional hold is like having a big fish on the hook and you almost pull it in, but at the last moment it gets away. "Please hold" means they will now totally forget about you. "Please hold" often means you have a few minutes left before the call is potentially dropped. (Almost as bad are the phony typing and clicking sounds they use to make you believe they are typing away as you speak.)

After thirty-five minutes of this torture, I had been pushed to the Tourette's syndrome point of the call where I started yelling the word "operator." Nonstop into my mouthpiece I yelled, "Operator, operator, operator!" No matter what they asked me from then on, I could not stop yelling it into the phone.

After forty-five minutes, someone from AT&T finally picked up. When he did, I immediately begged him to take my phone number in case we happened to get disconnected. They will always take the number and promise to call you back, but they rarely do.

I was told I was speaking with Eddie in India. I know that was not his real name. I said, "As you know, I am a valued customer." I then explained my situation to Eddie. He could not have been nicer. A good listener. A compassionate young fellow. Dopey me, I thought now we were getting somewhere.

After hearing me out for more than five minutes, Eddie said, "I am so sorry for your issue and that you can't get on the internet. You are a valued customer. You have been with AT&T since 1981 and we appreciate it. Unfortunately, you have reached the wrong department. You need to speak to technical. I'm in sales. I'll switch you right over." I screamed as if a rat just bit my toe.

"No, Eddie, don't switch me, please!" Too late! He hit a button and—bingo—disconnected me.

I then went back to my computer and figured I'd give it a try and hit the link to Amazon. Bingo, I was back on the internet. A modern-day miracle. Nothing better than being a valued customer.

As the World Turns

There's no place in this world where I'll belong when I'm gone
And I won't know the right from the wrong when I'm gone
And you won't find me singin' on this song when I'm gone
So, I guess I'll have to do it while I'm here.
—"When I'm Gone," lyrics by Phil Ochs

As the world turns dark, my job is to shine a light as best as I can and to try, if only a little, to brighten this ailing world back up. I have no illusions that I can fix the world. I am only one person. So perhaps the scope of that light won't shine much further than on my family, some of my neighbors, a few friends, and my audiences who come to laugh and forget, but that's OK. That's a start. At least I am doing something.

Two big Jewish holidays are Rosh Hashanah and Yom Kippur. When God decides who will live and who will die in the new year, hopefully I'll be given another chance and more time to fix the twisted and broken branches of this world. Then I will use the broom of wisdom to sweep clean the debris from this past year.

The consequence of doing nothing is a paralyzing thought. To do nothing is to give up my citizenship as a person. To do nothing is to forsake humanity. Not to correct is incorrect. We have seen where the world heads when people either do or say nothing, whether consciously or unconsciously. It's too late to do nothing. The clock will not tick backward. Every day we seem to be inching closer to the grip of another madman.

As hatred grows like unpulled weeds, it's choking the roots of a fragile civilization. As we are now witnessing, it's much easier to destroy than it is to build. Since I have become aware of these changes, my soul has been ignited. I have always cared about people, goodness, and fair play. I haven't always acted like I cared, though. I spent many years silently riding the merry-go-round, feeling proud just to pay my bills on time. I worried about my credit rating. But what about that ultimate rating—the one for your soul? The rabbis might say I was asleep, and that saddens me. I lost precious time. I personally feel somewhat responsible for the decay. But, thank God, caring was always in me, and I now recognize it. I finally hear an echo from the mountain. The supreme voice is angry when I sit still as if I have earned idle time. The voice asks that I do something. Something to show I care. Something that proves I am not just words. Something that shows I believe in Him and his children.

As the curtain recently closed on my sixties and I realized I have so little time left, my eyes snapped open. I feel the need to protect my family more now than ever. A day does not pass where I don't worry about their safety. I care more about being a good husband, father, grandfather, and friend. I care more about being helpful. I care more about helping to stop the madness—and it is madness. I care more about being a good Jew. I have never been prouder than I am today of my Jewish soul. I have never been more grateful for the gift I was given when I entered this world. It makes me think that, because of the depth of my love for being a Jew, the roots of these feelings, coupled with my anxieties for my people, are connected to the long, arduous, and treacherous roads my people have had to march down. Many times, to their deaths. These feelings are so strong it makes me think that this is not the first time my *neshamah* (soul) has entered the Jewish maze. It all feels so eerily familiar.

While the roots of our lives are being torn away, prayer, kindness, and especially your time are now more important than ever. A hello, a smile, a phone call asking how a person is has more power than ever before. People are scared. People are angry. People need assistance. A simple hello can reach the heart as quickly as any bullet.

The rabbis have told us that we can't solve this. We can't fix this. But we still must do our part. Mother Teresa never finished the job she was put on earth to do. The streets of Calcutta remain full of the sick and the dying. But she did what she could. The *Chofetz Chaim*[37] did not end *lashon hora* (negative speech), but he did what he could. The Jewish souls who walked their last steps, shoeless and into stone buildings, still believed, with the Shema[38] on their dying lips.

So now, God forbid, before the dark turns permanent and the door is sealed behind us on this Yom Kippur, I choose to light the few candles I still have left. A little light is better than none. I believe that each flicker of a candle is a wink from God to keep going. May you be inscribed for the next year of life.

---

37 Chofetz Chaim is Rabbi Yisrael Meir ha-Kohen Kagan (1838–1933). The subject of his famous book is "Laws of Clean Speech." He wrote against tale-mongering, gossip, and evil speech. Everything *The Enquirer* lives for. Did I just sin by saying that?

38 The Shema is regarded by many Jews as the most important prayer in Judaism. This is because it reminds them of the key principle of the faith: there is only one God. And if I do what my wife says, then that God will not smite me.

A Tight Twenty Minutes

It's 12:30 p.m. Summertime and at least 109 degrees. Downstairs at the craps table, a round man with a fat lip yells, "Come on, seven. Please God, one more time." People pray more in Las Vegas than in a Tibetan monastery. At a dimly lit bar a few feet away, a man in a silk shirt is trying to cut a hooker's price from $500 to $400 for an hour even though he only needs five minutes. She tells him OK, because she really likes him. He's slightly drunk, so he believes her.

Meanwhile, in a hotel room high above the Vegas strip, with a view of his name on the hotel marquee, comedian Avi Liberman washes his hands to say the hamotzi.[39] It's Shabbat in Las Vegas. Avi has a small pot of cholent (meat stew) that's been cooking since last night. You can smell it in the hallway as it mixes with the marijuana and cheap colognes from other guests walking by.

A few years ago, on May 23, 2021, at 7:54 p.m., the following message was sent to Avi's friend and fellow comedian El Lebowicz, who then forwarded it to me: "Hi. Sorry to message you like this, but I know you know Avi Liberman well and [I] would like you to know that he was in a car accident here in Miami. He is now in surgery and is in critical condition. Please pray for his *refuah*."[40] Like all of us comedians, Avi has died many times onstage, but this time he almost really died. He was a passenger in a car that got T-boned. The person driving walked away with a few broken ribs and spent no time in the hospital. Avi, on the other hand, was not so lucky. He remembers none of what happened to him, but fortunately, he was taken to the right hospital where the right doctor did the right operation. He

---

39 The hamotzi is the recital of the Hebrew benediction over bread before meals. We thank God for the bread before the meal because we know it will be good. The rest of the food we thank him for after the meal unless we crack a tooth on an olive pit. Then we start cursing.

40 You wish someone a *refuah* in times of sickness. The literal meaning is "a complete healing." If the sick person owes you a lot of money, you say this prayer day and night until he or she is either healed or dead.

underwent brain surgery, and thirty-five staples were put in his head. He was in the ICU for almost a week. Avi was told that if twenty more minutes had passed before he received medical care, he might have died.

Avi is a religious Jew and a journeyman comedian who travels nonstop from one end of the world to the other just to make people laugh. No matter how many flights and layovers are required to get him to a gig, he rarely complains. He's grateful for the work. He is grateful to be a comic. He is also a serial performer when it comes to benefits. All you have to do is ask him. Avi would work a fundraiser for a postnasal drip.

Avi was born in Israel and has dual citizenship with Israel and the United States. For many years, he has taken a few comedians twice a year to Israel to raise money by performing for the Koby Mandell Foundation. Koby Mandell was an Israeli-American who at the age of thirteen was murdered by Arab terrorists along with his friend Yosef Ishran in a canyon near their homes in Israel. Avi takes comedians who are not only Jewish, white, and straight but also Muslim, Christian, black, Asian, and gay. His only note to the comics is, "Easy on the lesbian stuff in Jerusalem." Avi believes that if he can get a comic who has never been to Israel to go to Israel, he will make a new friend for life. Much like the Rebbe (Rabbi Menachem Mendel Schneerson[41]), Avi is also changing the world one person at a time.

A few years ago, he collected *tzedakah* (charity) from his friends to distribute in Israel. Avi, three comedians, and I went on that trip. We visited the western city Sderot to distribute the money. At the time of our visit, Hamas was firing bombs into Sderot almost every day. We were warned that if the sirens went off, we would have only fifteen seconds to get to a bomb shelter. As part of our tour of Sderot, we were taken on a tour of a home that had been bombed the previous night. Because of the bombings, nobody was visiting Sderot and spending money there. So later that day,

---

41 The Lubavitcher rebbe, Rabbi Menachem Mendel Schneerson, of righteous memory (1902–1994), the seventh leader in the Chabad-Lubavitch dynasty, is considered to have been the most phenomenal Jewish personality of modern times. To hundreds of thousands of his followers and millions of sympathizers and admirers around the world, he was—and still is, despite his passing—"the Rebbe." Just like Elvis, according to many of his fans, is still making records.

bombings or no bombings, we all went to different storekeepers in Sderot and gave away the money Avi had collected. In his own way, Avi is a soldier for Israel and the Jewish people. He fights for Israel every day.

Avi was one of the first people I know who had COVID-19. Every night, for about two weeks, he would sweat so much that by morning his sheets would be soaking wet. The experience showed him what his audience feels like when he tries a new bit on them. He told me that right before one Shabbat, a couple of Chabad guys came into his hospital room to help him bring in Shabbat. He said, "I friggin' lost it and started crying."

I love working with Avi and missed our time together during COVID. He also works clean, which is rare for a comic these days, and in the next few months we are booked to do our stand-up acts together again in Las Vegas and Reno. Avi makes Las Vegas and Reno more than tolerable—he makes those cities fun. When Avi was unwell, I told him about a conversation I'd had with Harry Basil, the booker for the Las Vegas and Reno clubs. Harry had said he loves Avi and wanted to book us and that if Avi wasn't feeling well Harry would wait until the last minute to replace him, holding on to hope that Avi would feel well enough to perform. When I told Avi what Harry had said, he lost it again. The fact that a Las Vegas booker who does not have any obligation to be kind to him was showing him love was a big deal to Avi.

Avi is a believer in God. He told me that he thought his accident had a purpose—that it was meant to teach him something. He wasn't sure yet what the lesson was. What is clear is that through his recoveries he's had people praying for him worldwide. He's had people texting and calling and stopping by to see him. If he did not know it before, he sure knows it now: he is widely loved. Avi, you need to know you are one of the most beloved guys around. And that's a good thing. Maybe that's one part of what God is trying to tell you.

Avi's healing was slow for some time, with the left side of his face drooping a bit, but today Avi has his old face back and is just about healed.

He is performing in Vegas, cooking his stew, and traveling the world to make people laugh. Last we spoke, he was flying to Russia to do shows and for a date with a girl he met there. He then went to Ukraine for a week. When he left, he didn't know what was ahead for that beautiful country. The truth is we don't know what's ahead for any country, including our own. The same is true for our lives. We don't know what roadblocks we will face, and we must remember the importance of being there for one another.

Brother from a Different Mother

Some people arrive and make such a beautiful impact on your life, you can barely remember what life was like without them. —Anna Taylor

I met David Eichel in fifth grade. He was one of my oldest and dearest friends and he died recently. Some might say that with his death I lost my friend—but no, I did not lose him. He is as much with me now as he ever was.

First suffering a heart attack and then receiving lung cancer and emphysema diagnoses and being given only four to eight months to live, David didn't die when he was supposed to. Instead, he spent the next four years in hospice smoking Marlboros and playing online poker. Who knew the combination of Marlboros and online poker can add years to a cancer patient's life? When I'd visit him, we spoke about everything from our fifth-grade teacher to whether there was or was not a God. I said there was. He said he wasn't sure. I wish he could let me know. David was Jewish, but my bar mitzvah might have been the last time he ever stepped foot inside a shul.

David was the type of friend that if I did not see him for fifteen years, when we did meet again, we'd just picked up exactly where we left off. I think most of us have a few of those kinds of friends. Both of us were only children and both of us had tense childhoods. David was my brother from a different mother.

There is no relationship quite like the ones from your childhood. Friends from then know you in a way that others can't. For about six years, I spent seven hours a day five days a week with David, either in school or bolting from it, and many more hours playing together on weekends. Sometimes we rode bikes and sometimes we pitched nickels.

Long before doctors and parents dosed their depressed or hyper kids, David and I dosed each other with a deep friendship. Growing up, even when I felt down, and there were lots of those times, I always felt better after hanging out with him. Even when he was dying of cancer, just watching him puffing away and enjoying his Marlboro Reds somehow lifted my spirits.

When I went to visit him and if he felt OK, we would grab lunch and then take a short drive while listening to some of his favorites like Joni Mitchell. Amazingly, he could sing the lyrics to songs he had not heard in forty years. Good friends can also just sit together and say nothing; the safety of the friendship does it all.

For his first two years in hospice, I would visit him around once a month. Then one day, for reasons I still can't figure out, I just stopped going and calling. After a bit of time wondering where I was, he would call me. Guilty me, I would apologize for not visiting or calling more. And I meant it when I said I was sorry. David always, and I mean always, let me off the hook. No guilt, no shaming, always ending the call by telling me he loved me and when I had time, I should stop by. I made it back only once more.

The last time I went to see David, he told me he was going to marry his hospice nurse so she could get her green card and stay in the country. This turned out to be a God shot if I ever saw one. What happened was, after taking care of him for a while, she seemed to fall for the guy. I was told she loved him. It's true what they say, that you never know where you might find love. She was the last person to sit with him when he closed his eyes. She even bought a space next to him for after she passes.

It was a few weeks after his death that the mother of his only child called to give me the news. I wasn't shocked. I had expected him to die four years earlier. I am happy to know that in his final days, he was well taken care of and loved. To know that, to some degree it relieved some of my guilt for not paying him more attention. When the road gets narrow, we all deserve to be taken care of. Perhaps as he got closer to his final days and became more helpless and childlike, his wife was able to see in him what many others and I were attracted to, that David was just one hell of a good kid. Shalom, my friend.

I Want to Be Around for All of You

It is our attitude at the beginning of a difficult task which, more than anything else, will affect its successful outcome. —William James

I always knew my wife was a brave woman. After all, she has put up with me for over thirty years. But just how brave, we all recently found out. What she chose to go through and what many women choose to go through is a powerful lesson into the human spirit.

During her annual checkup, our internist suggested that my wife, Nancy, and I get a genetic test to see if there is anything lurking about. Ashkenazi Jews seem to be prone to a few horrible diseases. My immediate response to getting tested was an emphatic *no*. I am not big on finding out if I am going to die of something that I possibly cannot do squat about. If burnt toast can ruin my day, imagine if I found out I was coated with Charcot-Marie-Tooth disease.

My wife, on the other hand, without batting an eye, said she would take the test. She said it in such a nonchalant, carefree manner that it scared me. Her reasoning was if she found out she had something, maybe she could do something about it. My assumption was the opposite. She ended up making the right decision.

The doctor had her take a genetic test. A few weeks later, the results came back and all was good. But about three months later, she received a letter saying that she was the proud owner of the BRCA2 (breast cancer) gene. My immediate reaction to her new findings (which I kept to myself) was, *I knew this testing thing was a bad idea.*

According to cancer.org, a woman with the BRCA1 or BRCA2 gene has a seven in ten chance of getting breast cancer by the age of eighty. Also, the lucky ladies are at a much higher risk for ovarian cancer. Men with the BRCA gene can also get breast cancer and are at a higher risk for prostate cancer. Oy.

After finding BRCA2, the doctor put Nancy in touch with a geneticist. Because of COVID-19, all our meetings with the geneticist were over the phone. Her job was to find out about everyone that my wife is related to, what diseases they have or had, and what those who've passed away died of. As my mother would say, "She's a very nosy woman."

Being the doer she is, Nancy immediately proceeded to make her list of family members like she would any grocery list. Since the geneticist wanted to confirm the original findings, another box arrived with a genetic test containing the test tube and instructions on how to fill the tube. Nancy needed about an inch of spit. Gathering spit was hard for her. Being a New Yorker, spitting is second nature to me. I have been spitting since I was six. I can spit through the eye of a needle. Nancy has told me many times to stop spitting. And that's just in bed while watching *Jeopardy!* Unfortunately,

BRCA2 was reconfirmed with the new test. Eventually, I also stepped up to the plate and spit in my own tube. So far, so good.

So back again we went to our GP. It's good to have him steering the ship. Even though Nancy does not have cancer, he tells her she needs to see an oncologist. The doctor gives us a name, but Nancy asks for the GP's opinion as well. He tells her he thinks she should get a hysterectomy and a double mastectomy, but he is also clear that a lot of people may not agree with the second half of his assessment. Nancy is on board with the hysterectomy but not so much with the double mastectomy.

By the way, I went to every single meeting with every doctor and listened to every phone call during this whole shebang. That is how you can be most supportive of your partner's journey. You may not be able to cure her, but you can hold her hand. During all the doctor meetings, I would only speak if I thought she had forgotten something or if I felt I had something important to say. After thirty-plus years of marriage, you realize having something important to say is extremely rare.

The oncologist turned out to be a fine lady and agreed with our doctor that a hysterectomy and mastectomy were both good options. Nancy gave a thumbs-up for the hysterectomy but pooh-poohed the mastectomy. The doctor did not challenge her decision. After the doctor asked some questions, she gave her a breast exam. Her exam was not much different from the ones I give, except mine include dinner and a movie. Before leaving, the oncologist recommended some surgeons.

At home we looked up the potential surgeons on the internet. There is a sort of Rotten Tomatoes website for doctors. After reading a few bios, she picked a doctor who stuck out to her.

A week later we had a very pleasant one-hour meeting at Cedars-Sinai with a hysterectomy surgeon. My wife was clear that if he could not remove her uterus laparoscopically, she wanted to keep her friend intact. She wanted to get back to work as soon as possible and did not want a prolonged recovery time. He said he understood.

When we got back into the car, she said to me, "So what do you think of him?"

"What do I think?" I said. "He seems like a nice guy." I said the same thing about him that I might say about the guy who slices lox at the local fish store, "Seems like a nice guy." She said she had a good feeling about him and, coupled with good reviews and the oncologist's recommendation, she was going to use him. This is not unusual behavior for my wife. Ten minutes after we first met, she told me she thought she could marry me. Thirty-two years later and so far, so good. She seems to have a keen sense about people.

On September 30 at 5:30 a.m., I stood next to the "nice guy" surgeon, a few nurses, and the anesthesiologist. We were all surrounding Nancy's bed in pre-op. IVs were in place and the doctor looked at her and said, "We're ready if you are." I leaned over, gave her a kiss, and gently squeezed her hand. She looked a little sad. We had three boys delivered in that hospital. Now, some twenty-four years later, she was officially closing shop. As they started to roll her in, I said to the doctor and for everyone to hear, "Please be extra careful. You're working in one of my favorite areas." He was stunned. Nancy then told the doctor that I was a comedian. That helped to at least stop his hands from shaking, and he laughed.

A few hours later, I got a call from the doctor that he was done and Nancy was doing well. She came home that night and, thank God, healed up beautifully in a little less than six weeks. During those six weeks we took a daily walk, each day going a bit farther, and by the sixth week, she was back to walking two to three miles a day.

While recovering, Nancy received a call from a friend that her friend's sister, who is the same age as my wife, was diagnosed with breast cancer. The next day, Nancy decided to move ahead with the mastectomy. I told you she is a doer. She called her oncologist, who gave her the name of a well-known surgeon. She then called a few friends, and two of them had used this surgeon and liked him a lot. All this was happening during COVID-19 and at the speed of sound.

A week later, we were back at Cedars to meet the surgeon. He was about sixty years old, a Harvard-Yale guy with twenty-one years' experience. He has done countless mastectomies. Another hour-long meeting, where the doctor explains to us almost everything that he is going to do. It is not like the olden days when they would say, "Well, Max, we are all set to cut your head off Tuesday. Try to get some sleep." These days they tell you every hair-raising tidbit.

Nancy had done her research and told the doctor she was interested in something called DIEP (deep inferior epigastric perforator) flaps for the reconstruction. She did not want implants. With the DIEP flap surgery, fat, skin, and blood vessels are cut from the wall of the lower belly and moved up to your chest to rebuild your breast. It is an amazing surgery.

With each meeting and each phone call I realized just how brave the women are who make these gigantic decisions to subject themselves to this type of surgery when they are not at all ill. Thank you, Angelina Jolie, for shining a light by stepping up and sharing your experience, so that these potentially lifesaving procedures are normalized for more women.

The doctor said that because Nancy wanted the DIEP flaps, the surgery could take anywhere from ten to twelve hours. A possible twelve-hour operation for a relatively healthy person. I am up for days when I need so much as a tooth pulled. He then gave us the name of a young plastic surgeon who specializes in the DIEP flap procedure. There are very few surgeons in Los Angeles who perform this surgery. He said the woman is brilliant but that when we met her, if we thought she was too young, he would give us another name. I wanted to say to him, "Excuse me, but is she at least old enough to drive herself to the hospital?" But I kept quiet.

When we got outside and back in the car, my wife said to me, "So what do you think of him?"

I said, "What do I think? He seems great."

"Both my friends used him and gave him a thumbs-up. He has all five-star reviews. I like him. I'm going with him." I shrugged and said OK.

At that moment, this all got very real and scary at the same time. Two days later, we were back at Cedars to see the brilliant young plastic surgeon. We were brought into an exam room and they handed Nancy a robe. Nancy told me that out of all the robes so far, this was the nicest one. I agreed that it looked like a robe they would give you in a spa.

A few minutes later, the plastic surgeon came in. She looked young but also seemed super confident. Again we talked for an hour. She assured us that Nancy would be in good hands and she would be happy with the results.

Two days before the surgery, COVID-19 was roaring in Los Angeles and almost all nonessential operations were being canceled. Nancy checked with her doctor, who said so far, so good. Anyone who has ever waited for an operation of this magnitude knows this is a very trying time.

On December 15, 2020, the fifth day of Hanukkah, at 5:00 a.m., we got ready to leave for the hospital. Nancy had set up the Hanukkah candles and she reminded me to light them at home that night. I found that gesture so sweet.

As soon as we arrived, they took Nancy into pre-op. I was not allowed in until five minutes before she went into surgery, so for close to two hours, I sat and waited. At this point everything is completely out of your hands. If you are a praying person, this is a big part of your strength. If prayer is not your thing, you hope for the best.

Finally, they called me in to see her. I noticed her chest had lines drawn on it from a blue marker. I assumed these were drawn by the doctor and not some crazy tagger running around the hospital. I took her cold hand, gave her a kiss, told her I loved her and that I would see her later. I do not like to use the word "goodbye" at these moments. She quipped, "Is it too late to call this off?" I imagine there was a bit of truth in there somewhere.

The hardest part for me was getting through what turned out to be the next sixteen hours. A few texts from the hospital told me all was going well, but nothing else. I filled the time with a WhatsApp group my wife set up, a four-hour hike with one of my sons, writing, and talks with my kids on the phone.

Finally, a call from the surgeon came at about 7:30 p.m. He said he was sorry it took so long to call and that his part had gone well. The next call I got was from the plastic surgeon. She also said her part had gone well, and she said that Nancy would soon be out of the operating room and in recovery. She said the medical team was finishing up and I would hear from a nurse in about half an hour.

Two sweaty-palm hours later I got a call from a nurse who said it took longer than expected but that Nancy was fine and if I wanted to, I could come up for five minutes and say hello. I picked up my son and we went right over to the hospital. When we got upstairs, we were told only one person could go in to see her, so I went in.

When I finally saw her, as my mother would say, "*Oy yoy yoy.*" She looked very beaten up. She took my hand and started to cry, and I joined in. After five minutes, they asked me to leave. I begged them to let my son in for one minute, and they agreed to do so if I left. I told my son he could go in but he should be prepared. He said maybe he should not go in, but I said I thought he should, that it would be good for him and for her. He went in and she held his hand and cried.

COVID-19 was raging at the hospital. The ICU was almost filled. Thank God, she did not need the ICU. But Nancy wanted me to stay overnight with her at the hospital. She had a large suite. Normally, someone could sleep over in the patient's room, but at that time it was forbidden. I had my internist and rabbi both speak to the charge nurse and urge her to let me stay. They promised the nurse I would not leave Nancy's hospital room. The woman had a big heart and approved my staying, and I kept my word and remained in Nancy's room for four days straight without walking out the door. My wife was much calmer having me there, and I could advocate for her if needed. I helped her with everything from paging a nurse to drinking, eating, and getting her to do her painful lung exercises. If you can be there to advocate, do it.

The operations are now behind us, and Nancy has recovered beautifully. The pain from the surgery was not nearly as bad as she was warned that it might be. My hat is off to all women who choose to go through this. Both mentally and physically, this is an exceedingly difficult thing to do, and doubly so to those women who must go through it with cancer. We have three boys, two beautiful daughters-in-law, and a new grandchild. Nancy's words ring in our ears: "I want to be around for all of you."

On New Year's Eve 2021, Nancy and I were home and watched the wonderful movie *Bells Are Ringing* from 1960. It stars Judy Holliday and Dean Martin. Judy Holliday was a brilliant comedian who died at just forty-three years old. Nancy asked from what, and I told her Judy died of breast cancer. It was a bittersweet moment for us when we both realized how lucky we were that, in her sixties and with the BRCA gene, Nancy seemed to have dodged a big bullet. At midnight, as the Times Square ball dropped on TV, I walked over to her in the reclining chair that she had been sleeping in for a few weeks, gave her a kiss, and thanked her for what she did for herself and all of us. It truly was a happy new year for the Schiff family.

My Uncle Miltie

Cigar-smoking stand-up comedian and actor Mendel Berlinger—aka Milton Berle aka Uncle Miltie aka Mr. Television—was born on July 12, 1908, and passed away on March 27, 2002, at the age of ninety-three. Berle was once asked if he feared dying. He said, "No. I've died in Milwaukee, Philadelphia, and Omaha."

Berle was a giant in show business. He worked nonstop to make people laugh for eighty years. From 1948 to 1956, he was the biggest star in the country when he hosted the *Texaco Star Theatre* variety show. Each week, 24 million people tuned in to watch him. Berle had a joke for everything. For instance, it was well known that Berle had a large male member. Once approached by a young man who said his was bigger than Berle's, Berle was quoted as saying, "Show me yours and then I'll take out just enough to beat you."

I saw Berle work live twice. The first time was when he opened for Frank Sinatra. The other time was when I was on the bill with him in Montreal at the 1991 Just for Laughs Comedy Festival.

Since I first started performing in 1977, I have always had a battle with stage fright. It has gotten better, but it's far from gone. I never know if Mr. Fright will be coming to my show; he likes to show up unannounced. Some nights he's on vacation, and other nights I might be gripped.

People have asked why I torture myself. The answer is there is no other job I'd rather do. With all jobs, you pay a price. Mine is stage fright, a mere pittance. One night at Caesars Palace I was opening for Diana Ross and I was so scared that I thought I might choke or fall off the stage. The place was humming and spinning, but somehow I kept on keeping on.

The night I worked with Milton Berle, my stage fright was alive and well. Alone in my dressing room, I was short of breath and did not know whether I should run or hide. My rib cage was being punched from the inside. I sat scared to death that this might be the night my heart exploded. I still had a long thirty minutes before I went to the gallows.

Then something inside me said I should go and say hello to Mr. Berle. I thought it might take my mind off this horror. His dressing room was four doors down. His door was open, and I could see he was alone, sitting in his shirt and pants, smoking a cigar. When he would get the knock that it was showtime, all he had to do was slip on his suit jacket and go be funny. Rarely, if ever, are comedians' dressing rooms filled with laughter

and frivolity. We are not rock stars; the only time anyone was ever naked in my dressing room besides me is when my wife and baby were there, and the baby took off his diaper and started running around laughing. Comedians are worried neurotics. We are a desperate bunch begging for acceptance and hoping for a chance to spread lightness.

Mr. Berle saw me peering in and said, "Hey, kid, can I help you?"

I introduced myself. "Hi, Mr. Berle. My name is Mark Schiff and I'm on the show with you. I wanted to say hi." He gave me the wave to enter, and I did. I went over and shook his hand, and he looked at me. My hand must have felt like it had been locked in a meat freezer. He asked me how I was, and so I went for it and gushed, "Mr. Berle, it's an honor to work with you."

He said, "I know."

I then followed with, "I am scared. My heart is pounding. I've never worked a big theater like this." He looked at me, squinted, and gave me a big, toothy smile. I'm not sure, but I think he was genuinely touched by my honesty. When you open yourself to people, you take a chance—but on this night, it went the way it was supposed to go, which was perfect. In Yiddish, the word is *bashert*.[42]

He stood, dusted ash off his perfectly creased pants, walked over to me, and said, "I'm sure you're good because if you weren't, you wouldn't be here." I almost started crying. Here is Milton Berle, a legend, being not only kind but also gentle. "When are you on?" he asked.

"About fifteen minutes."

With a big smile, he replied, "I'm sure you'll be great. I'll try to watch." The thought that he might watch me made my sphincter tighten. He then picked up a cigar and said, "Here, kid, have a Montecristo." Thanks, Mr. Berle.

I walked to the door, turned, and thanked him again. I wish I could say his kind words relieved me of the stage fright, but it was quite the opposite.

---

42 *Bashert* refers to a person's soulmate, especially when considered as an ideal or predestined marriage partner. Some men and women are meant to be. But we also know that most people are incompatible and should live in different countries.

It was worse than before. Now not only did I need to prove myself to the audience but to a watching Mr. Berle as well. I was petrified, chilled to the bone. The Rosenbergs walking to the electric chair were less worried than I was. Why couldn't I keep my mouth closed? Why? Why? Why?

Mary Tyler Moore was hosting the show and had begun my introduction. I was holding on to the curtain so tight, I thought, *If I don't let go, I might pull it down and kill a few people*. I was seconds away from stepping into the lights when someone whispered to me, "This is Montreal. You need to say something in French. Otherwise, they will hate you." I walked out, grabbed the microphone, and launched into "*Bonjour*, folks." I then followed that with, "*Soupe du jour*. That's it for my French." I got a little laugh.

Short of breath, I jumped into my act. What I remember most was that I was scared but doing well. The audience was laughing at the right times. After my twelve minutes, I ended with my usual "Thank you, goodnight," and even tossed out a "*Bonsoir*."

Backstage, as my eyes refocused, I could see Mr. Berle was standing there. He had watched me. "Hey, kid, nice show. I told you that you were good." Again, I could have cried. He handed me another cigar and walked off into the backstage darkness. Because of his "Hey, kid nice show," I was now floating in the air like a helium balloon. It would be a decade later and the year before he died, when we would meet again.

Cut to the Hillcrest Country Club. The Hillcrest became a hangout for Jewish comedians because most other country clubs in Los Angeles were restricted. (Translation: no Jews allowed.) I was there to do a private show. I was my usual early self when I was told I could have lunch in the dining room. When I walked in, I heard laughter coming from the other side of the room. I looked over and there was Mr. Berle, holding court. Another *bashert* was handed to me. I was supposed to be here at this time. For some reason, I immediately flashed back to how kind he was to me in Montreal. I needed to thank him one more time. I was sure he wouldn't remember, but so what?

I walked over, and as I approached the table, Berle and the four people he was with turned and looked fixedly at me. Berle said, "Hey, kid, can I help you?"—exactly what he said when I stood outside his dressing room.

"Mr. Berle, my name is Mark Schiff."

He raised his hand to stop me from speaking. "Mark Schiff. I know you. You're that scared kid from Montreal."

"That's me." Ten years, a million miles, and thousands of people, how could he remember? I felt like I was trapped in some mentalist's act.

He then handed me a cigar and said, "Sit down and have some lunch, but don't butt in." Everyone laughed, but I laughed the hardest. We all need an Uncle Miltie.

Simon Says Do This

Shortly after my twelfth birthday, I started hearing things. At night, while I was trying to fall asleep, loud and scary symphonic music would explode in my head. I prayed, "Please, God, stop the music."

One day the music disappeared, and what replaced it was much more comforting and inspiring. My muse, or maybe my angel, got in touch with me. I would hear her quietly whispering in my head, "Write a play."

Her voice was friendly, caring, devoid of anger. She seemed to know me better than my parents, friends, or teachers. Though mostly nice people, they didn't understand what it meant to be called upon or to be a creative type. A normal life clocking in and out was their reality. My muse understood, and there were no judgments attached.

One morning at 4:00 a.m., when the house was dark except for one dull fluorescent light that was attached to a small desk where my mother sat to pay the bills, I slid into her seat. Until this night, I'd never had a reason to sit at this desk. But there I sat, in my kangaroo pajama bottoms and no top, clutching a BIC pen, and writing my first play. You ask, "Why a play?" Because that night, while I was in a deep sleep, the whisper came. My muse told me to write a play. Rubbing my eyes, I got out of bed, shuffled my feet to the desk, and began writing.

A half hour later, my father—on his way out to work—spotted me, a young Shakespeare, filling words in the blank white space of the black-lined paper. He asked, "What are you doing?"

I said quite casually, "I'm writing a play."

So as not to wake my mother, he whispered, "This is craziness. Go to bed. You have school in a few hours." He meant well, but meaning well has killed the call in many a budding artist.

I don't think I ever finished the play. But the memory of me sitting there writing it is indelibly rooted into my psyche and still one of the great moments of my life. That's the moment I came alive. That's the moment that I chose to write. That's the moment I now had something to do anytime I wanted. That's the moment my life suddenly had a purpose.

My grades were horrifying, and at that point, I hadn't even read one whole book. Many people already thought of me as a screwup, and they had a point. But what they didn't know was that I had a vision and a guide. I also knew three important words: *what the heck*. Sometimes, you just have to say what the heck. So I did, and followed my muse.

When I was eighteen, the muse started up again, telling me to do stand-up comedy. After an abysmal two-year business school experience, I began going to open mic nights. My muse turned out to be right: stand-up was my calling. I jumped in and never looked back.

For about twenty-five years, I wrote and performed stand-up comedy and mostly earned a good living. I had my own Showtime and HBO specials and performed on *The Tonight Show Starring Johnny Carson* and the *Late Show with David Letterman* several times. Then in 2000, my muse once again encouraged me to don my Shakespeare hat. I sat down and wrote a two-character play called *The Comic*. It was another what-the-heck moment.

The play was about an older Jewish comedian who checks into a cheap hotel to kill himself. At the lowest point of his life, he decides to do something nice for someone else. The point is that even in your darkest moments, you can still do something decent for someone.

The play was dark and bitingly funny. It was nothing short of a miracle when I found a few people who believed in the play. Almost every Friday and Saturday night for ten months, it went up at the Helms Bakery District's theater, a seventy-seater in what was once a giant bread factory on Venice Boulevard in Culver City, California. Someone knew Michael Patrick King, a major force behind the TV and movie adaptations of *Sex and the City* and our personal angel, and got him to back our venture. Every performance got rousing applause and most nights a standing ovation.

The play had two terrific actors: Henri Lubatti and Larry Miller. One night, Larry asked if I wouldn't mind if he brought Neil Simon in to see it. I said, "Are you kidding?"

"Are you kidding?" is the only possible response to that question. That's like asking an Orthodox rabbi if he believes in circumcision. Are you kidding? Larry had been in Neil Simon's play *The Dinner Party* and occasionally was in touch with Mr. Simon. Without a doubt, Mr. Simon has caused more audiences to convulse with laughter than anyone who has ever lived and probably ever will live. If I was offered an opportunity to go back in time for one night to see any play written between 1962 and 1990, it would be a Neil Simon play, hands down.

One Friday night, ten minutes before the curtain went up, I saw Neil Simon walk in by himself. If I were wearing glasses, I would have cleaned them to make sure I was seeing correctly. The host sat him on the aisle, five rows back. Moments later, lights faded to black. Larry Miller entered from stage left. Seconds later, it was lights up: the play had begun. As far as I could tell, it was going well.

An hour-plus flew by. Then the blackout, and the play ended. Amazingly, the people in the audience did what they did at every Neil Simon play. They stood, clapped, and hooted. Mr. Simon himself was also standing and clapping, though I wasn't sure if he was hooting. I wondered if he was clapping and standing just to be polite. Did he like the play? I was about to find out.

Five minutes went by and the audience had filed out, the theater emptied except for Neil Simon and Mark the playwright. Now began another of the greatest moments in my life. I was alone with arguably the greatest, most successful playwright who had ever lived, and he had just watched my play.

Now began what, without a doubt, was another living, breathing miracle. Neil Simon was about to discuss my play with me. Not my Broadway play or my West End London play. Not my fifteenth play or my sixth play. My first play—one held at a local theater.

If he had wanted to, he probably could have spent the evening discussing playwriting with such luminaries as Arthur Miller, Sam Shepard, Tom Stoppard, or Marsha Norman. But this was not their night. No, it was my night. It was the payoff for me gripping a ballpoint pen on an ordinary school night at 4:00 a.m.

I walked over to Mr. Simon, who was looking at the one-pager about the play, and went to shake his hand.

"Hello, Mr. Simon. I'm Mark Schiff," I said. "Thank you for coming this evening."

He looked back at the paper and then at me.

"Oh, hi, Mark. It's my pleasure. I see you wrote this play."

"Yes."

"Congratulations on writing this wonderful play."

"Thank you."

"I enjoyed it."

"Thank you. Aren't the actors great?"

"Terrific. The play is very funny. You could not make this play any funnier."

I couldn't believe what I was hearing. "Wow" was all I could say.

"Can I give you some advice?"

I couldn't believe what was about to happen: Neil Simon, *the* Neil Simon, was going to give me advice on playwriting.

"Yes. *Please.*"

"Your play, like my plays, gets into the most trouble when characters are just talking and not doing something. You need to make sure that they aren't just sitting and talking. They must be eating or moving or cleaning or something. They need to perform some action."

"I get that. I can do that."

It's a wonder I didn't have a stroke or jump up and kiss Neil Simon on the lips.

"Your ending isn't clear to me. Does your main character live or die?"

"I decided to leave that up to the audience. Let them decide."

"No. You must know. And you need to let the audience know. You can't leave that up to them. You need to make that decision."

"Really?"

"Yes."

"OK. I will. Thank you."

I handed Mr. Simon a copy of his play *The Odd Couple* and asked him if he wouldn't mind signing it and having his picture taken with me. He said, "Of course." He took out a pen and wrote something. He then posed for a photo, said goodbye, and exited the theater. I watched him go and then collapsed in a seat. I read aloud what he wrote on the cover of the playbook: "Congratulations on writing your wonderful play. Neil Simon." I put my hands over my face in disbelief at what had just occurred.

That night I went home to my desk and, just like Neil Simon had many times, I rewrote a new ending. There was now a definite resolve I chose for the audience.

The next performance of *The Comic* had a new ending and my characters moved a lot more. The audience now knew if Larry Miller's character lived or died. In the end, the play got even more applause (and more hoots) than before.

As I look back and think about that night, I have such gratitude for my muse, gratitude for everyone involved in the play, and gratitude for the ten minutes during which Neil Simon was willing to spend his precious time with me. When I heard he passed away, it was a very sad day for his family, the millions of fans who loved him, and me. Sometimes I think what happened to me that night could have easily happened to a character in one of his plays. And so, I think to myself, *How many people after writing their first play got input and the ending to their play from Neil Simon? There is only one person I know of.*

Curtain down.

8
HOPE

....

"B Positive" Is Not Just a Blood Type

Imagine you are thirty-two years old, and one day something seems off with your left eye. You go to your eye doctor, he sends you to someone else, and that person sends you to a specialist. Five weeks later, you are blind.

Welcome to Menachem Green's world. Menachem has Leber Hereditary Optic Neuropathy (LHON). It is an inherited form of vision loss, and as of right now there is no cure. This condition usually begins in a person's teens or twenties. Menachem told me that he is grateful that he had more years of vision than most people with LHON get.

I first met Menachem a few years ago, when he had his vision and worked at 613 The Mitzvah Store, a Jewish bookshop in Los Angeles. Then on Shabbas a few weeks ago, I was walking with my wife and I saw Menachem with a cane, Ray Charles–type sunglasses, and a young lady. I said, "Hey, Menachem. It's Mark Schiff."

With a big, toothy smile, he said, "The funny man. You want to hear a blind joke?"

"Sure do," I said. We traded blind jokes, and then he told me a little about what happened.

Menachem is a handsome young man with a great sense of humor who also happens to be a Torah-observant Jew. I could not stop thinking about how this young man, who had nearly perfect vision a little over two years ago, could be so upbeat. Was it because it was Shabbas and we are required to be joyful?

Over the next couple of weeks, I saw Menachem in shul a few times and then met with him at his apartment. I found out it wasn't just Shabbas. Menachem is a cheerful chap and remains positive in spite of losing his eyesight. He may have lost his vision, but he hasn't lost Menachem.

He told me he believes God will one day restore his sight, either through the medical world or through a miracle. He told me his faith in God is stronger now than before, and he continues to study Torah. He is being taught something called assistive technology. His teacher is also blind. This technology is specific to the person who needs it. The learning curve is tremendous, but Menachem is up for the task.

One big problem for Menachem is when you talk to him, he can't read your facial expressions. Yet he seems very in tune with the person he is talking with. It's important to him not to be a downer. He told me "B positive" is not just a blood type. He has friends who call him every day, and some stop by to help him around the house. He feels remarkably close to them.

Menachem grew up in Los Angeles. Sometimes when the Dodgers were on TV, his mother would watch with him and call the plays. Believe it or not, he's gone to the batting cages a few times. Why not? He's still Menachem.

I asked him if he was angry about losing his vision. He told me more disappointed than angry. When his family found out he would lose his vision, they got terribly upset, but Menachem told them, "Sometimes God throws you a curve ball and you have to learn how to hit it." He also told me he doesn't believe losing his vision is tragic. He said he's been dealt a difficult hand, but if you play it right, you can still win the game.

The organization Bosma Enterprises creates opportunities for people who are blind or visually impaired. Bosma reports that 70 percent of Americans who are visually impaired are unemployed. Menachem loves working and being around other people. When he's not working, his days get lonesome. He would much rather work and pay his own way. Last time we spoke, he shared the good news that the Dodgers had hired him to work in their offices. He needed a break and got one. He needed some *naches*,[43] and he got some. He needed someone to take a chance on him, and the Dodgers stepped up to the plate.

Even though at this moment the light is physically blocked from his eyes, Menachem knows God loves him and that his friends and family love him. He has hope. If you asked him what he'd like his life to be like in ten years, he would say to have his vision back, to be married, have a good job, be a good Torah teacher, and have box seats for the Dodgers. Go Menachem. See you at the batting cages.

The Perfect Circle

Back in the '80s I had a friend named Mickey who was very helpful and a fun guy, but he would pluck a person's one good eye out if he felt he could get cash for it. He was one tough, funny Jew, a *shtarker*.[44] When I was with him, I always felt protected. It was like being with a human German shepherd. Other than my father, he was the only Jew I knew with a tattoo, and a Star of David covered much of his upper right forearm. At my father's

---

43 *Naches* is Yiddish for "pride" or "gratification," especially at the achievements of one's children. This only applies if the child is a Jewish child who graduates medical school at the top of his or her class and becomes a specialist in any field except podiatry. In order to pronounce the word correctly, as with most Yiddish, one must produce an inordinate amount of phlegm.

44 *Shtarker* is a Yiddish word meaning "an extremely tough guy." Even though Mike Tyson is not Jewish, he is still a *shtarker*. Gilbert Gottfried was Jewish but not a *shtarker*.

funeral, Mickey locked arms with me and held me up when I got weak in the knees. Except for his thievery, he was a really great guy.

After moving to California, I kept my New York apartment for about fifteen years, just in case my career didn't work out. My mom said, "You always need a backup," even though she never had one. Periodically, I'd let friends stay for free. It was a tiny studio with no sink in the bathroom and a gas heater. If for some reason the heater's pilot light went out while you slept, there was a possibility you might sleep forever.

The apartment was too small for a bed, so I kept a foam mattress leaning against the wall and when I was living there I would plop it down on the cold floor each night. Occasionally, a mouse would run by my face as I was drifting off. Mice loved my apartment because I always had crumbs on the floor or an open package of something from Entenmann's. I kept a small TV, radio, and cable box in the apartment even after I moved, so that when people stayed there, there was some entertainment other than the mice sweeping up.

On a gig in Indianapolis, I met a jeweler named Marc Aronstam who quickly became a friend. One afternoon I mentioned to him that November 18, 1984, was an important date in my life. It was the day I started my life over, the day I stopped drinking and destroying myself. As of today, I've yet to have another drink. Marc suggested I let him make me a ring to commemorate the occasion. Some months later he handed me a beautiful ring that I cherished and wore almost all the time. Whenever I looked at it, I felt a surge of gratitude.

One day I got a call from a friend who was staying at my New York apartment. He said, "I thought there was a TV and cable box here." I said, "There isn't?" He said, "There is nothing here." I hung up and called Mickey, who admitted he'd gone shopping at my apartment. He eventually returned everything, and I eventually forgave him. Mickey was struggling with addiction and mental health issues. A few of us tried to help him, but ultimately to no avail. Five years later, I let Mickey stay with me in

California until he found a place. He swore to me he was done stealing. The day after he moved out, I realized my most precious ring was missing. I grilled him, but he never did cop to it. That said, I've always believed it was him.

Not long after, I heard he was caught stealing an expensive pair of sunglasses as well as many other things. I cut Mickey out of my life. Sometimes you have to get rid of people, even those you love.

Many times I've thought about the ring and how I wish I still had it. But I never tried to get another one. Then one day, I told my friend Roman Ward, a ninety-year-old Holocaust survivor, about my November 18 date and how important it was to me. When Roman came to America, he became a jeweler. He said, with his Polish accent, "Mark, my dear friend, I'd like to make you a ring as a gift." I told Roman I'd love it. He told me that he loved me.

Roman kept his promise and made me a ring. What's most amazing is that the ring he made is almost exactly like the old one, which Roman never saw. Just like with the original, every time I look at it I feel that same surge of gratitude. I finally don't miss my old ring anymore. I feel like this one is a gift from God through Roman. Like with the original finished ring, the circle is once again complete. As my friend Cubby once said, "It's good to know that miracles are possible without my consent."

Let There Be Light

I was on the phone talking to my friend Ryan when I heard a strange sound emanating from his end. I asked him what the sound was, and he told me it was a flood alert on his phone. I asked, "Where are you? Mississippi? The Mekong Delta?"

He replied, "82nd and Central Park West."

Growing up in the Bronx and Queens, not only did we not have flood alerts, we had no floods. Actually, we did have one once when my mother left the bathtub running and went to the supermarket to get me some Tang. That was when I was deciding whether or not I wanted to become an astronaut.

When I was growing up during that time, there were very few warnings about anything. The big one was the nuclear bomb warning. The children were told we would be safe by hiding under our school desks. I guess the kids in Hiroshima and Nagasaki didn't have school desks.

The only other big warnings were from my parents. Those were mostly about my behavior. "I'm warning you, you better start behaving." That was usually followed by the "or else" warning. I once asked what "or else" meant. "You'll see what 'or else' means." "You'll see" is ten times more frightening than "or else." Otherwise, a simple "Be careful" covered almost everything.

Now when I go to fill up my car with gas, there's a sign on the gas pump that warns me about the potential cancer I'm risking. I then need to decide whether to fill up or walk nineteen miles to work. On a family trip to Alaska, we had to take a bus from Seward to Anchorage. Before we took off, the driver gave us a ten-minute warning talk. She told us how to open and climb out the window in case the bus caught fire and was about to explode. She told us what to do if we were stopped and a grizzly bear boarded the bus and wanted to ride to Anchorage with us. She then proceeded to drive down a wet mountain road at about 50 mph with one hand on the steering wheel and the other hand holding a foot-long Subway meatball hero.

My favorite is the warning from the flight attendants who tell you, with a straight face, to tighten up your seat belt nice and snug so you're prepared in the event the plane engines conk out and you are heading in a downward spiral toward the earth at 500 mph.

I installed the Ring camera at my front door and half a dozen more around the perimeter of my home. I get ten to fifty warnings a day from

Ring about local home invasions, armed robberies, and car break-ins. Someone should have warned me how frightened I was going to be from all the warnings Ring would send me. A few times in the middle of the night in our backyard the camera filmed what I initially thought were masked burglars. It turned out there were no burglars, just a family of raccoons.

My first car had an oil light warning and that was it. I now have close to thirty different warning lights on my Kia. Most of the icons are impossible to interpret. One lets me know my suspension dampers are in trouble. Anyone know what a suspension damper is? There's even a warning light that reminds me that I've left my lights on.

No matter how many warning lights I have or how many times I'm told to be aware of potential dangers, few of them alleviate my fears. What I really need is a light to tell me when all is well. The truth is things are actually all right, so I need a way to let the good light in, the comforting light, the light that actually helps fix things. The light that warms my soul. We light Shabbas candles to bring more light into the world. Shabbas is good light. It's my faith and trust in God that allow me to relax, if at all, and that bring more good light to me. Loosely translated in Hebrew, it's known as *emunah*[45] and *bitachon*.[46]

Until I'm in touch with my *emunah* and *bitachon*, the negative lights and warnings are always burning brightly. For most people, *emunah* and *bitachon* are developed over a lifetime, and like lifting weights, they need to be worked on regularly so you can get stronger and better at it. Have some trust and faith and take care of what you can take care of. As Tom Bodett, owner of Motel 6, says, "We'll leave the light on for you." Just make sure it's the good light.

---

45 *Emunah* is generally translated as "faith" or the knowledge that God created and continues to run all of creation. My mother disagreed with the concept that God runs all of creation. When I was growing up, she was famous for saying, "I run this house. Me and nobody else. If God wants to run it, that's fine. Then let him pay the bills."

46 *Bitachon* is generally translated as "trust" and conveys a powerful sense of optimism. Optimism ran in my family. My parents were optimistic we would go broke and end up in the street.

The Blessing

When I was growing up, there wasn't much Jewishness in our home. My parents never shied away from being Jewish; we just never did much about it. I don't really remember ever having Shabbat dinner at home. Because of that, I never got the Friday-night blessing from my father:

May God bless you and keep you.

May God shine His face on you and be gracious to you.

May God turn His face toward you and grant you peace.

That's a small part of a beautiful blessing that people bestow on their children every Friday night.

In 1984 I had my first moment of clarity after I got sober and started cleaning up my past. Then came another moment of clarity. It was a knock at the door of my Jewish soul from the outreach group Aish HaTorah and their rabbis, Heller, Baars, Braverman, and Cohen, rebbetzins,[47] and so many others slowly and gently leading me out of the dark. One day I didn't know a single rabbi and the next day I knew ten of them. Even stranger was that almost all of them were younger than me and mostly beardless. This was a younger, hipper type of rabbi.

Then came the invitations. For practically every Friday night and Saturday lunch, some rabbi would ask me to come for a meal. All the rabbis seemed to love me. I grew up feeling that nobody liked me, and then suddenly rabbis from all over the world were flipping over me.

At the Friday-night meals, two things jumped out at me. Singing *Eishet Chayil* (Honoring of the Wives) and the Blessing of the Children. Boys and girls both got this blessing. Not just by the rabbis, but by everyday fathers and mothers who put their hands on their children's heads, closed their

---

47 Rebbetzin is the title used for the wife of a rabbi, typically from the Orthodox, Haredi, and Hasidic Jewish groups, or for a female Torah scholar or teacher. You know the saying, "Behind every great rabbi is a greater rebbetzin."

eyes, and prayed hard for them. Then when the prayer was over, the kids usually got a kiss. Most of the children seemed to appreciate it. Many of the little ones ran fast to their parents to get their blessing. They sensed this was special for them. When I saw the parents bless the kids, two things would happen to me. First, I'd smile. Then I would feel a tinge of sadness. I thought maybe it was because I wasn't married and didn't have kids.

Eight years later, I was married by Rabbi Aryeh Scheinberg, an Orthodox rabbi in my wife's hometown of San Antonio. Rabbi Scheinberg did have a big beard and was older than me. Boom—three boys later, I was now singing and giving out Friday-night blessings to all my boys. When I placed my hands on their heads, I could feel the love from my heart and soul pour out through my fingers directly into them. It really felt like a holy thing to do. Again, though, it was always tinged with some bittersweet and a touch of sadness.

Cut to thirty-seven years after the start of my journey, when my wife and I were at our friends Cathy and Lowell's for Friday-night Shabbat dinner and none of our kids were with us. Also at the table were Cathy and Lowell's three daughters; Rabbi Seidenfeld and his wife, Lolly; and one of their daughters. Lowell first blessed his three daughters. Then Rabbi Seidenfeld went to bless his daughter, who was sitting to my right. While watching Rabbi Seidenfeld bless his daughter, once again, I felt a sense of sadness hovering over me.

When Rabbi Seidenfeld was done, I asked him, "Can anyone get that blessing?" He said yes and that he wondered why I was asking.

Before I could say anything, God wrote the next line and passed it on to the rabbi. Rabbi Seidenfeld said to me, "Would you like a blessing?" In a heartbeat I nodded yes and bowed my head. He put his hands on my head, and I received what was my first ever Friday-night blessing. Not until that moment did I ever realize I had never been blessed.

I thanked him and told him I felt like my father had given me the blessing. It felt like my father was in the room guiding him to give me what my father would love to have given me but never knew how to. That blessing made up for all the ones I never got during my childhood. Now when I see people giving their kids this blessing, I feel happy for everyone.

Thank you, Rabbi Seidenfeld.

Sealed with a Kiss

A kiss is a secret told to the mouth instead of the ear; kisses are the messengers of love and tenderness. —Ingrid Bergman

Kissing is an amazing thing. Almost all of us have done it and had it done to us. Even COVID-19 never completely put an end to where lips meet. Lovers kiss, and mobsters kiss. Some kisses we like, and some not so much. When I was growing up, my grandmother would put her lips to my cheek and work up a suction that almost took off half my face when she pulled loose. I let her do it because I loved her and because I'd get three dollars if I let her. We kiss animals; some people kiss the ground after a flight, gravestones, mezuzahs,[48] or Torah scrolls[49]; and some even kiss a wall in Israel. We kiss hello, and we kiss goodbye. We kiss to congratulate, and we kiss to comfort. Some kiss the dead goodbye for the last time. We kiss photos of loved ones who are no longer with us. We kiss on one cheek. We kiss on two cheeks. We have candy chocolate KISSES. Sports stadiums have the "Kiss Cam." There's a rock band called KISS. There are long kisses and quick pecks. There's the good morning kiss and the goodnight kiss. There's

---

48 A mezuzah functions to remind you every time you enter or leave your house that you have a covenant with God. It also reminds you to make sure you turn your burglar alarm on and off when entering and leaving.

49 The Torah scroll is a long scroll containing the entire text of the five books of Moses, handwritten by a pious scribe in the original Hebrew. There are 304,805 letters inscribed with a quill by hand. It takes about a year to write a new Torah. That's the same amount of time it takes me to clean out my closet and desk drawers.

"kiss and make up." There's the "I love you more than anyone in the world" kiss. There's the "Let's go to bed" kiss.

If we don't want to deal with people, we tell them to kiss off. It's said some people even have the kiss of death. Everything they touch, they ruin. A deeply religious Jewish couple won't kiss for two weeks a month, and hardly ever in public.

When I was a kid, they told me that mononucleosis was the kissing disease. I always wanted to get mono. I just couldn't find anyone who wanted to give it to me.

I never knew how many kisses I had in me until we had our children. I don't know for sure, but I've probably kissed my kids a few hundred thousand times since they were born. I used to hold them as babies and would just keep kissing them. Anytime my wife handed one of them to me, I'd rev up the kiss machine. One time she went away for three days and I forgot to feed them because I was so busy kissing them. You can only do that with your own children, and to some extent with your grandchildren. If my neighbors asked me to hold their baby and I started kissing him for ten minutes straight, they would take the baby away from me and maybe even move out of the neighborhood. But with my kids, I was unstoppable.

It's not uncommon to kiss and nibble babies on their tush.[50] This usually stops by the child's third birthday then picks up again when they start dating in high school.

My kids are not big on kissing me back. If I want to kiss them even now, they will lower their heads and let me kiss them on the top of their skulls as if they are the pope, or I am.

A few months after my father died, I realized his birthday was coming up. I went out and bought a birthday card. I filled out the card wishing him a happy birthday, wrote that I hoped he was OK, and signed it "Love, Mark." I then put the card in the envelope, sealed it, found a mailbox, kissed

---

50 "Tush" comes from the Yiddish word *tuchus*. A tush is a person's behind. When someone says "Look at that tush," that can mean either it's a beautiful example of one or it's an enormous one. Plumbers are famous for exposing part of their tush when they climb under a person's sink.

the envelope, and dropped it in with no address. Most of us have at least one person we'd love to kiss one more time.

Most of all, it's just nice to be kissed by someone you love and to kiss someone you love. Some years ago, I had a breakfast appointment with my friend Irwin, who was in his eighties. Irwin and his wife, Dottie, were going on sixty years of marriage and lived in a second-floor apartment, up a long flight of stairs. At this time of his life, it was hard for Irwin to walk up and down the flight. Each step was difficult for him. We were about a half a block away when he told me he had to go back home because he had forgotten something. I told him I'd get it for him, but he wouldn't have it. He had to do it himself. When he finally got to the top of the stairs, he knocked. Dottie opened the door and said, "Did you forget something?" Irwin said, "Yes. I forgot to kiss you goodbye."

9
KINDNESS

....

Always Keep Your
Promises to Your Dog

When God created the world, He invested in man the power to elevate
the divine sparks or souls that are found throughout creation. It is for
this reason that in general, the way an animal's soul is elevated and
returned after its death to its divine source is through its positive and
spiritual interactions with man. —Rabbi Yehuda Shurpin

It's our responsibility to elevate our pets. Sometimes, though, I think it is
them elevating us. Like when I'm upset and my dog looks at me with that
face that says, "Easy does it, pal. Go chase a ball. You'll feel better."

My wife and I had a dog named Glendi. Glendi was a gift straight from
the heavens. My wife had been talking to me about getting a teacup Yorkie,
the only breed she was interested in. She had two as a child and always
wanted another.

One evening in 2009, we were dropping off something on our friend's
doorstep down on Glenville Drive. Running around on their doorstep was
a filthy little cold, wet, ratty animal. (Our friends weren't home.) Our gift

from God had been delivered. When I first saw this thing running around, I really wasn't sure what it was. Whatever it was, it was a real mess. My wife was still in the car. I said, "Come quick!" and she ran over and saw I was holding what turned out to be a teacup Yorkshire terrier that we eventually named Glendi after the street Glenville. Years earlier, while driving with my kids, we'd found a cockatiel on Pico Boulevard that we brought home and named Pico. Also, one afternoon I met this supermodel at a bus stop. She was twenty-four and gorgeous. I was not allowed to bring her home. You can't have everything.

The next day we took Glendi to our vet and found out she was not microchipped. We then searched for her owners, advertising her finding and looking for lost dogs in newspapers and online. Nothing. The vet said she was in good health except for a slightly messed-up back left leg and some bad teeth. I wish I got a report that good from my doctor.

Glendi turned out to be the sweetest, most loving, dumbest dog on the planet. After ten years, she still didn't understand the command "Sit." Now that I think about it, my boys also took about ten years to learn to sit. And it's taken me twenty years to learn to pick my socks up off the floor. I guess it runs in the family.

We once hired Glendi a trainer, and to quote him: "Glendi is not the brightest star in the sky." Most dogs enjoy playing ball or running around. Not Glendi. Her thing was lying in bed and staring at us. She was also a painfully slow walker. In fact, we didn't walk her; we'd take her out for a drag. She could sleep eighteen hours a day and still be up for another nap. Adult Yorkies have forty-two teeth. Glendi had six scattered about her mouth, like some kind of hillbilly dog. But we loved her, and she loved us.

I know Glendi knew that we saved her life, and since her first day with us, Glendi spent her entire existence following my wife from one room to the next. I'm sure Glendi never thought, *What am I doing with my life?* or *Is this all there is?* She never wanted or needed to be anything more than a friend. On Friday nights, Glendi would wait for her chicken soup, and at

Shabbas lunch she had her own chair at our table. After a few morsels of people food, she would fall asleep and take her long Shabbas nap, sometimes in her chair and sometimes in my wife's lap.

After ten years of pretty robust health, Glendi got sick. It seemed her kidneys might be failing. She was in the hospital for four days. We went to visit her every day. It was like visiting a relative. We brought her brisket and chicken. The only thing we didn't bring her was the daily newspaper. Her doctor said it's wait-and-see. We prayed she would bounce back, but if not we'd make sure she never had to suffer.

The rabbis say it's our job to elevate animals, but I've learned a lot from Glendi. I've learned it's important to give a hearty hello when someone you love comes back home. I've learned it's important to snuggle next to someone you love. I've learned it's important to eat your meals with gusto. I've learned it's important to enjoy what you have and not complain about what you don't have.

When we had to put our first dog, Star, down years ago, the vet asked me if I wanted to come into the room when he gave Star the injection. I didn't go in. It seemed too painful to me. To this day I regret not going in. I wish my face was the last thing Star saw when she closed her eyes for the final time. I secretly promised Glendi I would be there when that time came. And it's important to keep those promises. I vowed to be there, and I showed up.

I am well aware about homelessness, wars, and people dying, losing their jobs, losing their homes, losing their minds. So what right do I have to get all bent out of shape when my two-and-a-half-pound Yorkie dies?

Well, every right in the world. I know a dog is not a human being, but that doesn't mean she isn't part of the family, and it doesn't mean that it isn't terribly painful to lose her.

The few days before Glendi's passing, she started getting weaker and weaker, and when she tried to walk, she would fall over. It was very painful to watch. She was not the same happy-go-lucky dog anymore. We asked the vet how we would know when it was time. He said we would know. When that day did come, we knew. We knew it was the right thing to do. My only job at this point was to be there for her. This was the kindest thing I could do. There was no amount of money or time that was going to change this.

Her passing has left a giant hole in our hearts. We were attached to her, and she was attached to us. I'm pleased to report that after not being there for Star, I kept my promise with Glendi. I went in during the ordeal. I held her paw, pet her, and cried bitter tears. I believe it was the first time she ever saw me cry. I kept saying over and over, "I love you, Glendi. I love you." The doctor asked me if I was ready. I nodded. The doctor then gave her two shots, one to make her sleep and the other to stop her heart. With the second shot, her eyes went from bright and clear to dull and cloudy. Even after she was gone, I kept telling her I loved her. She died with her eyes wide open, looking right at me. It was one of the saddest and most tender moments of my life. I kissed her before leaving the room. My only regret is that I did not close her eyes before I left her for the last time. As I walked out I said, "Goodbye, sweet Glendi. We love you." I cried all the way home.

I kept my promise that I would be with her at the end, but I have also realized that, in the past, I've lied to all my dogs. I've told them that I would take them out for a walk and then made them wait. I told them I would feed them in five minutes only to realize an hour later that I hadn't.

How many times have I told my wife I'll take out the garbage in one minute and did not? How many times have I promised myself not to eat something bad only to find myself chewing on it an hour later? I recently promised God I would learn two prayers by heart and have not moved on it at all. Fill in your own blank.

I realized our relationship with God is remarkably similar to our relationship with animals. As we are dependent on God, our pets are dependent on us. Like with a baby, if we forget about them too long, the results could be catastrophic. When my little dog barked for dinner, it was her prayer to me that I would hear her need. When I pray to God, it's my prayer that He will hear me. Just like I hope God doesn't make me wait too long, my dogs all hoped the same from me. If you have a pet, there is a good chance you will be called upon one day to do what I had to do. Do it. Do it for you. Do it for your pet. I promise you that you won't regret it.

How a Christmas Gift Changed a Young Jewish Boy's Life Forever

My mother was constantly telling my father how much she hated the Bronx and wanted to move. So when I was seven years old, my mother, father, and Peachy, our parakeet, and I took a Greyhound bus from the Bronx to Los Angeles. I remember our driver stopping for lunch at an Indian reservation in Arizona and announcing to be careful not to get scalped. Being scalped would be the least of his worries if he said that today.

After arriving in Los Angeles, my mom and I walked one afternoon to Ralphs supermarket. As we entered the supermarket, I didn't know it, but my outlook on life and people was about to change forever from a chance meeting I was about to have.

While I was pushing the cart (to this day, I always love to push the cart) up an aisle, I spotted Captain Huxley pushing his grocery cart. Captain Huxley was the name of the character that actor Roy Roberts played on the 1950s TV show *Oh Susanna!* Those were the days when the entire family could watch the same TV show. I screamed to my mother, "There's Captain Huxley!" and with the speed of light, I ran over to him. He was tall, with a pencil-thin mustache. This was my first time meeting a real actor.

I said, "Are you Captain Huxley?"

He said, "Yes I am, son." I could not have been more excited.

"Can I have an autographed picture of you?"

He smiled and said, "I don't carry them with me, but if you give me your address, I'll mail you one."

"Really?"

"Absolutely." I had my doubts.

I was wrong. That night around 8:00 p.m., there was a knock at our door. I said, "Who is it?" and the unmistakable voice said, "It's Captain Huxley."

I screamed, "Mom, Dad, Captain Huxley is here! Captain Huxley is here!"

My mother yelled back, "Captain Huxley?" She opened the door, and there he was with a big smile, holding a gift-wrapped package. And there I was in my briefs and T-shirt.

He handed me the package and said, "Merry Christmas, Mark." I ripped off the paper and saw a beautifully framed eight-by-ten autographed picture of Captain Huxley dressed in his TV captain's uniform. "This seemed to mean a lot to you, and with this being Christmas week, I knew if I mailed it, you might not get it for a while. So Merry Christmas, son."

This was my first ever Christmas gift. I thought, *I hope Jews are allowed to keep Christmas gifts.* It meant the world to me, and he knew it. He then said he had to run. I can still see him standing there. We wished him a Merry Christmas, thanked him profusely, and said goodbye.

Some fifty-five years later, I still have the photo hanging up. Every time I see it, I smile. It was one of the kindest things anyone has ever done for me. The whole event changed my perception of humanity. Up until that point, I had a great deal of mistrust for most adults. People would promise me things and many times not deliver. With a simple act of kindness, the Captain turned it all around. The Captain may not have been Jewish, but to me he was a great teacher of character traits. He taught me that some people are good, some people are decent, and that sea captains are the best. He had what the sages call a *lev tov.*[51]

---

51 *Lev tov* is Hebrew for "a good heart." It is a way of expressing a basic core value of Jewish life. Blintzes and sour cream and chopped liver made with chicken or goose schmaltz (fat) will clog any *lev tov* or good heart from here to Timbuktu. Just as an aside, have you ever heard of a less Jewish place than Timbuktu?

How does one thank someone for such an act of kindness? By doing the same thing if called upon. Thanks to the Captain, when a child asks me for something, I try to keep in mind that this might be more important to the kid than I'll ever know. The Captain long ago passed on, but his kind deed is very much alive inside me.

The Candy Man

The candy man can 'cause he mixes it with love and makes the world taste good. —Leslie Bricusse and Anthony Newley, "The Candy Man"

A few years ago, I went to the funeral of Lori Gilbert Kaye at the Chabad in Poway near San Diego. She was the one person who died when the synagogue was the scene of a terrorist attack. The funeral was filled with every possible emotion you could imagine, including hope.

I learned how important Lori was to her community. She changed so many things in this small community, including securing the loan for the shul building at a time when banks were not giving loans to nonprofits. She also bought food and handed it out to the homeless. She dropped off flowers at the homes of lonely people. Lori cared about her life and the lives of others.

At the funeral the rabbis and Lori's family and friends all agreed on two things: terrorism will not stop us from our commitment to being Jews, and we must use her murder to bring more light into the world. I didn't hear any talk of hate or retribution; instead I heard talk of doing more mitzvahs and lighting candles on Hanukkah and Shabbas. I also heard about how people risked their lives to save the children who were in the synagogue. The rabbi's four-and-a-half-year-old granddaughter was in the room at the time of the shooting. She saw her grandfather bleeding and screaming, "Get out, get out," while losing blood from a finger that was shot off. The rabbi said afterward that maybe we have to go back and look at what we're teaching our children when they are young. Perhaps if they are taught the right things when they are little, it might prevent these sorts of tragedies.

The following week, my wife and I went to North Hollywood to stay with friends who are members of the Shaarey Zedek congregation there. Friday night we shared the Shabbas table with Norm and his wife, Bonnie, and Saturday lunch, two other couples came and joined us. We talked about Poway, we talked some politics, we talked about making a better world, and we talked about security at synagogues. I think many people are scared because none of us know who will be next, but I think we all agree that there will be a next, and a next, and a next.

While we were having breakfast with Norm at his home, he said he needed to get to shul early in case they didn't have enough people to form a ten-person minyan[52] for those saying kaddish. While we walked the four or five blocks, Norm greeted many people who were going to his shul. When we got to shul, Norm asked the security guard if he fixed his flat tire from the night before, and a short conversation ensued about how wonderful AAA is. Norm then went inside, took his aisle seat, and started to pray along with the congregation. And that's when I saw my friend Norm doing exactly what the rabbi asked us all to do: teach the kids goodness. Every few minutes, a couple of kids would approach Norm for a lollipop. Before they got their lollipop, they had to do a few things. First, they had to wish Norm a good Shabbas and shake his hand while looking into his eyes. The handshake had to be a hearty handshake, not a dead fish handshake. Then, when they got the lollipop, they had to say "Thank you."

With the children, I saw in action the man that Norm is, as one child at a time, his interactions changed the world for the better. To fight hatred

52 A minyan is the quorum of ten men (or, in some synagogues, men and women) over the age of thirteen required for traditional Jewish public worship. Orthodox Jewish law strictly forbids women in the minyan because it could lead to dancing.

and lack of hope, his weapon of choice is a bag of lollipops. He was teaching them important lessons such as to wish people good things, to let someone know you mean it when shaking hands, and, most importantly, to always say thank you. Norm is helping to send good people into the world. I can't think of many things more important than that.

After shul, Norm, the Candy Man, and I were walking back to his house when he spotted a twenty-year-old across the street. Norm waved to him, said hello, and wished him a good Shabbas. The young man waved back, said hello, and gave us a good Shabbas back. Then Norm turned to me and said, "I have known him since he was a little kid at the shul. I used to give him lollipops. You should feel his handshake now. It's really something."

The Haircut

There is a Jewish tradition called *upsherin*,[53] in which a Jewish boy gets his first haircut when he's three years old. Afterward, friends and family gather at a party, tell him how good he looks, and, of course, eat and eat and eat.

With every dog we've ever had, when the dog got a haircut, everyone in my family compliments the dog. "Look how pretty you look." "You're so pretty." They want to know where the dog gets her hair cut, as if they're considering going to the same place. But I get a haircut, no one comments, or if they do, it's mostly negative. "Why did you cut it so short?" or "It looks so uneven" or "I hope you didn't have to pay a lot for that."

The truth is the dog always gets a better haircut than me. The best explanation I have is that people who give dogs haircuts don't have a conversation with the dogs. They stay focused. They don't ask the dogs where

---

53 *Upsherin* is the ceremony when traditional Jews give a boy his first haircut following his third birthday. Thank God they do not wait three years to circumcise.

they were born or how they keep trim. When I get a haircut, I feel obligated to talk to my barber. I need to know if he's going to tattoo the other side of his face or just leave it the way it is.

I've always taken my dogs to a groomer, a word far classier than "barber." When I'd pick up the dogs, they always looked happy and relaxed. One time I dropped off my dog at home and walked the five blocks back to the groomer. I said, "Do you have time to give another haircut?"

The groomer said that her 3:30 had just canceled and that she had an hour. Then she said, "Where's the dog?"

"No dog," I replied. "It's me. I want you to cut my hair. I want to compare the haircut you give to the one my barber gives. The dog always gets a better haircut than me."

The groomer smiled and said she would do it as long as she didn't have to give me a bath or express my anal glands. I agreed and said, "Most importantly, I want you to treat me like I'm any old schnauzer. No special treatment just because I have two legs and know how to use a fork. That means no questions."

She gave me a thumbs-up and then scratched me under my chin. I reached into my bag and pulled out my morning cereal bowl and asked her to fill it with water in case I got thirsty. "Let's do it," she said.

I was about to climb up on the table she uses for dogs, but she screamed, "No!" Then, "No. No table. Down, boy." I quickly backed off and hung my head in shame. I was beginning to really like this woman. She then lifted me onto the table like I was a two hundred-pound English mastiff and put me on all fours. She fastened a leather collar around my neck so I couldn't jump off the table.

First, she checked me for fleas, pinching something off my neck and smacking it dead on the table. I guess that was her little flea joke. The whole haircut took about thirty minutes. She then finished the job, using a stiff boar's-head bristle brush that brought blood to parts of my scalp where there hadn't been any blood for decades.

During the haircut, she didn't say one word to me, just kept shearing, snipping, and petting my head while whistling various army, navy, and marine tunes. Except for having to stay in the all-fours position for thirty minutes, it was by far the most relaxing haircut of my life. I loved every minute of it. The only drawback was that she didn't have a mirror, because dogs never want to see the back of their head like we do.

Afterward, she texted my wife to pick me up. Ten minutes later, my wife walked in, and before I could explain to her what went down, she looked at me and said, "You look so pretty. It's nice and even." I then jumped in the passenger seat of the car and hung my head out the window during the ride home. After I got home, I laid down on the floor and took a nap.

The next morning, I made an appointment with the groomer for the following month.

Pause When Agitated

Does this need to be said? Does this need to be said by me? Does this need to be said by me now? —Craig Ferguson

The goal is not to be better than the other man, but your previous self. —Dalai Lama

A while back I received an email that was chock-full of hatred and anger. It was sent to me by a friend of more than thirty years. He knew I had stopped drinking three decades earlier, but in the email he offered to buy me a drink. He went on to suggest that I was funnier and smarter when I was fat and drunk. My friend is also a member of the tribe.

My initial reaction was anger, which is not abnormal. I considered sending the email out to everyone he knows as well as the industry he works in. *I will show him*, I thought to myself. But there are two rules I try to live by: (1) never trust your first thought when you are angry, and (2) pause when agitated.

The "pause when agitated" rule can save marriages, jobs, and friendships. It can also stop waiters from spitting in your meals. It might even save your life. So instead of reacting, I phoned a few wise folks. Hands down, across the board, I was counseled not to respond. The consensus was to dump the email and not lower myself.

For the next few months, I did nothing. Wings spread and lark happy, I was extremely proud of the new spiritual heights from which I was looking down on others. But *Mishlei*, the Book of Proverbs, warns us that "Pride goes before destruction." Since I would never forget how awful this guy was, I decided to hang on to the email. Big mistake.

Months later, I received a stupid political email that twenty-five other people were included on. As I was reading it, I started feeling agitated. When I saw that one of the names on the email was that of my drink-buying ex-friend, it was as if someone had waved a matador's muleta in my face. A resentment I did not know was there came barreling out of its cave as I tumbled off my spiritual perch, hit the ground, and in half a tick, my anger fuse was lit. Before you could say "what," I disseminated his nasty email to the whole group. Even though I did not know 98 percent of the people on the email chain, my arrogance convinced me they would all take my side.

Within a second of hitting the send button, I knew I had made a mistake. Again I called my wise friends for counseling, only this time it was after the fact. Remember, it's important to make the call before you shoot yourself in the head. As I stood in the mud, I could see my high horse had taken off without me. It was decided among my friends that what was necessary was an "amends" email to the whole group of people that I had thoughtlessly dragged into my *mishegoss*.[54]

---

54 *Mishegoss* (Yiddish) is craziness: senseless folly, indulgence, lunacy, tomfoolery, and foolishness. This is the way most Jewish children act at Sunday school and at their bar and bat mitzvah lessons.

Well over thirty years ago, in a men's room, this ex-friend was peeing at a urinal. I called his name, and he turned just enough for me to snap a photo of him holding his penis. Luckily for me, I eventually got rid of the photo, or I might have also posted that too. Anger has destroyed many a life.

The next day, after taking a deep breath, I sent out a group apology email. I quickly heard back from two people. One condemned me, and one applauded me. Then after a closer look the next day, I sent a heartfelt email to my ex-friend to apologize to him. I made absolutely no mention of his part in any of this. This effort was just about clearing my own side of the street. I really was sorry. I've yet to hear from him.

A few days later, my friend Sheryl Neuman stopped by our house to give us a gift for being hosts of a *Sheva Brachot*[55] for her son and daughter-in-law. The gift was the book *Positivity Bias* by Mendel Kalmenson. Something inside me said, *Read this book now.* Using Sheryl as his emissary, God had sent me this book of stories about how the Lubavitcher rebbe, Rabbi Schneerson, lifted people up instead of bringing them down. The glass is always half-full in the rebbe's world. Sending the group email was the exact opposite of what the rebbe would have done, although the rebbe likely would have found something positive in what I had done as well. The rebbe believed in finding the good in people even when they let you down and even when they hurt you. Kalmenson writes, "Viewing other people through the lens of a good eye endows us with a certain degree of optimism."

Two weeks later, my friend Maz sent a book called *The War of Art* by Steven Pressfield. I had had such good luck with the last book I figured, hey, why not? This book is about the resistance we experience when we are growing and changing. Pressfield writes, "Resistance obstructs movement when you pursue a calling like the arts, launch an enterprise, or try and move to a higher station morally, ethically, or spiritually." I find that to be

---

55 In Jewish tradition, during the week following a wedding, festive get-togethers are held in honor of the couple. Each of these events—usually an elegant dinner—is called a *Sheva Brachot*. Offering free food is the only way to get young newlyweds to come out of the bedroom.

totally true for me. When I am trying to be more honest, more helpful, a better person, or closer to God, nine out of ten times, I will do something to block the path. The Leviticus warning not to "put a stumbling block before the blind" most certainly includes self-sabotage. But I try to be thankful even for the setbacks. The setbacks are painful but necessary reminders that I am not perfect and that I still have a long, long way to go. Setbacks, when viewed correctly, can be eye-opening gifts.

In football, when a team loses yardage, they immediately huddle and try to retrieve the lost yardage and then some. Guess who is there to stop them? Resistance. The same is true with our life setbacks. If you make a mistake, never beat or quit on yourself. Get right back up. Not only to get back to where you just were, but to move ahead to a higher place, the place that now belongs to you, but until now, you were not ready to occupy.

A Period of Transition

Transitioning isn't pretty, but stagnation is hideous. —Nikki Rowe

People love throwing sayings at you when you are going through life's trials and tribulations. For instance, "When life hands you lemons, make lemonade." OK. Suppose, like me, you don't like lemonade. I've been handed lemons and did nothing with them. Most of my lemons turn mushy with white and green mold on their bottoms.

Here's another: "You made your bed; now lie in it." Worst advice for someone depressed or out of work. "Get out of bed and do something with your life" should be the advice.

And that's where I was at in 2020 and 2021. For over a year, I had basically been out of paying work. I'd written a book and pitched some ideas, but not much dough had been coming in. When people asked me if my work had returned, if I told them the truth, they didn't have much to say.

Sometimes there is nothing to say. Sometimes the person just needs to hang tight and see what will be revealed. We've heard "When God closes one door, he opens another." True. But the waiting in the hallway for that other door to open can be painful. So while waiting for that door to open, don't forget that it's important to keep knocking.

Just recently, as I was walking slowly to get my mail (no need to walk fast when you are out of work), I bumped into a neighbor who told me his business of many years is now on life support. I asked him what he might do. He said he thinks he might enjoy flipping houses. I said good idea, but start small. "First try flipping pancakes." Generally, injecting a little humor never hurts. He mumbled something about being in transition, then quickly walked off without the usual smile and see you later.

Like him I thought, *Well, I'm in a period of transition. In fact, isn't all of life transitioning from one thing to another thing? Breakfast to lunch. House to car. Emotion to emotion. Until, eventually, the ultimate transition.* "Transition" is a nice word if you believe you're transitioning to somewhere better. If not, the t-word could be scary.

An extremely uncomfortable conversation is when my wife asks me, "What are you going to do about work if things dry up?" I hate the sound of that. "Dry up" sounds so fatalistic. When I think hard, what comes to me is that I am not really cut out to do most other things, especially now that I have aged like a good porterhouse, slightly marbleized on the inside and out. I have been a comedian for almost forty years. My plan B was my plan A.

My friend George Stanley is ninety-six years old. I speak with him maybe three times a week. George is also out of work. I tell him for his sanity and the sake of his marriage, he should go back to school and get a new career. He agrees. He and his wife, Sandra, who is only in her eighties (a mere spring chicken compared to him), sing together each day, and occasionally they will sing to me on the phone. When I am down, hearing those two belting it out can really cheer me up.

George is a warehouse of aphorisms. Somehow words coming from George make me feel like they're coming straight from above. He always reminds me of three things: (1) Each day, just put one foot in front of the other and make sure you do something to move yourself forward. That will make you feel better. (2) Don't take yourself so damn seriously. Getting too serious can depress and immobilize you. (3) Let go or be dragged. The more you hold on, the more you might get hurt. Those things have made a big difference. They have pulled me out of many a pit that I had begun to dig for myself and even started to furnish. George reminds me that I have always landed on my feet. (My question is, what do you tell someone with no feet that he or she will land on? Just asking.)

Daily I am left with two choices, plow on or buckle under. I choose to plow on. And I try not to worry more than a little. I bet doctors tell patients not to worry more than almost anything else. Someone told me that I should let God do the worrying and that I should just do the work.

But if I ever show up at your office and you see me floating around and are wondering what I might be doing there, it's a good possibility that I might be in a period of transition.

Ruby: A Lesson in Kindness

Who is wise? He who learns from every person.
—Ben Zoma, *Pirkei Avot* (Ethics of the Fathers)

Like most kids, I had a secret life that my parents knew nothing about. I was about fifteen years old when I met Ruby. I think he was about fifty. Ruby was Jewish, round, and bald. He always wore an old, out-of-style sport coat. He was also a divorced gambler. Not an uncommon combination.

When we first met, he described himself as a loser with hope. At fifteen, I also felt like a loser, but without hope. Ruby was a petty crook. He always had a few stolen credit cards in his wallet. He would buy them from pickpockets and muggers. He hated using his gambling money to pay his bills, but then, all money was gambling money to him.

I met Ruby at the House of Lords, a poolroom on Queens Boulevard in Forest Hills. I was fourteen years old when I started hanging out at Lords and shooting pool for money—money I often stole from my parents' wallets. Money that they never mentioned was missing, which was strange considering my mother only took down about a C-note a week. Me grabbing a double sawbuck from her purse was considerable. I guess you could also call me a thief.

By law, you had to be sixteen to get into a poolroom without a guardian. I had a phony ID that said I was eighteen even though I looked a young twelve. Rocky, the owner of Lords, was a short, dumpy, foul-mouthed bookie.

Whenever Ruby popped in, he was looking for action. Gamblers never stop in anywhere just to say hello and see how your mother is doing. Ruby did not shoot pool himself, just bet on the game.

Like me, Ruby was a lonesome soul. Lonely people recognize each other. But he had a kindness to him, and I needed that. He had an eloquent tone to his voice, and even though he was a street guy, he sounded intelligent. When we talked, he was always soft-spoken and gentle. Even when he lost all his money, which was often, he never got angry at me.

I met him at a time when I was heading in the wrong direction. Kindness is something I always craved, but at the time, kindness at home or from my friends was at an all-time low. I have a soul that seems to cry out for it. If this were a movie pitch, I would say, "Ruby was a crook with a big heart."

Ruby was exciting to hang with. Two days a week I would cut school and meet him at his Rego Park apartment around 10:00 a.m. Then we headed out to either the Aqueduct or Belmont racetrack to play the horses, depending on which one was open. Before we went, Ruby would always take me to breakfast on one of the hot credit cards. He would say, "Get anything you want, kid." I always loved the track. In some ways, the track was a big part of my schooling. It was at the track that I really learned how to add, subtract, divide, multiply, and figure out fractions all in my head and all within seconds. Not bad for a fifteen-year-old track bum.

Ruby and I would ride out to the track in his 1964 Bengal Ivory AMC Rambler. One time on the way, he stopped at a tire shop and put four new ones on. He gave them the hot card. When it was declined and he saw them calling it in, he said, "Hey, kid. Get in fast." We jumped back in the car, and with the new tires he tore out as fast as a '64 Rambler could tear out.

During our rides Ruby would share stories about how hard life was for him, how sad he was, and how his wife screwed him over and "took the kid." He always called his son "the kid." I never learned his real name. Out of nowhere he might blurt out, "I haven't seen the kid in years" and "I wonder how the kid is doing." There was a real honesty and pain when he would say those things. Before Ruby, I'd never heard anyone talk like him. I'd never heard anyone tell me how hurt he or she was except my mother, and that was usually followed by something about how it was because of me.

Ruby never asked me about my home life. And you know what? I was fine with that. He was an open wound, an unhealed, hurt child, and he was never shy to admit it. He never drank or used drugs to kill the pain. He just lived in his own personal hell and let the pain take him wherever the pain wanted to take him.

On our rides back from the track, I could always tell if he lost or won. If he won, he would be so excited about how his luck was finally about to turn. He might say, "No more black clouds for me." If he lost, he was as quiet as a stone. When we got back to town, we would stop for dinner at some fancy restaurant he had never been to. He would run up a big bill and pay with a bad card. We never went anywhere twice.

The Mishnah says you can learn from everybody. In a strange way, I learned a lot from Ruby. And I am not unhappy for having had the experience. I learned that I did not want to be a gambler or a thief. I learned that stealing never felt good to me, that I felt ashamed to be part of such a thing. I learned that it scared me. I learned losing money by gambling made me sick to my stomach—that it made me angry and caused me to feel stupid, that losing made me mean. I learned I never wanted to get divorced and have a child that I only called "the kid," and that if I lived a life like Ruby, the closest I might get to my son or daughter might be a dusty four-by-six framed photo.

But I also learned kindness. Ruby had a big heart. He had the soul of a poet. The man could not have been more accepting of me if he tried. More than a few times, he said that I should finish school and that I should make something of myself; otherwise, I might end up like him. At a time in my life when I did not feel accepted anywhere, by anybody, Ruby was a friend.

I wish I could say I learned these lessons and straightened up right away. I did not. I had to go through my own personal little trip through hell first. One morning, I cut school and went to call on Ruby. When I got there, I found his apartment door unlocked. I cracked the door, peeked in, and went inside. There was nothing left, and it was swept army-barracks clean.

I went up to Lords and asked Rocky if he had seen Ruby. "Ain't seen the MF in a week," he told me. Nobody I asked knew anything. They were as quiet as a graveyard at midnight. I kept going back to the poolroom hoping to one day see Ruby again. That day never came. Maybe he went back to see "the kid." Maybe he was in jail. Maybe someone dumped him. Maybe, maybe, maybe.

In hindsight, I consider his disappearing from my life an act of kindness. I cannot see how it would have ended well. Years later, after getting my first credit card, one day I realized I had lost it. When I got my statement I saw someone had charged three expensive dinners. I thought to myself, *Nah, couldn't be . . .*

The Rumor Mill

Like most schools, mine were rumor mills. There was no social media—just kids talking about other kids and saying cruel things about them. When we heard things about other kids, not knowing if they were true or false, we rolled out the filth anyway. I didn't know it was wrong to say things about other kids. I did know it hurt when they said things about me. I just didn't put the two together. I didn't know that in Judaism, it was up there with murder.

Here's the slogan: "Rumors hurt people." Now that I know the extent of the pain it can cause, I have regrets.

When I was growing up, most everyone had a mother and a father, but then there was Nat. Nat was the one black kid in our school, and as far as we knew, Nat had no parents. Nat lived in a place that was once called the Brooklyn Industrial School Association and Home for Destitute Children. It eventually changed its name to the Brooklyn Home for Children and later to Forestdale. The home was once an orphanage and initially didn't mix its kids with the local public school kids, but at some point, we were all mixed together.

Most if not all the kids from my school didn't know any black kids besides Nat, and most knew very little about him. What we did know was that he was amazing at punchball, had lightning speed, and could go from amused to very angry in a second. If he was angered, his fists would quickly spring into loaded position. (I don't think he ever actually used his fists.)

None of us ever went to visit Nat at the home, nor do I remember Nat ever coming to any of our homes. We knew where he lived. and when we would walk past someone would say, "That's where Nat lives," but beyond trying to peek through the fence, we never went in.

I imagine it was lonely for him. And it must have been hard for Nat seeing all of us, mostly white Jewish kids, dressed well and going back to our nice homes. Some of these nice homes were hell for a lot of us, possibly worse than Nat's situation, but he didn't know that.

There were rumors that many of the kids who lived at the home were bad kids. Dangerous kids. We assumed Nat might have been one of those. We never knew that by spreading this rumor, we became dangerous kids. We never knew how we might be hurting Nat and others in the rumor mill. Those rumors made us all afraid of Nat, and we kept our distance.

Once, one of the teachers made Nat an assistant school crossing guard, a coveted position. The guards got to wear a white plastic strap across their chest with a shiny tin AAA Safety Patrol badge. Nat looked cool and was proud of his job. However, one day one of us got into an argument with Nat. He was incredibly upset at us and took the plastic strap off his chest and threw it at us. Because of the freezing temperature, when the plastic belt hit the ground, like frozen Turkish taffy slapped down hard on a table, it broke into a dozen pieces. Nat was responsible for the belt. He had to return it in good condition or pay for it. He lost the crossing guard job, the one job that made him feel special. After he threw the belt, all I remember was Nat running back home. If it were me, I'd have been crying.

I am not sure most of our parents knew of Nat. Nat was simply not one of us. I know he knew it. How could he not?

When we all moved on to junior high and went to different classes, I didn't hear much about Nat. Then, when moving on to high school, I don't remember ever seeing him again. Did he get sick? Did they locate a parent of his? Did he change schools? None of us has any idea how his life turned out. When I speak to my classmates and Nat's name comes up, we all hope

Nat has had a good life. I hope he found the love he deserved.

Lashon hara (evil speech) is one of the areas I have gravitated toward correcting in my life. I know how much rumors hurt me as a kid. I know how people saying nasty things about me felt, how it made me cry. Some are with me to this day. Nat, wherever you are, I am truly sorry for my part in it.

10
LOVE

....

Don't Fence Me In

I can't think of many things these days that are not locked up, fenced in, or otherwise protected. We have jails, guard dogs, alarms, cameras, moats, bars, and border walls. We lock up guns and ammo. We lock our phones, computers, and meds. Hotel rooms have safes that warn you that the people they hire might be thieves. One place I know locked up the defibrillator, and when someone keeled over and they couldn't find the key, they had to break it open with a hammer. Luckily for them, the hammer wasn't locked up.

Growing up, I remember hearing about chastity belts. Imagine these days some guy saying to his wife or girlfriend, "Sure, I trust you, but wear this when I'm out of town. Plus, I'm taking the key with me." We told women we don't trust you, but you'll have to trust us. And look how well that worked out. No problem there, right guys?

In the 1950s most people in America didn't lock their front doors. When I was a kid, if I wanted to visit a friend, I would just show up at his house unannounced. Today, except for Jehovah's Witnesses, no one shows up unannounced anymore. Nowadays, it would be considered rude and scary. When I was twelve, one Sunday morning at around six, I went to see if my friend David wanted to go for a bike ride. David's family lived in an apartment on the fourth floor and never locked their door, so I tiptoed into the apartment and woke him up. A few weeks later, I went back, got off the elevator, and walked into his apartment but first stopped in the kitchen for a glass of milk only to realize I was in the apartment one floor below. I finished the milk and left.

Fences can be wonderful things. They keep what's inside protected and what's unwanted at a safe distance. Throughout Jewish history, our rabbis and leaders have erected fences to protect Jewish tradition, Jewish custom, and Jewish communities and to keep out the unwanted influences. These fences are called *siyagot laTorah*.[56] On Shabbas, we are not supposed to spend money. To keep us far from transgressing, the rabbis erected a fence teaching us that we should not even touch money. That's why I take my wife to malls and jewelry stores on Shabbas. I know she can't touch any money.

I'm a married guy so I don't usually chat with or spend much time alone with other women. A handsome guy like me is very vulnerable to who knows what. So there's a fence around me, and I love it.

About a week ago, my wife caught me stealing. She had baked some cookies and told me not to take any. When she wasn't looking, I snatched one. Our indoor camera caught it. Now there's a fence around the cookies.

One place we should be careful but also open is with our hearts. That's a tricky one. We need to protect them, but we also need to keep them open enough to let people in. If you're human, you've had your heart broken. If we lock up our hearts, we lock out many of life's possibilities. Our hearts have to remain open and be ready to greet the next person, place, or thing. That's why we give people we trust the key to our heart. A closed heart can lead to a small, sad, unhappy life. Getting hurt is part of being human. I've been hurt and I've done the hurting. It's never fun, but it didn't kill me either.

---

56 *Siyagot laTorah* are fences around the Torah. A fence around the Torah is a theoretical Jewish principle to prevent Jews from doing forbidden things. It is similar to the old chastity belt to prevent certain things from occurring. You get the picture.

So pop by anytime. I won't think you're rude. The door will be locked, but if I'm home, I'll be happy to let you in.

The Good Old Days

Dear God, you made many, many poor people.
I realize, of course, that it's no shame to be poor.
But it's no great honor either!
—*Fiddler on the Roof*, by Jerry Bock and Sheldon Harnick

California's crime rate has gone through the roof. Though I guess if you are going to be murdered, Los Angeles is one of the nicer places for it to take place. My wife asked me once, "If we were to move, where would you want to move to?"

I quickly answered, "I'm not sure where, but I'll need two things: to live in a Jewish neighborhood and to be near a hospital." All Jews need to live near an MRI. However, if I could only pick one, I'd pick a Jewish neighborhood.

Even though my parents were not religious, they always liked living in Jewish neighborhoods. Although it was not strictly Jewish, the Bronx was cheap and it was New York, so there was a smattering of all types. It was a vibrant, noisy, one-step-up-from-poverty neighborhood. To this day, I have never lived anywhere quiet.

We lived in a six-floor walkup. That means there was no elevator in the building. You had a choice: walk up or sleep in the street. When I was five, I fell down three of those flights. I fell down one flight, got up, then fell down another, got up, and down again I went. Buster Keaton had nothing on me. My mother took me to get stitches in my head from someone up the block.

I think the person was a doctor—or at least a seamstress.

Just like Abe Lincoln, no matter what the weather was like, I walked to school. I remember many mornings when the snow was higher than me and I would beg my mother to let me stay home. Her answer was always the same: "Too bad. Wear boots and gloves."

I am an only child, but I had plenty of friends in the form of roaches, water bugs, mosquitos in the summer, and something that looked eerily like a giant fly and I later found out is called a Gauromydas heros. No matter how clean my mother kept the apartment—and she did keep it clean—we could not get rid of the bugs that lived behind the walls and down our pipes. Sometimes, if my father was trying to kill a bug and missed, he'd yell, "Come here, you! Come here, you!"

We had no air-conditioning. In the summer, in order to stay cool, we opened fire hydrants or went to the city swimming pools (which doubled as urinals) that were open from June until September. So were our screenless windows. If the mosquitos were hungry, they knew they could always pop in for a quick bite. My mother, being a good Jewish mother, said she hated seeing even the mosquitos fly on an empty stomach.

Our sinks never stopped dripping. There was a perpetual brown stain where the water dripped, making the sink look like it was a heavy Camel smoker. When you took a glass of water from the sink, you had to wait for it to clear up. We lived in a virtual petri dish.

In the frozen New York winters, occasionally the superintendent would send up some steam heat. To get the heat sent up, we had to bang on the pipes, so the superintendent got the message people upstairs were popsicle-izing. But steam heat sucks all the moisture from your skin, and my poor father had to get a third job to keep my mother supplied with lotions. She would scare me half to death when she would tell me her skin was about to fall off.

To get rid of our garbage, we had something called a dumbwaiter in the apartment. A dumbwaiter is a small platform made of wood, attached to a pulley system, and located behind a small door inside a brick chute that you pulled up and down by hand. If you had garbage, you pulled the platform to your floor, put the garbage on the platform, then lowered it back down. Sometimes during the day, the superintendent would pull the garbage out from the chute. If it was one of those days when he was shorting you on heat, you might drop a bag of soaking wet garbage on his head.

All our water pipes were made of lead. Our bathroom and kitchen were always covered with lead paint. I drank lead-based water and ate lead paint chips that fell into my cereal and my mother's cake batter. The lead flakes looked like dried coconut shavings. In school, I would chew on number 2 lead pencils. And when my father gassed up the car, I stood near the exhaust pipe and sucked in the lead fumes. Because of my high lead content, my doctor had me stand in front of his patients while x-raying them instead of making them wear the lead vest.

When I was growing up, the only reason I knew we were semi-poor was that my mother always complained about it. My father's answer was "What do you want me to do? I'm already working sixteen hours a day."

When I look back, I remember the Bronx as a powerful place to grow up. The Bronx was my little Isaac Bashevis Singer moment. Singer had Warsaw. I had the Bronx and the cast of characters who came along with it. My mother's refrain was "One day I want to get the hell out of the Bronx. I have had it with the roaches."

Like the Jeffersons, my parents eventually did move out and moved on up a few notches to Forest Hills (also in a Jewish neighborhood). No roaches, no water bugs, and a much nicer place. We had screens on the windows and an elevator to our fourth-floor apartment. I was skinny in the Bronx and got fatter when I started riding the elevator instead of walking twenty-five flights a day.

Today, my parents are gone and the Bronx is a fading memory. I now live with my wife in a lovely one-hundred-plus-year-old cottage-house in Los Angeles. Until I moved to California, I never lived in anything with more than one door. My little house has two. Like my parents, I live in a mixed but mostly Jewish neighborhood. When I walk my neighborhood, I feel very much at home and feel a surge of gratitude for what I have. Seeing tzitzit hanging out of a shirt lowers my blood pressure. My life has somehow worked out much better than I could ever have imagined.

Occasionally, when it gets extremely hot and has not rained for a long period of time, we might spot a water bug or three come up through the pipes looking for something to eat. Before I kill it to stop it from crawling into my mouth, I first smile and remember the Bronx, especially my father chasing the bugs in his underwear, yelling, "Come here, you! Come here, you!" Ah, the good old days.

I'm Proud of You

Every child wants his or her parents to say, "I'm proud of you." Even though my folks have been gone for decades, I would still love to hear my mom or dad say just once more, "I am proud of you, Mark." Nothing wrong with that.

When your children tell you something good that is going on in their life, you can feel the beat that they take while they wait for the sign from you that you heard them. That you care. That what they said is important and meaningful. A book I read and loved is called *I'm Proud of You: My Friendship with Fred Rogers*, by Tim Madigan. It's about the relationship between the author and television show host Mr. Rogers. Mr. Rogers would sign "IPOY" for "I'm proud of you" in his letters to Tim. It was a phrase Tim had never heard from his dad.

We can all do that for each other. There is a big difference between saying "Good job" and "I'm proud of you."

I am proud of each of my three sons. Each one is unique, funny, interesting, and, most importantly, good. A day does not go by that I am not thankful for them. I wish I gave my parents half the *naches* that my sons have given me.

One day I received a text from my favorite son that stopped me in my tracks. (Just kidding—they are all my favorites!) It was from my oldest son, Jacob. He said, "On Shabbat, I am throwing a kiddush[57] in honor of my wife's birthday." That is pretty darn cool on multiple levels. The little boy whose hand I used to hold while walking to shul, who I told not to step off the curb, who, when I had to punish him, just broke my heart. That boy was now married with a son and making a kiddush to honor his wife; his growth is a real mindblower. And it gets better. Jacob then told me that because of COVID-19, the minyan would be outdoors and mask-friendly. And here is the kicker: he wanted the "old man" (or "Pops") to come. (Depending on how he feels, he calls me either "old man" or "Pops." When he first started calling me Pops, I found it slightly annoying. Pops to me was Pa Kettle. But now I love it. Like my wife's cooking, it grew on me.) He wanted me to hang with him and his friends. I was honored.

That Shabbat morning at 8:55 a.m., I met Jacob and his friend Dan and we sauntered over a few blocks to the minyan. It was in a backyard with no grass, just dirt, folding chairs, and a few collapsible tables. There were about two dozen young men, mostly in their late twenties and early thirties. I was easily the oldest by thirty-four and one-eighth years (but who's counting). These days when I go places, if I am the oldest, I feel weird; this time, though, I felt no such thing. I felt blessed and happy, and in the right place. The backyard dirt floor was holy ground, as holy as any cathedral. These young men, most of them already married with kids, were keeping Judaism and Shabbat alive and having a good time doing it. This was truly the definition of a happy minyan.

---

57 Kiddush, literally "sanctification," is a blessing recited over wine or grape juice to sanctify the Shabbat and Jewish holidays. The word also refers to a small repast held on Shabbat or festival mornings after the prayer services and before the main meal. It is the ten-thousand-calorie pre-lunch Jews ingest before they have their actual lunch.

After the davening ended, they put a few of the tables together for the kiddush food to sit on. Amazingly, these guys used tablecloths. It was beautiful. Sitting next to my son and looking at all that was going on, not only was I proud of him, I was proud of all these kids. I also thought of my wife and was proud of her for being an *eishet chayil.*[58] That was a big part of getting Jacob to this point. And I thought of his wife, Anna, who helped make sure he continued this journey. Even though none of his grandparents are here to say IPOY, I could say it for them. Jacob: Bubbe, Grandpa, Nana, and Zaide would be proud of you.

IPOY, Jewish people who came before us, many of whom died or suffered endlessly to keep Judaism alive and well for us. Keep it going, Jacob and friends. We need you. Judaism needs you so we can all be in the right place.

---

58 The exquisite and multilayered poem "*Eishet Chayil*" (Woman of Valor) was written by King Solomon as part of *Proverbs*. We sing this ode to women before kiddush on Friday evening. "A woman of valor, who can find? Far beyond pearls is her value. Her husband's heart trusts in her." Those beautiful words written by King Solomon must mean he was in deep doodoo with his wife and tried to write his way out of it.

11
MARRIAGE

....

Proof There Is a God

Therefore, shall a man leave his father and mother, and shall cleave to his wife, and they shall be as one flesh. —*Genesis 2:24*

There's an old joke: Before a man gets married, he is incomplete. After he's married, he's finished. Yet so many people do it. And keep doing it.

The fact that I got married and have stayed married is proof there is a God. When I asked my rabbi what God was doing these days, he said, "Arranging marriages." He also said that arranging marriages is harder than splitting the Red Sea.

To have continued marital bliss, all I have to do is forget most of what I saw and heard while growing up. My parents, aunts, and uncles, though nice enough people, were not the best examples of happy and healthy marriages. I remember being at my aunt and uncle's fifty-fifth wedding anniversary. I said, "Uncle Louie, congratulations."

He said, "I haven't killed her yet."

She fired back, "Go ahead and try."

I think I'm a different person today than I was when I got married. Hopefully, a better one. I credit my wife and many other people with helping me make a lot of the necessary changes. For me to have stayed married for close to thirty years, I had to grow up. My mother warned me that I had a lot of work to do if I ever wanted to live with another person. She would say:

- You'd better grow up and grow up quickly.

- You'll shape up or you'll ship out.

- One day you're going to get married, and I'm telling you now, she won't put up with your nonsense.

- You'd better marry a maid.

- Keep acting like you are now and you'll be alone an awfully long time.

And my favorite:

- I've never seen anything like you.

After careful deliberation, here are some of the areas I believe I was deficient in before I got married: Taking care of my health, dress, neatness, attitude, and cleanliness; clipping my toenails; paying attention; smiling; minding my manners; washing and drying dishes; brushing all my teeth instead of just the bottom ones; barging into rooms unannounced; saying thank you; eating all the food in the refrigerator and not telling anyone when we were out of things; blasting my music; yelling across the room for things instead of getting up and getting them; hogging the remote control; grabbing food off people's plates without asking; releasing gas in bed and lying about it; putting my underwear on inside out and not fixing it; taking phone messages and not passing them on; taking the garbage only as far as the back door; finishing my dinner before the other people even started;

walking a block ahead of everyone; leaving the toilet seat up; not replacing toilet paper rolls; using the same face towel until it was as stiff as a board; constantly asking questions to things I know the answers to. Amazingly, even with all of that, I was the pick of the litter.

The good news is that God created women so that when they look at a man, they see an unfinished project that needs shaping. And women feel it's their job to try to save this poor soul from rack and ruin. It's Torah: "You are not obligated to complete the work, but neither are you free to desist from it."

There are two types of married men: one who always wants to be right—God bless him for trying, but he ends up divorced or murdered—and one who realizes that the other person has his best interests at heart. The latter type surrenders and stays married.

My wife and I sent three boys into the world. They are in much better shape than I was when I was released. But to be quite honest, like all men, they still need a good overhaul.

Seinfeld, Bradley Cooper, and My Wife

My wife and I were invited to Jerry Seinfeld's sixty-fifth birthday party. What a great night. I'd love to show you a photo from it, but no one was allowed to take pictures except the photographers who were hired, which was a wonderful idea. Nobody was bothering Steve Martin or Howard Stern for a selfie. No one was asking David Letterman or Martin Short to line up for a group shot or bothering Julia Louis-Dreyfus or Amy Schumer to say happy birthday to their Uncle Milt on their iPhone.

Bradley Cooper was there and wow, is he good looking. You know they say a woman likes a man with a good sense of humor. If I weren't funnier than Bradley, I'd be very worried. Being the good husband that I am, I dragged my wife over by the tippy tip of her left pinky and introduced her to Bradley, who could not have been nicer. Amazingly, two weeks after meeting my wife, Bradley broke up with his girlfriend. Coincidence? Maybe, maybe not. Bradley has yet to call my house. I guess he fears being rejected by my sweetie even though I'm sure she'd let him down easy.

There was one other striking moment that stood out for me. It was when Jerry's wife, Jessica, got up and toasted all the comedians' wives in the room. There were also plenty of women comedians there. But this reflected a special bond Jessica has with the wives of the comics. She gave a shout-out to all of them by name. And there was a lot of meaning in the toast; Jessica got it right. Comedian wives have to endure an awful lot. One requirement necessary in order to be a comedian is that you have to have the skin of an alligator and so do the wives, which ends up costing a fortune in plastic surgery.

Comedian husbands have to travel, and the wives are left home to hold down the fort. And then there is all the alone time, which some wives like and some hate. You might say, "Hey, Mark. Many men travel these days and leave their wives at home. What's so different here?" Here's where it differs: When most men go to work, they do whatever they do, maybe have a business lunch, and maybe go out with friends after work. But when a comedian goes on stage night after night in town after town, he makes jokes about his wife in front of total strangers. No other job allows a guy to sit in a boardroom and get huge laughs about his wife for half an hour every day. Male comics have always joked about their wives and female comics about their husbands. It's always been a big part of a stand-up act.

Not all women can take it, though. Some of the comedians even mention their wives by name, and the range of jokes about these relationships varies. Some of the jokes are light and good-natured, and some are brutal. Richard Pryor talked about how he tried to shoot his wife when she was in his car. Woody Allen talked about his wife being frigid. Don Rickles said his wife almost drowned when she fell into the pool with all her jewelry on.

When my wife is in the audience and people know she's there, it's not uncommon for them to ask her if the jokes bother her. She always says no, and I believe her.

Sometimes if the comic is too rough on his wife or too open about their relationship, it can endanger the marriage. A comedian has to understand where to draw the line between funny and hurtful. Most comics have to learn that lesson by trial and error. Many jokes are born out of truth, but exactly how truthful should a comedian be onstage? The stage is not a therapy session for the comic to work out his problems. It's a place to make people laugh and leave them feeling better than when they came in.

So if you don't mind, here's the comedian's version of marriage advice for the guys. If you're not a professional comedian, I would tell you to go easy on the wife jokes. When I'm done talking about my wife onstage, I get a check handed to me. If you try it, you might get your head handed to you. Thank you very much and goodnight. I'll be here all week.

$2 Million

I've been to dozens of weddings, and I still tear up almost every time. Outside of a birth, few events match the amount of hope and potential love that a wedding does. With all my heart, I hope and pray for the best for the new couple. I hope they last forever. I wish them *shalom bayit*,[59] peace of the home.

But as we know, sometimes it doesn't work out. At certain times being married is like riding a bucking bronco. You just have to hold on for dear

---

59 *Shalom* means "peace," and a *bayit* is "a home." Maintaining peace in one's home is especially important. What we also need is *shalom me'chon'it*. *Me'chon'it* means "car." All bets seem to be off when married couples take long car rides to visit in-laws.

life. Otherwise, you might end up with brain damage. No other relationship comes close to the depth of marriage.

Sometimes people find out that they want or need to call it quits. Sometimes it gets so bad, people almost (or actually do) kill each other. Sometimes all that's left is police tape and a chalk outline.

If a couple does call it quits, I think some of their close friends and family members who attended the wedding should be invited to some part of the divorce proceedings. And these people should be able to take sides. After all, most of us take sides anyway. We spent years listening to how horrible someone was, so we should get some reward for time served.

Divorce proceedings tend to be much more dramatic and interesting than weddings. There's yelling and screaming and crying—and that's just the lawyers trying to get their money. Plus, I love that many times the people involved don't hide how much money the divorce is costing them. It's one of those rare moments in life when someone tells you exactly how they're feeling and puts a dollar amount on it. "This SOB is costing me close to $2 million." That becomes the mantra, "$2 million." Every few minutes they mumble "$2 million."

Perhaps at their final court appearance, their mothers, if they're still alive, should once again break a plate,[60] but this time over each other's head. If not that, then maybe the couple should consider stepping on each other's wedding ring finger. If they get divorced within the first six months of marriage, all of the gifts they received should be put onto a website and wedding guests should be able to pick something nice for themselves. Also, friends and family should be privy to what went wrong in the marriage so the "I told you not to marry him or her" group gets some satisfaction.

At almost every wedding I've been to, the clergy will give a talk about what an incredible person either the bride or groom is and how lucky the other person is to have found this eighth wonder of the world. If this turns

---

60 At a Jewish wedding, the mothers of the bride and groom stand together and break a plate to represent the seriousness of the commitment their children are taking. Like a broken relationship, a broken plate can never be completely repaired. It also represents the humongous amount of ball breaking and chops busting that are going to occur over the next fifty-plus years.

out to be a crock, the clergy should be fined between $28,000 and $41,000 to cover the cost of the much-needed therapy.

For many people, instead of marital bliss, they have marital blisters, but you can learn to maneuver. There is actually someone in my community who gives private talks to men who are about to make the big leap. The talk lasts six hours over a two-day period. It explains to the groom that he is probably marrying a person who might go insane part of the time but that eventually this will all make sense, and marital bliss will hopefully return soon. Women don't need a six-hour talk. They intuitively understand that they are marrying someone who has been screwed up by his parents and part of her job is to take this person apart and then patiently reassemble. But like anytime you assemble something, you might find that there is a missing piece or two, and you'll have to live with that.

One thing that does help a marriage is to have a common goal and a moral system you both agree on. If both spouses are dedicated to becoming better people and living some sort of holy life, this can help. The rabbis are clear that if you want a good marriage, you need to incorporate God into the mix. After all, he put you two together, so he just might know how to keep you together.

Marriage is so tough that the rabbis tell us God actually comes down and is under the chuppah with you. Anytime God personally shows up, it's a big deal, so you better get cracking. Living with a person is like living in a foxhole. So like in a foxhole, keep praying, keep your head down, do the necessary hard work, and God willing, it will work out for both of you. You know what they say: "There are no atheists in a foxhole."

You Look Marvelous

If my son called and said, "I'm getting married in an hour," I could be shaved, showered, dressed, napped, and still be fifteen minutes early. That's most guys. My son is getting married and my wife, my son's fiancée, and her mother need at least five months.

When I was a kid, people would accost me about the way I looked. I would get, "Who dressed you?" and "You're not really going out looking like that?" To them, I must have looked like one of the kids out of *Oliver Twist*. My mother was fond of calling me a ragamuffin or street urchin. My answer to her and everyone else was to shrug my shoulders.

Once a man decides on his permanent twenty-two-piece wardrobe collection (twenty-four pieces if you include underwear and socks), he then locks those in and rides them into eternity. In my closet, I have one of the first suits I ever bought. To me, it still looks good. To others, it looks like something Ben Franklin might have worn. Even the moths won't nibble on it for fear of getting the splashes.

Sure, our wives and kids occasionally try to spruce us up with a new shirt or more modern-day sport coat. But they are aware that getting us to make changes in our appearance is like trying to piece back together someone who fell off the Empire State Building. Our response is "I don't need any more clothes" or "Where am I going?"

I hate to admit it, but I could get dressed without looking in a mirror. The main reason I ever look in a mirror is to see what part of my lunch might be hanging off my face: pieces of rice, chocolate, or dried tomato sauce.

Most women, in my observation, take a long time to get ready. Even going to bed. I could be in my PJs, done brushing my remaining teeth, and under the covers in less than three minutes. My wife? Forty minutes later.

With all the creams and lotions she applies nightly, it's a miracle she doesn't slide out of bed and onto the floor.

My youngest son, Noah, got married a few years back. I remember my wife waiting for her seventh dress option to be delivered. When it arrived I suspected she would try it on and then ask for my opinion. I would then tell her I liked it and that she looked great. She would then proceed to pack it back up and send me to UPS to ship it back. Why even ask me? Who does she think I am, Christian Lacroix? For me, it's a five-minute deal. My friend Jack told me where I could get a brand-new tux for less than $200. I asked him if they were negotiable. Fait accompli.

I had fun listening to my wife, my son's fiancée, Chloe, and her mother, Donna, talk about the color of the dresses, the length of the sleeves, the shoes, earrings, jewelry, nails, makeup, and of course, hair. When my wife goes to the hair salon, it takes hours to get it right. It takes a man no more than six seconds to comb his hair and check the bottom of his shoes for gum or four-legged excretions. When I go for a haircut, I say the same thing to my barber that I told my kids when they spilled milk: "Please clean it up." Thinking about this, for the first time in my life, I understand the line in the prayer book that reads "Thank you, God, for not making me a woman." I could not take the pressure they are under. This was all being done for a party that would last no more than six hours, which is about the time it'd take for my cheap suit to start unraveling and splitting at the seams.

Like magic, these women appeared looking as beautiful as a Hawaiian sunset. All I had to do was hand over a few hundred checks and say four words over and over: "Yes ... sure ... of course." Then on the big day, I lift the young couple up in their chairs while we all danced and yelled, "Mazel tov!"

12
PARENTING

....

Great Catch, Champ

When a father helps a son, both smile; when a son must help his father, both cry. —Yiddish proverb

My father gave me the greatest gift anyone could give another person: he believed in me. —Jim Valvano

For the last few months I've had the pleasure of watching my neighbor Aaron teach his kids how to catch a ball. When a father is playing catch with his son or daughter, there are few things in life that bring more happiness. It's total enjoyment to the max. To see the smile on a child's face when he or she looks into the baseball glove and unexpectedly sees the ball sitting there is amazing. Then when the child grabs it and holds it up in the air in triumph, it is unbelievable. What's better than that?

Once a child learns how to catch a ball or ride a bike, life moves very quickly from there. In a short amount of time, my neighbor's children will be even with him, if not better than he is, at whatever games they play. That's the way it is, and that's the way it's supposed to be. Soon after teaching my kids ping-pong, they were all beating me at the game. I rarely win when we play a game of Rummikub. And if I'm honest about it, I hate losing to them and they hate losing to me. So at least we are even at something.

When my kids were little, on Saturday mornings we would have a fifteen- to twenty-minute walk to shul depending on the amount of fighting, crying, and refusing to walk that took place. Fifteen to twenty minutes' alone time with my children is priceless. When your kids are older, how much private time do you get with them anymore? Generally, not a lot.

I know it's a cliché that childhood goes fast, but it's true. Our sons and daughters are children for around six thousand days (unless they go to college and graduate school, then maybe fifteen thousand days). In a blink of an eye, they are all grown up.

I only have sons, and it's hard to think of a better feeling than for a father to watch his sons grow up, become *menschen*,[61] and take care of themselves. It's beyond comforting and beyond belief. It's one of those "maybe I did something right" moments. Then when they get married and you see them not only take care of themselves but also help take care of another person, you get the warm feeling that maybe you did something right.

One of my rabbis, who has nine kids with his wife, once said to me, "There has to be a God. We could not have done all this on our own." He meant that to raise a bunch of kids and get them all out into the world as good and decent people is a miracle and demands assistance from above. I believe that.

I think the greatest thing I got from my father is that I knew, with every fiber of my being, that he loved me. If you're a father and you can transmit that to your kids, you've done a lot. Knowing a parent loves you can take you extremely far in this world.

My father didn't spend much time with me. He was busy working. But the time he did spend, he was *there*. When I was growing up, there weren't a lot of distractions. In the car, we had no cell phones, no iPads, nothing. Our

---

61 *Menschen* (singular: *mensch*) are people who can be relied on to act with honor and integrity. Bernie Madoff, for example, need not apply.

entertainment was the front window. When we got into the car, we had a bad-sounding AM radio and did something called talking. That's how two people find out things about each other. Today, you can see people doing that on YouTube.

Hey, dads, I have an idea for you: Have what I call a 1960s day. Have a day where you leave all the electronics at home and take the children out for a ride, or to a ball game, or a movie and lunch. Then maybe one day your kids will look back and say to their kids, "One of my favorite things to do was when my dad and I left our cell phones at home and went out for the afternoon." Then one day they can get into their driverless cars, look out the front window, and see things they've never seen before.

Never Talk While Eating Fish

I'm an only child, so I was the whole ball of wax. In many ways, I was my parents' life. My parents tried to have more children but could not, and for some reason I was never privy to why.

My mother was an extremely nervous woman. Asking her why she was so nervous made her even more nervous. She spent much of her life saying things like, "I'm a nervous wreck," "I can't sleep, I can't eat," and, of course, "Nobody cares about me." I'm sad to say I believe she really did feel that no one cared. She was never able to see what was magical about life. Life always seemed to be a chore to her.

My mother was much more worried about something happening to me than my father was. He was concerned but knew I could take care of myself. When I would go from one room to another, my mother told me to call her when I got there. When I was in the bathroom a long time, she would ask me a half a dozen times if I was all right. My father would just yell, "Did you fall in?"

When my mother made soup and it was hot, she did everything short of putting a warning label on the bowl to remind me not to burn my delicate tongue. She would tell me to blow on the soup to cool it down, and if she saw I didn't blow on it, she would offer to do it for me. If my mother served fish, she would warn me numerous times about the possibility of bones and choking to death. She would say, "Never ever talk when you're eating fish. You could choke." I became very scared of eating fish and swimming in the ocean. How come when fish eat other fish they never choke?

If my parents were alive today, my mother would probably own a small home x-ray machine to run the fish through, looking for hidden bones before serving them up to me. (To be fair, I have twice as an adult almost choked on fish bones.)

My father, on the other hand, was much more loosey-goosey. He would say to my mother, "Leave him alone," "Let him live in peace," and "You're getting him crazy."

My mother would shoot back. "Fine. He can do anything he wants. And if anything happens to him, I'm holding you personally responsible." And so it went on like this for most of my childhood. I was constantly told of terrible things that might happen to me. "Don't climb on ladders—you might fall." "Don't sit in front of an air conditioner if your hair is wet— you'll get pneumonia." "Don't change a light bulb with wet hands—you'll electrocute yourself." "Don't sit too close to the TV—you'll hurt your eyes." "Don't make faces—your face will stay like that." "Don't go on terraces— you might fall off." If a glass broke, my mother would yell, "Get away from the glass-you'll cut yourself." Don't, don't, don't, don't, don't. Almost everything had disaster tied to it.

According to the way my mother saw life, there was only a small chance of anything working out. For years after moving out of my parents' house, I felt helpless in many areas. I was afraid of touching things because I might get hurt or I might break something. I had to learn almost everything from the ground up, and so began my journey of learning how to survive.

I understand she meant well and loved me and didn't want anything to happen to me, but a steady diet of "you can't" was not always to my benefit. I struggled for a long time and had many more insecurities than perhaps I would otherwise have had. To this day, I still check every rim of every glass I'm drinking from, every jar that I open, because I'm frightened of swallowing glass. A few times, when I thought I might have swallowed some glass, I would just patiently sit and wait to see if I was going to bleed to death internally. So far, so good.

I accept that that's life. That's the way it is. Truth be told, I'm fine with it. The lessons I needed to learn from my upbringing were the lessons I needed to learn in life. It's that simple. You get what you get and you deal with it. And if you don't, it deals with you. I also think sometimes people have to go through certain things in order to be able to help other people who are going through similar things. It's the old "I've been where you are." It's identification. "I know what you're going through. I understand." That can go a long way in helping people.

What I really wonder is, what have I put my kids through? What have I done to them? So far, they won't tell me, and they have yet to write anything about me. But this is Hollywood, so I'm sure one of them will think of something to pin on me and make a few bucks for it (if they don't spend it all on the shrink's couch).

They Are Back

After my three sons graduated college, within a short amount of time, each landed a job and had his own place. My wife and I became empty nesters and were living the life. For dinner, if we wanted, we were free to eat Frosted Flakes fricassee. Then, like a couple of old winos, we could fall asleep on the couch with the TV blasting away. I could shower without someone banging on the bathroom door with stupid questions to which I had to reply, "I'm glad you asked that."

One day, darkness prevailed upon us. While I was picking out a pair of underwear that was less than two weeks away from becoming an oil rag for my car, the phone rang. It was Jacob. He wanted to move back in for a few months (which would turn out to be closer to a year and a half) before he got married. He said we would be saving him a fortune on rent. He always comes up with some way I can save him a fortune that costs me a fortune. His room in the house, though, had already been converted into a Costco and 99 Cents storage locker. I told him he would have to sleep surrounded by jars of mustard, bottles of tomato sauce, a case of Windex, and a twenty-four pack of toilet paper. With unbelievable chutzpah,[62] he asked if we could move the stuff to another room in the house.

Jacob's first day back, while I was showering, he banged on the bathroom door so hard I thought the house was on fire. He yelled, "How much longer till you're done?" Thank God he is now married and back out.

Noah, our youngest, was living in New York when COVID first hit. We were worried because of quarantine and airport closures, so we had him come to Los Angeles and he also moved into our Costco storeroom. He said we needed to double our internet speed so he could work from our house. So, forty-five dollars more a month, and our internet was flying faster than a peregrine falcon.

By now we had also added to the room multiple cases of microwavable brown rice, forty-eight bottles of water, a case of pink salmon, and three five-pound jars of mixed nuts. Like a rat, Noah would sit in the room, virtually flying around on our lightning-speed internet, and snacking all day on the nuts, selectively picking out all the cashews and leaving the garbage nuts for us.

---

62 Chutzpah is Yiddish for "courage" or someone with a lot of nerve or gall. Chutzpah in a more modern language means he or she has some set of balls.

One morning Noah sweetly asked me if I would make him those great breakfast potatoes I made when he was little. He hit me in my soft spot. I used Yukon Gold potatoes, diced small, green pepper, onion, garlic, olive oil, salt, pepper, oregano, and smoked paprika. Lots and lots of imported smoked paprika. With a little olive oil and a cast-iron pan, I cooked it all together until the potatoes became soft and wonderful. Then for the next four months while Noah lived with us, every morning I served him up my special potatoes, eggs, and coffee. One morning as I was cooking breakfast and wearing an apron that read "Kitchen Help," he put his arm around me, thanked me, and asked if I could add a small bowl of berries to his morning order.

My middle son, Eli, recently switched jobs and is now back with us for a few months. When the boys were younger, they shared a room. One night we went in to put them to bed, and before we left, Jacob asked, "Hey, Dad, will I ever have to move out of the house?"

I remember looking at my wife for the permission nod to answer him. I got the nod and said, "Jacob, great question. Yes, one day when you get older and get married, you will move out and get your own place." He seemed satisfied with that answer, but then Eli asked the same question. The middle kids are the rough ones.

"Dad, will I also have to move out and get married?" I looked to my wife again, but this time, the yes nod came a little slower.

"Eli, when you get older, you will have to move out too," I responded.

He pulled the covers up to his neck, looked at all of us, and declared, "I am never leaving. You can't make me leave." He then proceeded to cry like I had never seen him cry before.

The good news is that, thank God, he eventually moved out. We love him, but this meant no more forty-five-minute showers with me banging on the bathroom door. The bad news is that when he left, he took with him all of our pickles, three hundred dollars' worth of frozen steaks, and my Bose Bluetooth speaker. Still, that's a small price to pay for peace.

The Nineteen Boxes

My mother died July 9, 1999. I remember coming home that Friday afternoon from picking up Shabbas flowers. I was parking my car when I saw my wife walking out of the house to greet me. I knew right away that something awful had happened, because she never comes out of the house to say hello. I could see in her face that something was wrong. "What's the matter?" I asked. Taking a deep breath, she said, "Your mother is gone."

With the release of those words, my life has never been the same. There are certain sentences that change your life forever. We all have them. Within seconds of the delivery of that sentence from my wife, I was struck numb. It was as if I had just had a dose of Novocain delivered into my brain. When I looked at my wife standing there, I could see her in front of me, but even as we hugged, I could only feel stillness all around. It was like the earth had stopped rotating. It was as if my forty-five-year-old brain, with all its knowledge and experience, had been emptied out and now knew only one word: gone.

I proceeded to pick up the flowers, grabbed my laptop off the back seat, and for the first time walked into my house an orphan. When I walked out that morning to go to the office, I had a mother. When I walked back in that afternoon, I did not.

Ten months later, and the reality of it was very slowly sinking in. I still thought every Sunday, *Hey, Mark. Call your mother.* However, if you ever heard any of my conversations with my mother, you'd think, why is he even bothering to call? My mother and I loved each other very much. It's just that, at certain times in our lives, we didn't act like it, and rarely did we talk about our feelings. Is it a male thing? Maybe. A typical phone conversation with my mother went something like this: "Hello, Mom, it's me. Good. Everyone's good. And how are you? Not good. What's the matter?

Everything. You'll feel better soon. Oh, you won't. OK, I'll call you next week. Love you, bye."

If you've lost someone close to you, you'll agree that one of the hardest things about the death of a loved one is that you can't hear the person's voice anymore. On one level, I know that's true. But on another level, I can say that sometimes I now hear my mother louder and clearer than ever.

After my mother died, my wife and I went down to Fort Lauderdale and spent three days packing up her one-bedroom apartment. Then I went to Mailbox Express, and for a mere $800, I sent home nineteen boxes. It took me seven months to open them. What I didn't know was that inside those boxes, my mother was waiting to talk to me in a way I had always yearned for and was never able to hear from her. One of the first things I found was her ninth-grade autograph book. The book contained thoughts on her future, dreams, and hopes. Her friends wished her luck with one day having a family and becoming an actress. Opening that book was our first real conversation since her death. I was hearing about her dreams as a child to become an actress and perform on Broadway. She sounded so happy and excited. I told her I was sorry it never happened for her, but I was sure she would have been great if it had. I meant every word of it. Never before was I able to express such empathy to my mom.

Then I found her class picture from ninth grade, and I heard her ask me to pick her out of the photo. I said sure and found her picture right away. I told her how beautiful she looked and how she really hadn't changed all that much. She thanked me for the compliment.

The most exciting moment for me was when I found my baby book. My mom had saved a few dozen cards that people had sent her and my dad to congratulate them on my birth. She had meticulously placed them in a baby book with some of the greatest black-and-white baby photos ever developed. This book had dates, events, even a strand of my hair. It was my mother at her best. What I was hearing now was coming from the deepest part of her soul. She now roared with happiness and love for the young family that was just beginning. I heard my mother's heart overflowing with love. My mother was far from gone. She was here more than ever. I had never heard her sound so good and seem so happy.

Smell My New Car

When I was growing up in New York in the late fifties and early sixties, if a neighbor got a new car, it was a big deal. Back then you got married forever and you kept your car forever. But if you did get a new car, the whole neighborhood knew it. And if you were a kid and you wanted to check it out and if your hands were sparkling clean and if you didn't have mud on your shoes, your neighbor might let you sit in it. However, if they got the gold standard, a Cadillac, it wasn't worth even trying to get near it. If I got too close to a new Caddy, my parents would tell me to stand back and not touch it. They acted like I might pull out a hammer and start banging on the windshield.

Because of the icy winters and heavily salted roads, a new car looked like an old rusted can of Heinz beans in a short amount of time. Plus, New Yorkers parked by squeezing into parking spaces using the "bang into the next car's bumper thirty-eight times" method. When the bumper was hanging off the car, they were done parking.

My father didn't get his first new car until he was forty-two. When he did, he was such a happy man driving around in his brand-spanking-new $3,000 1970 Dodge Swinger with AC and a vinyl roof. For months after getting the car, he could not stop talking about the new-car smell. "Smell it. Smell it. Smell it" was his mantra. One time, when he was about to get a ticket, he asked the cop to stick his head in the window and smell it. The cop laughed so hard, he let him go.

Back then, very few people ate or drank coffee in their cars. Cars did not have cup holders. Now with cup holders you have a place to keep your pens and loose change, and once I even saw a set of false teeth with what looked like bubble gum stuck to them. Some folks even got pregnant in the old cars. That's why they had lots of ashtrays, for people who enjoyed smoking after sex. But eating in the car was out of the question. It was considered rude. I recently told my friend I wanted to get a slice of pizza. He said there was one in his glove compartment.

Back then when you sold your car, no one ever asked if it was a non-smoker's car. There was no such thing. The nonsmoker car had not even been invented yet. In fact, the nonsmoker hadn't even been invented yet. You could still smoke in your hospital bed an hour after having lung surgery.

When I started to drive, my parents occasionally let me borrow their car, which when I think back on it was an incredible act of love considering the kind of lunatic I was back then. At the end of the night, I always put between fifty cents' and a dollar's worth of gas back in. Gas was thirty-six cents a gallon back then.

Practically everything my father taught me about a car, you could apply to living a better life. My father took great care of his car. How one drives and takes care of a car says a lot about a person and who he or she is. If the inside of your car looks like a storage bin turned upside down, then there's a good chance that your insides are also a mess. My father would remind me, "If you want to keep nice things nice, it takes work." We all know people who have to clear the front seat and floor of their car before you can get in and put your feet down without possibly stepping on something that was once alive.

My father taught me how to put air in the tires and how to check the oil. We're Jewish, so we only check the oil, we don't change it. These days most people I know couldn't find their oil stick because they don't know where the hood release is. He also taught me how to use hand signals, even the ones that let people know exactly what you think of them.

His marriage tip was: if I saw a woman and her car was broken down, I should stop and help her. She could be the one. When he was single, he worked at an auto school that my mother came into one day for driving lessons. A year later, they got married. She passed her driving test and then proceeded to drive him crazy for the next thirty-nine years.

The Nearness of You

It isn't sweet conversation
That brings this sensation, oh no
It's just the nearness of you
—Hoagy Carmichael and Ned Washington, "The Nearness of You"

A while back I was at the funeral of a good friend. His wife and three children all got up and spoke about his virtues as a husband and father. It was an absolutely beautiful and moving event. They spoke of how much he meant to them and how he was a friend to all who met him. They spoke of his unwavering support for them and their dreams in life. They spoke of how they would not be who they were without him. They spoke about how much they loved him and how much they missed him already, just one day after his death. They already missed not being near him. Almost everyone was crying.

My father died when I was thirty-six. He died before he met my wife. He died before I got married. He died before he got to see his grandchildren. He died before he got to really see the type of husband and father I was to become. He died not really knowing who I was or what I was capable of.

Did I really get to know him? No. I knew only a few facts about his childhood and adolescence. My father was a quiet man with a quiet soul. He didn't say much, and he didn't get involved in any big events. He worked, came home, ate dinner, watched a little TV, and then went to sleep. He did that five days a week, fifty weeks a year, until he died.

When I was a kid, I only saw him for about an hour and a half a day. Sometimes we'd both sit in bed in our boxers and polish off a pint of ice cream while watching TV. Anytime spent with him was valuable to me. We really didn't need to talk. He was Dad, and I was Mark. That's it. We just needed to be together, near each other. My leg over his leg, watching the tube.

The bottom line is that sometimes you just need to be near the people you love. It's what my friend's wife and kids were saying at his funeral. For this reason, when one of my kids calls and asks me to go for a ride with him to get a haircut, I go. When the other kid asks me to go to a ball game, I go. When my wife asks if I want to go to Ralphs supermarket with her, I go. Not because I think any huge event is going to happen. Not because I'm going to get an answer to a life problem that's been plaguing me for years. Not because I need to find out anything new about them. I go just so I can be near them. I go so I can be the first to see the new haircut. I go to share a bag of peanuts at the ball game. I go so I can hear a question like "Do we need pickles?" I go because one day I won't be able to go anymore. I know it and they know it. We don't talk about it, but we know it.

The main reason I go to the cemetery to visit my parents is to try to be near them one more time. Try all you want, it's not the same. Be near your loved ones now, while you can.

Pay Attention

The soul is healed by being with children. —Fyodor Dostoevsky

If you've ever seen an old prison movie, you know the scene where they are strapping a convicted murderer into the electric chair and he is screaming, "I'm telling you, I didn't do it." Standing next to him is a priest (never a rabbi, unless they're the Rosenbergs). Then there would be a shot of a wall clock ticktocking away. Next, a shot of a phone not ringing. The convicted murderer is asking if the governor has called. An important phone call, don't you think?

Nowadays, many people act as if every tweet and text is of a similar magnitude. In the old horror movies, you would see normal-looking people walking around like zombies being controlled by outside forces. Like a woodworm beetle, the mobile phone has bored a hole into our brains. We now live our lives waiting for moment-to-moment commands from the digital galaxy. Our prayer is that one day our tweets go viral.

Once in a while, I'll ask rude people to put their phone away. My family warns me that one day I'll be shot. I was once at a doctor's office, waiting to get an important blood test result. I was nervous. Across from me was this yakety-yak gabbing away at a pitch Pavarotti might attempt when trying to reach the rafters at Lincoln Center. I politely asked yackety to please take the call outside and then pointed to a "NO CELL PHONE CALLS PERMITTED" sign. A look of hatred poured out of her eyes. When she would not stop, I asked her once again. Yackety then said to her friend, "Some man is being very, very rude to me." Even at funerals, shiva houses, and weddings, it's not uncommon to hear phones go off and to see people hunched over them talking.

Have you ever taken a phone away from your child? They go berserk. They're practically suicidal. I once realized that I left my phone home and immediately felt like I left the house without pants. I know that feeling, because I once did leave without my pants. I was at a Passover program with my family. I went out to get them some drinks from the tearoom. While standing at the elevator, I looked in the mirror and saw that I had nothing on but my boxers. Fifteen years later, they still mock me.

What I'm most concerned about are the new batch of people being born. When I was a kid and went out with my parents, they would talk to me, point things out, scream at me, and, of course, threaten me. But at least they were paying attention to me. Seemingly, that's happening less and less. I don't know about at home, but in the streets, fewer adults seem to be paying attention to their little ones. Many times I'll see parents, grandparents, or nannies talking or texting while pushing strollers across busy streets while the lonesome kid is told to be quiet and stares off into outer space.

On Shabbas, what's better than talking to your child while walking to shul? Every so often I'll see parents who are running late, rushing the kids to walk faster while they have their faces buried in the siddur. All they've done is replace the phone with the siddur. Instead of walking and talking to the kids, they are walking and talking to God. Once more, the kid is asked to be quiet.

What is more important to you, praying for your children or answering their question about whether or not there are bugs on clouds? Talk to them now, or they may not want to talk to you later. Remember this: they're only going to be young once.

Granted, paying attention is not easy. Multitasking has cut all our attention spans. Paying attention takes practice. It means getting out of yourself and really finding out about someone else, and there is a price for that. That's why they call it "paying attention." You are paying for it with your attention, something of which you have a finite quantity to give.

Welcome to the Club

In the middle of the marches, riots, tearing down of statues, curfews, and coronavirus of 2020, the phone rang. It was our oldest son, Jacob, telling us he thought his wife, Anna, was in labor. I asked him how he knew, and he said, "When we were lying in bed watching TV, I saw a teeny tiny hand reach out from under the covers for the remote control."

When I heard those words "in labor," it was as if my world had come to a complete halt. For nine months, like bounty hunters, we'd been tracking this kid's every move with sonogram photos. Every second in life is always an "Oh my God" moment. But this was an in-your-face—with a new face—"Oh my God" moment. We were being called upon to witness a miracle.

And then the greatest magic trick of them all: "Now you don't see him, now you do." Six-plus hours later, Anna gave birth to a boy. Their first child and our first grandchild. The mazel tovs started pouring in. Every grandparent we talked to said the same thing, "Welcome to the club. You'll see it's the best club in the world."

If only this little baby knew how much happiness he has already brought into this broken world. This baby is so important that as coronavirus raged on, family members risked their lives by flying in to get a firsthand look at all six and a half pounds of him. My religious friends were asking when the bris was, and my secular friends were asking what his name was. In my secular world, I was one of the first to have a grandchild. In my religious world, I was one of the last.

When he was five days old, the young parents had hardly slept. They both looked like they had exophthalmos, also known as proptosis (the medical term for protruding or bulging eyeballs).

Babies are for the young. If my wife gave birth to a baby a week ago, by now, one or both of us would be in a coma. And be happy to be in it. So buckle up, kids—it's payback time. It's now your kid's turn to get a taste of what all parents have gone through since babies were invented. My son complained that the baby screamed for hours without stopping. That's a good baby. Keep screaming, little guy. Rock the walls. This is your time. Blow your horn. As grandparents, we smile and say, "What a set of lungs on that kid." I hate to say it, but it all makes me laugh. It makes most grandparents laugh.

When we noticed that the new parents' eyes started glazing over and they started taking on that suicidal look and the other tenants in their apartment building were secretly gathering enough signatures so they could serve the happy new parents with an eviction notice, we "club members" went home to our nice peace and quiet and our oatmeal-and-banana dinner. When you get older, you start eating like a baby again.

Next day back at their house, they asked me if I wanted to hold the baby. It's been twenty-four years since I held a newborn. I took the baby and cradled him in the crook of my arm. At first, I didn't feel anything. In fact, I felt numb. But I just kept looking at him and staring at this beautiful new face. I was enamored by his brand-new soft skin. It went on like this for a few days. I had hardly any feeling except numbness. It slightly worried me.

Then it happened. I was on the treadmill exercising, and suddenly I felt wobbly and unsure of my footing. A gush of sadness and heaviness came over me. My old life was once again being exorcised from my soul, and a new life was being injected. And then the dam broke. I started to cry. Deep, deep sobbing. I started to feel a huge gush of emotion. I was being infused with new love. It was startling. I started to feel real love. He had entered my heart. I had to step to the side of the treadmill and hold on. When my wife found out that they named the baby after her father, she too got weak in the knees. That's a big honor.

Last week our kids dropped the baby off for us to babysit. The second they left, he started crying and screaming till the second they came back.

When they returned, they asked, "How was he?" We responded, "Just perfect. He's a little angel."

We have now been grandparents for a couple of years. I think we're just beginning to understand what everyone means by "Welcome to the club." The word "happy" is insufficient to describe the feelings of elation we felt when we first became grandparents to a beautiful, bouncing baby boy named Ben, and we feel even stronger now. (I don't know why they call new babies "bouncing babies." Not only did Ben not bounce, he hardly even moved for the first few months.) Ben is now a nonstop bouncer along with his parents, who at times are bouncing off the walls themselves. One big, happy bouncing family. The parents' eyes are also still bulging out of their heads.

For me, this kid has been a *mechayeh*,[63] and for reasons you might not expect. Sure, having a new person to love is amazing. Sure, watching my son and daughter-in-law blossom is amazing. Sure, spending thousands of dollars on a person who will never know you spent thousands of dollars on him is amazing, although according to Maimonides, aka the Rambam, this is an extremely high form of giving. But for me, that's all a pittance compared to what I am about to tell you. The best of all—and I mean the absolute best—is knowing that this new family member is a much bigger slob than I am. I've always been a slob, but this kid takes the cake and then spits it back out all over the place. I am so grateful that God, in His infinite wisdom, has decided to take some of the heat off me.

My beautiful wife constantly complains that my hands are wet. After I wash them, I try to dry them, but no matter how much I towel them off, water seems to stick to them like it's been Krazy Glued on. Not only are Ben's hands always wet from nonstop sucking on them, but he can also put practically his whole hand down his throat. Also his cute little face is always drenched. If you did not know better, you'd think he'd just climbed

---

63 *Mechayeh* refers to pleasure and enjoyment, a real joy. When the dentist pulls an abscessed tooth, that's a real *mechayeh*. When the dentist pulls the wrong tooth, that's a lawsuit, which is also a *mechayeh*.

out of a swimming pool. Then there is the perpetual thick drool that constantly hangs from his chin that does not seem to bother him. He is a drool machine. From a distance, if you stare at the drool, it looks eerily like razor-sharp icicles hanging from an underpass in the dead of winter. He also acts as if this is the year 1509 and he is Henry VIII; if he does not like his food, he throws it on the floor, grunts, and bangs on his high chair.

Then there is his gas problem. This kid releases more gas in one afternoon than the United States has produced since 1915. But when he toots one out, he is never asked to say he's sorry. He is never asked to leave the room. In fact, quite the opposite. Everyone is incredibly happy to hear the foghorn. Some even clap. I, on the other hand, if I should do such a thing, am practically sent to Outer Mongolia. I am not proud of it, but more than twice, I tossed blame his way for what I should have taken ownership of. I wonder if God considers that a lie. Write me and let me know if I need to make amends at www.markschiff.com.

When I ask the family how come it's OK for him to do these things but not me, their stock answer is "He's a baby and doesn't know any better." Yes, I do know better. Yes, I do act civilized ("act" being the operative word). But really civilized? Come, come. The rabbis teach that who you are as a person is how you act when you are alone. I know how I eat and what sounds come out of me when nobody else is around. Enough said. You get my drift.

But dear parents of beautiful bouncing Ben, you can hope, and you can pray, and we all know you will be the greatest, most loving parents possible. But this is a boulder that quite possibly cannot be stopped. Not so many years from now, some unsuspecting sweet woman will, God willing, marry Ben, and like every woman who marries a guy, at some point in the relationship there will come the day when she asks herself the question, Who the heck raised this animal?

13
SELF-HELP

....

How to Accomplish Getting Nothing Done

Procrastination always gives you something to look forward to.
—Joan Konner

Ever since I was a kid, I've always bought self-help books, or maybe I should say "shelf-help" books. The first self-help book I remember buying was Evelyn Wood's *The Evelyn Wood Seven-Day Speed Reading and Learning Program*. The book explains how you can learn to read *Moby-Dick* in an hour and retain it all. I bought Wood's book in 1996 and I've yet to finish it. In fact, buying the speed-reading book kept me from reading other books I wanted to read. Plus, it made me very aware of how slow a reader I am. Just buying the book and not finishing it I believe lowered my self-esteem.

Another one I bought was *Feel the Fear and Do It Anyway*. That book took me over a year to read because I was afraid to feel the fear. Eventually I did finish it, and it turned out to be an excellent book. The author, Susan

Jeffers, believes that, with the exception of a few people, most people are capable of breaking through their fears. I was afraid I was one of the people who are incapable of it. Plus, most of these books you have to keep reading over and over. I'm afraid that I probably won't go back to the fear book.

A few years ago I purchased *The Memory Book* by Harry Lorayne and Jerry Lucas. If my memory serves me right, and I'm not sure that it does, Jerry was a basketball player. Ever since I was a child, people have always questioned my memory. Here are a few by my mother: "I must have told you ten times to get your feet off the chair." "Do you not remember that I asked you to clean up your room and take the garbage out?" "When was the last time you did what I asked you to do?" I never had an answer for that one.

My teachers questioned my memory too. "How can someone forget to bring in their homework three days in a row?" "You said you read *Tom Sawyer* and the only thing you remember about the book is that there is a guy named Tom in it?"

When I got married, my wife joined in by telling me she doesn't believe that I have a bad memory, but rather I have what she calls a "selective memory." She says that I only remember the things I want to remember. For instance, it seems that I tend to forget when we are going out to dinner with other people. Or before I come home, I'll call her and ask her if she needs anything. If she does, I'll ask her to text the list to me. Then, like clockwork, I'll forget to look at her text in the store and I'll go home without the items. That leads to "Don't call me to see if I need anything if you're not going to pick it up."

My wife also claims that I'm a procrastinator, so I bought Steve Scott's book *How to Stop Procrastinating*. But I found that rather than reading the book, I was wasting so much time doing other things. When my wife would see the book just sitting around unopened for weeks, this would cause us to fight, so I ran right out and bought Alicia Muñoz's book *No More Fighting*, which is a self-help book for married couples to learn to stop fighting before they start. When my wife threw Muñoz's book into the barbecue pit, I knew that wasn't the right one for us.

One of my wife's biggest complaints is that I am messy and have things strewn all over the place. So off I went and got Sunny Schlenger and Roberta Roesch's *How to Be Organized in Spite of Yourself*. You guessed it: I can't seem to find the book.

The one book that did help me organize was *The Life-Changing Magic of Tidying Up* by Marie Kondo. Her thesis, and it works, is if you don't love an item in your possession, you should either give it away or throw it away. You do this by taking whatever objects are causing you clutter and getting in your way and then gathering them all in one area. You then pick up each item individually, look at it, and if you don't feel love for it, you toss it.

I gathered up every self-help book I had and put them all on my dining room table. There were 158 of them. I then picked up each book one at a time, looked at it, and if I didn't feel the love for it, I got rid of it. I ended up tossing every one of them except for my Evelyn Wood *Speed Reading* book. The only reason I kept good old Evelyn was that if one day I do learn to speed read and by chance I do buy another self-help book, I can read it then get rid of it an hour after I buy it. As of today, I have yet to read a single word of Evelyn Wood. But it's not a total loss. It's an old hardcover book that holds a hot cup of coffee on top of it very nicely. I'm thinking of writing a book called *How to Not Buy Self-Help Books*. I hope to see you at my signing.

I Love Your Smile

A smile is an inexpensive way to change your looks. —Charles Gordy

I'm a stand-up comedian, a profession that causes, if you're good at what you do, people to heap praise on you. Before I step onstage, a person introduces me with "And now, ladies and gentlemen, please welcome . . ." and then says my name and applause follows. Afterward, if I have had a good show, the applause repeats, and this time even louder.

How many people get an introduction and applause when they show up for work? "And now, ladies and gentlemen, the law firm of Crumb, Bing, and Wallace wants you to welcome back to the office Karen Lipmanshbybivberg. You saw her yesterday, and she'll be here all week. So put your hands together for Karen." Applause.

Wouldn't that be nice? Instead, Karen arrives without announcement, and when she finishes for the day, maybe one or two people might say good-night to her. When I'm done with my set, people want to hang out with me. Many people take work home with them. Nobody ever calls me at home or at my hotel after my show and says, "Hey, Mark, tell me one more joke."

Most people get very little applause or actual recognition in life, but many deserve it far more than I do. Have you ever gone by yourself to visit someone who is in a coma? Unless you told someone you were going to do this, no one knows you were even there. Even Moses, with all he did for the Jews in leading them out of Egypt, not only got no applause, but he was also left out of the Passover Haggadah.[64] In fact, many good things people do at or outside their jobs are done in private and in silence. Which is a good thing. It's between them and God.

---

64 The Haggadah is the book we read at Passover. The word *Haggadah* means "telling," as its primary purpose is to facilitate the retelling of the story of the exodus of the Jews from Egypt. Also important is that the children and adults get to ask questions about things they do not understand or do not agree with. To liven up the seder, it's a good idea to invite at least one belligerent atheist to disagree with almost everything meaningful.

If you ask most people if they need applause or recognition, they might say, "It might be nice occasionally." Many, however, will say no, that they chose the life they lead and if they have a happy and healthy family, then that's applause and recognition enough for them. And that's true. But occasionally telling people that they are doing a good job or that they look good or you like them or you're happy to see them is not a bad thing. Just be careful what compliments you give people these days.

When I look in the mirror, I don't think I'm the best judge of how I look. In fact, quite the opposite. I hardly ever think I look good. I need people to correct my vision.

I have a cousin who's in his midseventies. He's a nice guy, but he looks a little weather-beaten. I was with him recently and I told him that I thought he looked good, and by the way I really did think that. In less than a second, he said, "Really?"

I said, "Yeah, you look healthy."

Again he asked, "Really?" I would bet the house that no one has told him that he looked good in many years. When I told him, he perked right up. His eyes seemed to look a bit less sad. Someone saw him. He wasn't the invisible man for a minute. When I tell people that I was just thinking about them, most of the time they don't believe it. How about saying something to brighten a person's day? "I love your smile." "It's good to see you." "Those are nice shoes." There are hundreds of things you could say to brighten someone's day, especially people in your family, who often are taken for granted. I once told my cousin she was my favorite cousin, and she told me how much that meant to her.

So try it. Try saying two nice things to at least two people every day—especially to your spouse and kids. They'll appreciate it. And maybe, just maybe, after ten years of doing this, they may say something nice to you. Then let me know you did it, and I promise I'll stand up and applaud you for it.

Lost and Found

It's a requirement to be happy all the time. —Rabbi Nachman of Breslov

I have your final grades here. Some of you are not going to be happy.
—My sixth-grade teacher, Mr. D

I was miserable as a child and stayed that way until my midthirties. I thought this might be my destiny. But I was wrong.

Growing up, I was told that if you give people a chance, they will step all over you; if you trust people, you're an idiot; and don't complain to waiters or they'll spit in your food. (In some restaurants, that might add flavor.) At times I felt so sad that even my eyelids hurt. The few friends I had were as troubled as I was. "Birds of a Feather" syndrome.

When I was a kid, there was so much yelling and threatening at home, it was maddening. I vividly remember sitting on my bed at around ten years old, asking God to stop the screaming. I begged God to bring peace to my family. I always believed in God, which brought me some sense of security. Other than that, I had hardly any.

The thing that got me feeling halfway OK was when I'd ride my bicycle like a madman. I peddled hard and fast and would jump the curbs while screaming at the top of my lungs. At sixteen I decided on my own to enter therapy, and I stayed in it for the next seventeen years. In my midthirties, still gloomy and doomy, I decided, though I didn't actually know it, to clean up my life. Baby steps. Slowly, one by one, I kept dropping people, places, and things that I deemed were bad for me. I was freeing myself. When it came to dropping bad habits, I was the original Marie Kondo. Marie Kondo invented the KonMari method. The difference here is bad habits don't get donated or hopefully passed on. Bad habits should get thrown out. And hopefully you never buy them back again.

Eventually I stopped drinking and smoking, and slowly I started eating better. Occasionally I even added exercise. For the first time in my life, I was starting to take care of myself. After I quit smoking, I quickly gained about forty pounds. I needed a protective layer to shield me from whatever hurt might come my way. I was not quite ready to feel yet. But even with the weight gain, I felt I was getting better.

It took me almost fifteen years to get rid of those pounds. But I did it. There were even bursts of occasional happiness. When I told my therapist how much booze I drank, she suggested that I join a recovery group, so I got into recovery. Then ten months later, I joined a shul. I'm now hooked on both. This year, it will be thirty-five years of my doing recovery work and being a member of a shul. If you wonder what I'm trying to recover, it's those parts of myself that were lost early on, or that I never knew I had. My happiness and self-worth for one.

A giant lesson I learned since hitting the road to healing is that there are people you can trust. Life started to show some real possibilities. I even got married. That's a big deal for someone with trust issues.

One day I made a big decision. I had been complaining about my parents and my childhood for so long I was sick of it. It bored me and it bored others. It was a hopeless maze. I decided that I would no longer complain about my parents or my childhood. I was officially done doing so. I was done with that part of my story. "What was, was" and "So what. Now what?" were my new mottos.

This one decision started me on an open road with endless possibilities. I felt free, light. At times I still get sad, but it's not a daily occurrence. I've found sometimes just taking a simple action is all you need to get the ball rolling. Just open the door a crack and let some light in. The trick is to get rid of your old story and start a new one. A new life.

It's risky, but worth it. The rabbis teach us *kol hatchalot kashot*[65]—all beginnings are hard. Your new story should have hope and love. Lift the

---

65 *Kol hatchalot kashot*: All beginnings are hard (Mechilta, Yitro). It's a statement that we intuitively know to be true. Any desire we might have to start something new inherently comes with risk. My oil stocks are proof of this.

curtain onto your new life. In my new story, I'm not the victim anymore. Occasionally I still need to ride my bike and scream my head off when I go flying off of a curb. Some things are just fun. Let me know if you want to join me for a ride.

Nap Time

At almost any play, movie, event, or talk that I attend, I fall sound asleep during at least some of it. I've paid hundreds of dollars to go see Broadway shows and gone right to sleep within minutes of the lights going down. I've fallen asleep during a World Series game at Yankee Stadium.

I also fall asleep every time I open a book and start reading in bed. I have one book I've been reading for about twelve years. I pick up the book, start to read, and about a paragraph or two in my eyes start banging up and down like a broken garage door. I then drop the book out of my hands, and I'm gone.

The good news is I don't ever feel like I've wasted my money or missed out on anything by falling asleep. I'm always happy and grateful after a solid nap. If there is something good to be found in my falling asleep, it is that I don't snore or bob my head up and down like some junkie in a crack house stairwell. I just sit with my head down, generally holding a book or Playbill or a bag of nuts. I also am considerate enough not to ask people what I missed when I wake up. The truth is I don't care what I missed. I got a good nap and that's all that matters. The few times I've gone to the opera I'm sorry to say the opposite has happened. I could not fall asleep. That, to me, is a horror. Staying awake while pudgy Italians are screaming for three hours to me is the equivalent of being waterboarded.

But what about when you go to hear your rabbi or priest or some other spiritual leader who is trying to pass on to you the deep meaning of life? Should you still go to hear him or her if you know you're definitely going to fall asleep? Is it disrespectful to go? Is it rude? When we lived in San Antonio, I remember saying to our rabbi, "Rabbi Scheinberg, I want to come hear you, but I need to tell you that more than likely, I will fall asleep during part of or possibly all of your talk."

He laughed because he thought I was joking with him. He said, "You won't be alone."

I asked again, "Do you still want me to come?"

"Absolutely, please come."

I went every week and fell asleep every time. As soon as he opened his book to begin teaching, it was like I was being hypnotized. My eyes would start to glaze over, and bingo, I was gone.

I'm not alone with this. I remember Rabbi Marvin Hier, the head of the Simon Wiesenthal Center, once telling someone that when he was a pulpit rabbi in Canada, the police came to his shul and asked, "In case of emergency, how many could you sleep here if necessary?" He said, "I sleep three hundred and fifty here every Saturday morning." Going to hear a rabbi is the best of both worlds. I learn a little and get a good, solid nap.

For the record, whatever event I go to, my intention is to stay awake. Unfortunately, I rarely win that battle. In this respect, I'm very much like a dog. I can fall asleep any time or place. I can remember as far back as fourth grade when my teacher asked me to wake up and pay attention. I don't know that being awake and paying attention always go hand in hand, at least not for me. You can ask my wife about that one. Many times I've been awake and suddenly heard her say, "Are you listening to me?"

I was born with a dumb look on my face, and it has stuck. I also have an uncanny ability to repeat back word for word what people say to me without paying the slightest attention to what they are actually saying. When people talk to me it's almost like having the radio on in the background. My mother would say, "Living with you is like living with a parrot. Because you can repeat back what I'm saying, but it doesn't mean you've heard anything I've said."

Doctors tell you if you're tired, you should get some rest because you probably need it. Well, I'm tired. Goodnight!

I Don't Want to Exercise

Do you know who cares if you exercise? The people who sell exercise equipment. After that, pretty much zilch. That includes your parents, children, friends, and spouse. Most of the time, they just don't care. Two reasons exercisers are hated is that they whine about every ache and pain, and because they *hock*[66] you to death about why you're not living up to their standards. Of course, your friends and family are proud of you and want you to be healthy; they just don't want to hear the speed you got your heart rate up to today. How would you like to hear about every time they eat chocolate, drink Coke, and nap? Leave them alone.

I have been exercising at least six days a week—sometimes seven—for close to ten years. Hot, cold, fat, thin, I get it done. And I don't talk to my family about it, especially the ones who never exercise, unless of course I'm in the mood for some eye rolling. When I first started exercising, I hated it as much as Nancy Pelosi would hate being married to Donald Trump (imagine those fights), but I did it.

My mother had a favorite expression. "Like it or lump it, but just do it." Most mornings I get up and the first thought in my head is, *I don't want to exercise. I hate exercising. I'm going to kill myself.* Thought number two is, *I don't want to get up. I am so tired. I'm going to kill myself.* I then walk zombielike to the bathroom to do my business, wash up, and put on my

---

66 *Hock* is a Yiddish word that means "to nag or pester." It's mostly used by the waitstaff in kosher restaurants about their customers who put all the Sweet'N Low in their bags and keep asking for more.

workout gear. Putting on your gear sends a clear message to the anti-exercise voices that you're serious. (The voices hate that.)

Now here's the left turn. Before exercising, I make breakfast for my wife. I do that seven days a week. A lot of times I don't want to do it, but like it or lump it, I do it, even if the night before we had a fight. Sure, I might think about poisoning her, but my rabbi said thinking and doing are two different things. I also always try to make sure not to leave a mess even though she always finds something. Then I walk the dog, which I also don't like to do. I've come to realize that no matter how much I don't want to do something, I can still do it.

To me, Disneyland was a torture chamber, but I went and smiled. You cannot maintain a marriage, friendship, or relationship with your children if you only do the things that you want to do. Even when you do nice things for people, it doesn't matter. I remember doing a million things for my kids and guess what: at times, they still hated me.

I beg, I implore you to never ever bring up what you've done for someone else. It doesn't work, because they'll just throw back in your face what they've done for you. Except my kids. They can't seem to come up with anything that they've done for me.

So here's the deal. If possible, in the mornings try to do something for someone else before you do something for yourself, even if it's feeding a stray cat. It gets you out of yourself. Most mothers intuitively know this. I had to learn it. My experience is that when I do something for someone else, it sets a nice tone, especially in the morning. Then after that's done, it can become more about me. I can now exercise, shower, do my prayers, and meditate. And I can do all of that pretty much guilt-free (when you're Jewish, there is no 100 percent guilt-free).

If I wake up and it's only about my needs and my wants, then I might stay that way for the rest of the day. Thinking about someone else is freeing. Plus, by my making breakfast for her, my wife can never say, "You never do anything for me." Actually, she could, but it's harder.

Find that lucky person or persons you are going to do something nice for tomorrow morning. And if you can't find them, you can always drop breakfast at my house. Incidentally, I take my coffee black, no sugar or cream.

Keep Your Two Cents to Yourself

It's only words, and words are all I have to take your heart away.
—The Bee Gees, "Words"

Louann Brizendine, a practicing physician at the University of California–San Francisco, suggested in her book, *The Female Brain*, that women speak 20,000 words per day on average. That would amount to 489,100,000 words in the average lifetime. Men, she suggested, speak an average of 7,000 words a day, so that is 171,185,000 words in a lifetime. Then there is the Jewish husband. He speaks 12 words a day unless you include all his uses of "Yes, dear," and the begging. With these included, the Jewish husbands are approaching the 489,000,000 mark.

Some people, when you say something to them and they do not like what you said, depending on the type of person they are, they will respond in various ways. They might politely say, "Why would you say something like that?" or "That wasn't very nice." If they are from the Bronx, you might hear, "You're lucky I don't put my fist down your throat." My favorite is "Say that again and I'll jam my foot up your ass." How that last one stops someone from talking, I am not exactly sure, but clearly it is an attention getter.

Being careful with your words is a key ingredient to a happy life. Say the wrong thing and pay the price. I cannot tell you how many times I have said something that I wished I could take back, especially to people I love and who love me. Seeing someone who you have hurt by saying the wrong thing can be a painful experience. So many times, thank God, I caught myself about to say something and clamped my mouth shut.

About twenty-five years ago, some friends of mine had a child who was born with many health issues. Still to this day it gives me the shivers to think that I almost said something to them about the way they were raising their child. I, who had no understanding of their pain and knew nothing at all about what they were going through, almost opened my big mouth.

My mother would tell me many times in my life to keep my trap shut. Trust me, they do not call your mouth a trap for nothing. Remember the words are trapped until you let them out. Once they are out, they are like sperm cells. And like the one sperm cell that makes it through and can create an entire life, a harsh word at the wrong moment to a sensitive person can cause pain and humiliation that also have a life of their own.

Not too long ago, I received an email from a person who had started hating me a few years ago. Before that, we were friends for over forty years. I had written an email where I mentioned how lucky we were that the president got the vaccine going so quickly. Here is how quickly words can escalate:

He wrote, "Yeah, God bless the fireman who burned down the White House and then pissed on it to put out the fire—your ignorance is stunning."

I then let myself get sucked in after his ignorance line.

I wrote, "Still as happy as ever, aren't you? Your name-calling is becoming of someone of your stature."

Here is where it escalated to the next level.

He wrote, "You were smarter when you were fat, drunk, and high, you hypocritical Jew fuck."

If you're trying to guess who sent these words, no, it wasn't my rabbi or my mother. But it could have been the latter.

I was slightly upset for a few hours. More shocked than upset. And then I said to myself, "Do I want to enter this world of hate with him?" The answer was no. My first mistake was falling for his ignorance line. So

I cashed out. If I had stayed in, I'd have had to raise the stakes even more. I thought about it and I knew I would have to get real mean. I'd have to bring up his dead sister, his rotten relationships with women, and how he would be lonely for the rest of his life. I even thought of telling him how few people would probably show up to his funeral.

But you know what? I folded and felt great that I did. It felt like a major accomplishment, because if I'm not careful, anger will always get the best of me. Anger is corrosive to both the body and the soul. Anger destroys. Anger is a great thief. Anger can shut me out from the sunlight of the spirit. Anger can get a person to say some real mean things.

The code I try to live by (but still often fall short on) is "restraint of pen and tongue." I might write the nasty email, but I don't send it. I might think I need to strike back, but I try like hell not to, because if someone hurts me, it does not mean I have to hurt him or her back. I can tell the person that I'm hurt and leave it at that. The good news is the bad feelings almost always pass.

Before you send that email or you say to that person what you really think of him or her, do what Regis Philbin suggested people do on *Who Wants to be a Millionaire?* Use your lifeline and call a friend first. Tell the person what you're thinking. Tell him or her how you want to destroy that person. Or better yet, put a penny in your mouth and suck on it until it melts. Only when it melts and is all gone, can you send an email. But even then, I would think twice about putting in your two cents.

14
FAMOUS FRIENDS

....

The Day Bob Dylan Came to My House

Do you ever wonder just what God requires? You think He's just an
errand boy to satisfy your wandering desires? —Bob Dylan, "When
You Gonna Wake Up?"

You call that singing? Shut that garbage off. —My mother

Bob Dylan, just a Jewish boy from Minnesota. I've listened to Dylan
nonstop for over fifty years.

In 1976 I was living in Greenwich Village, begging for money and
writing poetry. I even had a poet's beard. One evening I was at a rock club
called The Bottom Line with my lifelong buddy, Bernie Ferrera. Seated
three tables away from us were Bob Dylan, his wife at the time, Sara, and
a friend, Louie Kemp. I grabbed the menu off our table and went over for
an autograph. He gladly signed it. Without taking a beat, I said, "After
the show, would you and your friends like to come over for a cup of tea?"
Mind you, I had never done this before. He then asked where I lived, and
I mumbled, "Six blocks away." He stared at me as if he were x-raying my
soul. He told me to write down my address and he would be there. I said,

"Really?" He nodded yes, and my head exploded. For the next two hours, while sitting through the show, all I could think of was that Bob Dylan was coming over.

After the show, Bernie and I ran to my apartment that I shared with my two roommates. My gay roommate happened to be home, and when I told him that Dylan was coming over, he snapped, "Why didn't you call me? I would have baked a cake."

An hour passed and no Dylan. Maybe he wasn't coming. Maybe I was dreaming. People probably invite him places every day. Why was this night different from all other nights? The answer is because it was. The doorbell rang. I looked out the window, and there the three of them were. I ran down to let them in. When someone you deeply respect keeps his promise, like Dylan did, it means the world to you.

Up the long flight of stairs, the four of us trekked. All I could think about was, *Bob Dylan is at my house—now what?* Sara and Louie sat on my old couch (that I had found on the street), and Bob stood leaning against a small stepladder, tapping his fingers. He would not answer any questions about himself but rather kept asking about me. "What do you do, man?" "How long have you been writing poetry, man?" Bob Dylan was interviewing me. Pretty cool. Then just like that, after forty minutes, Bob said, "We got to go, man. See you again." And puff, they were gone. I can only imagine that our conversation had to have been one of the least interesting experiences of his life. I found I had nothing to say. Yet it was amazing.

A few months later, I was back at the same club, and this time John Lennon was sitting with Maria Muldaur. I asked him over for tea and he politely declined. Maybe he spoke to Dylan.

Cut to twenty years later. It's Shabbas and I'm in shul at kiddush talking to a guy who introduces himself as Louie Kemp. I said, "I know that name." Then I remembered. I said, "Louie, you, Bob, and Sara came to my house in Greenwich Village." He kind of remembered the night and said I was lucky to have caught Dylan at an incredibly open time in his life. Since then, Louie and I have been friends.

A few years later, Louie and I were on our way to see Dylan perform in Los Angeles. Louie turned to me and said, "First we have to stop and pick up Joni Mitchell at her house." Pretty cool. When we got there, Joni asked me if I wanted a cup of tea while she got ready. Sure do.

Sometime after that, I saw Dylan at Young Israel of Century City at his grandson's bar mitzvah. It was good to see him again. I did not say hello, though, because I sensed that he wanted to be left alone. But thank you, God, for Bob Dylan. And thank God, I like tea. All I can tell you is "Never be afraid to ask. You just might receive."

Katharine Hepburn and Me

When I first started out in show business, I had one of the all-time greatest jobs. I was a candy and drink guy for Broadway shows at the Broadhurst Theatre on 44th Street between 7th and 8th avenues. I got paid $7.50 a show, and what was great about the job, especially for comedians, were the hours, 7:00 p.m. to 9:00 p.m. The comedy clubs didn't get rolling until 10:00 p.m., so that was perfect. I eventually got fired for pilfering and jerking around. Losing a high-paying job like that is a real kick in the gut.

The real pay from it was that you could get into any of the other Broadway theaters for free. There was an unwritten law that they let you into their theater and you let them into yours. At my theater was the play *A Matter of Gravity* starring Katharine Hepburn and Christopher Reeve. And believe it or not, this candy guy got to be friends with Katharine Hepburn. I also had the honor of watching Ms. Hepburn and Christopher Reeve act live for close to seventy performances. What an honor that was. You would think it would have made me a better actor. It didn't.

One afternoon early in the run of the play, I came in two hours before showtime to make sure we had enough Goobers, Chuckles, and Orangeade for the evening performance. I looked up and there was Katharine Hepburn, by herself, running around the theater opening every door upstairs and downstairs. She wanted to cool off the theater. After finishing, she quickly disappeared backstage. One of the workers said to me, "She comes in every day at five and opens the doors. She won't perform in a hot theater."

The next day, even though I didn't have to, I came in at 4:50 p.m. Five on the dot, she comes and starts opening all the doors. With courage I never knew I had, I walked over to her and said, "Ms. Hepburn, can I help you with the doors?"

"Who are you?" she barked.

"I'm Mark. I run the candy concession if you ever want anything."

"No, thank you." she said. And then she said, "You need a cold theater to keep the people awake."

"Why don't you get someone to do it for you?"

"Can't take the chance. They might forget."

So practically every day for the next two months, I would come in two hours early and meet with Katharine Hepburn. Eventually she trusted me enough and let me open the upstairs doors for her. Believe me, I was honored. After all the doors were open, she would say, "Good job." Every once in a while, she would even tip me. When I said no, she made me take it. Then, amazingly, every day she would delight me for five or ten minutes with stories about James Cagney, Humphrey Bogart, Spencer Tracy, and many others. Nice stories. Nothing nasty. No gossip. Just sweet recollections. It was truly a mind-blowing experience to hear the First Lady of Cinema in her New Englander accent say, "How are you, Mark?"

Then one day, out of nowhere, she came running in and yelled, "Come here." She then handed me a copy of James Cagney's autobiography *Cagney by Cagney.* On the inside of the book, she had written the most beautiful inscription.

About two weeks later, I again hear "Come here." She said, "Here, I did this last night." She handed me a wrapped package. After removing the wrapping paper, I unveiled what was about to become one of my life's most treasured possessions. An original ink self-portrait drawing of her character in full costume. A signed drawing by Katharine Hepburn of herself for me. Double mind-blowing. I imagined her sitting in bed wearing Chinese silk pajamas, mumbling out loud, "Mark will love this." The last time she said "Come here," she handed me her home phone number. She said, "Give me a call if you ever want to talk."

Now, I'm twenty-three years old and earning $7.50 a night with no career prospects. I'm living in a mouse-ridden, $150-a-month slum and Katharine Hepburn hands me a self-portrait and her home phone number. That would be the equivalent of the Lubavitcher rebbe telling a new convert to come to his house to play some pinochle and have dinner with him.

Later that night, in my freezing-cold apartment, staring at her number in disbelief, I think, *Call her and talk about what?* What do I have to say to Katharine Hepburn? Perhaps, "Hi, Kate. It's Mark the candy guy. I'm fine, thanks. Listen, tonight after your standing ovations from twelve hundred people, can we grab some Raisinets, and then what do you say we hit a movie? Why don't you call Cagney and Henry Fonda and see if they also want to come? Then after the movie, let's stop at Lauren Bacall's house for some drinks. I'm sure she'd love to meet me." Or should I say, "My father just got a new Bell and Howell 8mm camera. You want to be in some of our home movies? I'll direct."

I didn't make those calls, but the day I did call Ms. Hepburn, peeing in my pants from nerves was the least of my problems. As her phone rang, all I could think was, *What are you doing? What, are you crazy? Who are you to call Katharine Hepburn?*

Then I heard that unmistakable voice. "Who is it?"

"Hello. Hi, Ms. Hepburn. It's Mark from the theater."

"Mark, how can I help you?"

"I just called [choke] to [choke] say hi."

"Hi to you," she said. Then, very sweetly, "That's nice of you to call. I'm having a party at my house tonight for some friends. Why don't you come by?"

The word "OK" flew out of my mouth. I then hung up and thought, *What was that?* I'd just been invited to a party at Katharine Hepburn's house by Katharine Hepburn. Believe me when I tell you, that was the last time I wore those pants.

I can't tell you how scared I was going by myself to a party at Katharine Hepburn's house. Who am I? What is going on? She lived on East 49th Street in a four-story town house in Turtle Bay. I didn't feel worthy to even walk into her home.

She greeted me at the front door and with a hardy handshake said, "Glad you're here. Go in and have a good time." I was in such a haze that night that I can't remember much of anything from the evening. One thing I do remember is standing on a spiral staircase looking at four little statues just sitting there, very much out of plain sight. She saw me looking and I asked, "What are those?"

"My Academy Awards," she responded. She still holds the record of most Academy Awards of anyone for acting. In another corner was a bust of her head by, I believe, either Picasso or some other artist of that stature.

After the run of the play, I lost touch with her. If I didn't have the book and the drawing, I might have thought I dreamt up the whole thing. The relationship, like the play, was a limited run. I felt incredibly grateful for the experience, but something inside told me it was over, and I respected that voice. I certainly didn't want to ask her for help. When you're given a gift, it's not polite to ask for another one.

It was the type of relationship where you wonder, why is this person being so nice to me? I had absolutely nothing to give her in return. I would just sit and listen to one of the greatest actresses who ever lived regale me with stories. Ms. Hepburn was exceedingly kind to me. What's even more amazing was that she seemed to really enjoy talking to me. What a great actress. I think she understood I was a young kid in a difficult world trying hard to become something and get a grip on this life. It was written all over my face, and she read it perfectly.

The first day we met she could have easily told me that she was busy and had no time to talk, and I would have totally understood. But instead she availed herself to me a few minutes every day. You don't have to be Katharine Hepburn to be kind to a new kid on the block. You just have to be sensitive. And who was more sensitive than the First Lady of Cinema? She died at ninety-six. It's nice when kind people live a long time. We know way too many who don't. Thank you, Ms. Hepburn. If I could have, I'd have given you an Academy Award for Kindness. I hope I can pay it forward in my own small way. After all, you can't keep it if you don't give it away.

Hey, Carl, Don't Forget Your Toupee

If there were a Mount Rushmore of comedy, one of the heads up there would be that of Carl Reiner. Less than two weeks before Carl died, he tweeted, "Watching Trump methodically implode while having my all-time favorite meal, Pink's Hot Dogs, Boston baked beans, and hot sauerkraut, rounded out an almost perfect day for me!" Funny and timely right up until the end.

Carl Reiner was born on March 20, 1922, and died on June 29, 2020, at the age of ninety-eight. Carl created so much comedy that he and his best friend, Mel Brooks, could have had their own comedy museum. To list just a few of his credits, he worked on *Your Show of Shows*, "2000-Year-Old

Man" (with Mel Brooks), and the *Dick Van Dyke Show* (which he wrote the first season of by himself; he also played the temperamental show host Alan Brady); he costarred in *The Russians Are Coming, The Russians Are Coming*; and he directed two of my favorite films, *Where's Poppa?* and *Oh, God!* Carl also directed and cowrote *The Jerk, Dead Men Don't Wear Plaid, The Man with Two Brains*, and *All of Me*. These last four films helped launch Steve Martin's early career. In 2019, at the age of ninety-six, Carl was in *Toy Story 4*. His credits are endless.

The first time I met Carl was through the famed manager George Shapiro. George is Jerry Seinfeld's manager and had been Carl Reiner's manager for many years. Carl was also George's uncle. George called and told me that Carl was hosting a benefit at La Costa and asked if I would like to do a set to help raise money for a children's organization. I jumped at it, and two weeks later Carl was introducing me. It was an amazing moment for me to be introduced by this icon of comedy. After the set, he could not have been more complimentary, and he asked me to please do it again in the future. I told him that to be recognized by him as a funny person was like telling Moses a piece of Torah and he said, "That is really good. I never thought of that."

I told Carl I'd love to take him to lunch one day and chat comedy. He said of course and gave me his home address and phone number. Soon after that, I called him to make the date. He asked where I wanted to go, and I suggested a restaurant called Milk and Honey on Pico Boulevard in Los Angeles. We picked a date and he met me there. After being seated, he noticed all the yarmulkes around the restaurant. He asked me if I kept kosher, to which I replied, "I do my best." That led us to a discussion on God. I told him I believed in God, and he told me that he did not. In an interview from 2009, Carl said, "My take on God is that I'm a nonbeliever, as Nat Nolan is. Man invented God 'cause he needed it. God is in our head."

All I know is, Carl Reiner had a gift. Whether or not you believe it came from God or from somewhere else, he was coded with the comedy gene his entire life. Wherever it came from, I am grateful he had it. After the God talk, like all Jews, we talked about the food in the restaurant, which he seemed to really like. I told him that I knew his son Rob and he asked me if I could help Rob lose weight. Is that not the most Jewish conversation you've ever heard? First, we talked food, then God, and then how his son could lose weight. Carl, wherever you may or may not be, the world is a lot less funny without you. Shalom, my friend.

What's a Kid from the Bronx Doing Hanging Out with Sir Anthony Hopkins?

Born and raised in New York, I had the good fortune of being able to go to lots of Broadway shows, and like a lot of people, I kept the Playbills and T-shirts from almost all of them. One day I decided to go through some old boxes and found one from the play *Equus*. But *Equus* was not just another play that I went to. *Equus* and its star, Anthony Hopkins, changed my life.

Like most Bronx kids, I was given the gift of chutzpah. Bronx kids learn early that if you don't ask, you don't get. And if you don't get, you're miserable.

One big "yes" I got from asking was from Sir Anthony Hopkins. In 1975, Sir Hopkins was starring in the hit Broadway play *Equus*, a searing drama about a stable boy who blinds six horses. In other words, not a big yuck fest. I went back at least six times.

At the time, I was also a member of a Jewish theater company called Theatre EXP 3. We performed Yiddish plays in English. My big role was as Berel in *Chassidic Rhapsody*. It was an awful play with awful actors and a largely deaf, geriatric audience.

One night my acting company went to see *Equus*. Soon after the play ended, our artistic director asked me to ask Sir Hopkins if he would come and speak to our group. So a few nights later, after Tony's performance (eventually, he asked me to call him Tony), I cornered him at the stage door. He had no idea who or what I was.

"Mr. Hopkins, I'm Mark Schiff. I'm in a small theater company, and we'd love if you would speak to our group." Tony was still sweating from an almost three-hour performance. Half startled, he stared at me with his baby blues and said in his rolling Welsh accent, "What? What's your name? What do you want?" I explained again, and, lo and behold, he agreed! He then handed me his home phone number.

We agreed that the following Sunday, he would come down and speak to us. When Tony came, he brought with him a stack of Xeroxed scenes from Chekhov plays. He handed each actor a scene to study. A few minutes later, he directed all of us, one by one. Tony came back two or three times more to follow our progress. I imagine being directed by Anthony Hopkins was like being directed by Orson Welles or Laurence Olivier. Like them, when he spoke, he was full of passion, depth. You knew intuitively you were hearing from a real artist who knew things that you needed to know.

Tony also spent time talking to and getting to know our artistic director. One night, around two in the morning, my phone made a jing-a-ling sound. (Jing-a-ling was the sound phones made back then.) It was Tony. He had been drinking, and he was mad. He went on for about fifteen minutes about our artistic director and what a cruel and mean man he thought he was. He was also very worried that the director might cause some sort of emotional damage to us young actors. He didn't like the man, and he was scared for us. He wanted us to get away from him. Without really knowing any of us, he was trying to protect us. It's a rare moment in life when you meet someone who hardly knows you but cares so much that he tries to help you, especially a person of his stature.

After that call, I would worm my way in and periodically join Sir Hopkins and other *Equus* actors for drinks at Charley's, a Broadway bar. Each time, he reiterated to me that my troupe should get away from our artistic director. None of us in the group were able to see what Tony saw, but then one afternoon at a rehearsal, the director snapped. He started yelling, cursing, and belittling us. He even started grabbing people tightly by the wrists and dragging them around. At each rehearsal, he kept getting worse. Tony was right. The man was a lunatic.

Tony saw what none of us could see. His level of reflection and intuitiveness are two reasons why he's such a great actor. Thanks to him, a few of us soon quit the company. Over the years I've seen Tony a few times, and in a most gentle voice, he reminds me how worried he was about us kids. Sir Anthony Hopkins is not only a good man, but he's a courageous man. In this world, that's a rare bird that usually flies alone.

Free Cars

My first free car was a 1952 Chevy Deluxe with three speeds on the column that my uncle Phil gave to my father in 1966. Three years later, my father gave it to me. I loved that car. It weighed more than an Israeli tank and was about as strong as one. When I was eighteen, I was driving to Washington, DC, from New York to participate in a sit-in. A sit-in is like a baby tantrum. You sit there until you get what you want or until you're out of pizza.

When I got to Maryland, a red light on the dashboard blinked on. I tried to make it to a service station, but a few minutes later my engine seized. In the car with me were my friend Ricky and a one-armed hitchhiker named Stumpy whom we had picked up on the New Jersey Turnpike. Sans the car, the three of us hitchhiked to Washington.

The sit-in was to free the jailed Bobby Seale and Angela Davis. I marched and sat and yelled, "Free Angela! Free Bobby!" having no idea who or what they were. As it turned out, they were members of the Black Panther Party, and communists. I was an uneducated kid thinking I was doing the right thing but not really understanding either way.

My second free car was a 1964 Oldsmobile Jetstar I. Again, someone gave my parents a car, and when they were done with it they handed it to me. The Jetstar was truly a thing of beauty, but it was a gas-guzzler. If a car could be an alcoholic, this was it. When you needed gas, what you did was pull into a gas station, fill it up, pull out onto the road, and then pull into another gas station to fill it again. Once a year my family would get a Hanukkah card from the Saudis, thanking us. Two days after my parents gave this beautiful car to me, a woman ran a stop sign and totaled it. *C'est la vie.*

My third free car was a gift from my uncle Harold in 1983, a '76 Toyota Corolla. One night, while driving on the West Side Highway in New York, one car after another kept coming up behind me, honking and flashing their lights as they sped by. I pulled to the side of the road and saw that my trunk was ablaze. My spare tire had melted into something resembling the La Brea Tar Pits. I probably should have run instead of waiting for the car to explode like something out of a mafia movie. Luckily, my uncle had left a fire extinguisher in the car, and I was able to put the flames out, but not before much of the trunk's steel had melted. I later found out one of the wires had shorted out. I drove it trunkless for the next two years. Whenever I was in the car for more than ten minutes, my clothes smelled like I had just pulled people from a burning building. The car was towed three times because it looked like an abandoned car that had caught fire.

My next free car was again from Uncle Harold, this time in 1998. He shipped the car to me in Los Angeles by rail from the Bronx. Despite already having a car, I took it as a backup, just in case. This was a real loser of a car. It was a 1980 Nissan "something." It was such a piece of junk that I don't think Nissan could even come up with a name for it. The passenger side door had been hit a few years back and couldn't be opened anymore. If you had to exit that side of the car quickly, you needed to call a friend who owned a Jaws of Life to help cut you out of the window. I once went to pick up a date, and after she realized she had to climb across the driver's seat, she refused to get in. The car also had trouble making it up a steep hill and sounded severely asthmatic as it tried.

Now we climb up a few notches. My friend Jerry Seinfeld is a huge fan of cars. He knows cars. He loves cars. If reincarnation exists, he has a good shot at coming back as a car. He has Porsches, Volkswagens, and the old classic diesel Mercedes.

Around 2010, Jerry and I were in Indianapolis on tour with Kevin Dochtermann, the tour producer. The three of us had gone for our usual afternoon walk. Whatever town we were in, we always took a thirty-minute walk. Jerry and I have gone for walks everywhere, from big cities to giant cornfields to casino parking lots. It's our private chat time. We are always amazed, wherever we are. How many people could say "It's great to be in Ogden, Utah, for five hours"?

One afternoon we passed a showroom that sold mostly 1960s and 1970s American muscle cars, cars like Mustangs, GTOs, Camaros, Chargers, and Stingrays. Jerry said, "Let's go in."

These cars may not have been Jerry's style, but I loved everything about them. There were about thirty of them on the showroom floor. When we went in, the owner recognized Jerry and struck up a conversation with him. I browsed the showroom on my own. If it were possible to fall in love with a car, I was falling for everything I eyed. Each was pristine and looked like it had just rolled off the assembly line in Detroit. To me, this was great American art. To Jerry, a Porsche owner, these were donkeys. He owned Thoroughbreds.

After a few minutes in the showroom, Jerry walked over to me and said,

"Pick one out for yourself."

"What?"

"Pick one out."

"Really?" I was about to wet myself for the first time since I was four.

"Yeah, any one you want. My treat." Then he walked away.

With mouth agape and brain numb, I stood there in shock. A minute or so later I came to and started looking around. After sitting in half a dozen or more of these beauties, I landed on my dream car: a 1965 Pontiac LeMans GTO convertible. Yes, I had been given old cars before. Yes, I was grateful for each one. But none of them were anything like this killer GTO.

Sitting behind the steering wheel was heaven. This car seemed so perfect. I felt like a kid in it, like this was the car I'd been waiting to own my whole life. To this day, there has never been a bigger smile on my face. This car was me. I pictured myself driving it all 2,079 miles back to Los Angeles with the top down. There would be beautiful girls running alongside it, begging to jump in with me. I exited the car, stepped back, and took one more look-see. It was perfect. I had hit the lottery without buying a ticket.

I walked over to Jerry and said, "Thanks, man. This is one of the nicest offers ever. I love the car, but I'm going to pass."

He said, "OK. Let's go and have lunch." Just like that. Let's have lunch.

He never questioned my decision, and we never spoke of it again. I waved goodbye to the car. My heart dropped as we exited the showroom. I felt like I had made a gigantic mistake, but I couldn't bring myself to tell him I'd changed my mind and that I wanted the car. If I were in better shape I would have kicked my own ass for being so stupid. Something in me wouldn't let me accept a gift of this magnitude. A beat-up car with dented doors on its last legs, though? Hand me the keys! A magnificent '65 GTO was just too much of a gift. Too much to grasp. Too big to accept.

I was sad for the next few weeks. I could not shake my malaise. If you let it, low self-esteem will rob you of great moments. At the time, I didn't feel worthy to say yes. Who was I to accept this?

When I got back to my hotel room, I called a close friend to tell him the story. He said, "Listen, Mark, from now on, if someone wants to do something nice for you, let them do it. They like you and want to do this for you. You robbed Jerry of some happiness. Your not accepting the gift is denying him a certain pleasure. If he ever offers you another car, say yes."

I thought, "Yeah, sure. Nobody offers a car twice."

Fast-forward to 2014. Jerry and I were on the 405 Freeway in Los Angeles, heading to the Santa Monica airport for a show that night in Atlantic City. Jerry was driving his mint 1982 Mercedes 300D Diesel. It's a stunning example of an era gone by, and one of the best cars Mercedes ever made. It only had thirty-five hundred original miles on it. Many of these cars can easily clock over a million.

Jerry said, "I know you like these cars."

"Love them," I said.

"I'm thinking of selling it. You want to buy it?"

"I wish I could afford it. I'd love to have it."

Jerry flicked the blinker and changed lanes. "If you want it, I'll give it to you."

"Really?" I thought to myself, *Here we go again. This time you say yes. Do not turn this down. It will make him happy to give it to me.*

"Yeah."

"I'll take it."

"Great. It's yours."

I was so excited, I'm not sure if I even said thank you.

"The radio isn't working well," said Jerry. "Do you want to take it like this, or do you want me to have it fixed?"

"You know what? Why don't you fix it."

Two weeks later, I got a call from Jerry's assistant, Robert. He said, "The car is ready. Come and get it." He seemed very happy for me.

Whoever said lightning doesn't strike twice doesn't know Jerry. It does, and I still have the car to prove it.

I was ready this time. For fun and for free, I was able to accept what was given to me. I knew it would make him happy, and it indeed did make Jerry happy to give it to me. Over the years, we've talked about this car and other ones he has just like it. He is always happy to hear that I am still driving the 300D, and I'm always happy to be driving it. It's a great car. Occasionally, I'll send him short videos of me rolling along, having a blast. He also knows how much I like the station wagon version of the 300D. I need to again ride the 405 Freeway with him when he's driving one of his wagons. You never know. If I can get one more, it's a collection.

15
STAND-UP

....

The Night

Dwell on the beauty of life. Watch the stars and see yourself running with them. —Marcus Aurelius

I have always loved the night. I've always found it wonderful. When most people have pajama-ed up and are tightly tucked in, I'm out roaming in the shimmer of the evening. When the sun quits, my heart starts ticking. For jazz artists and comics, the night is king. That's when we hear the music. That's when our souls start to dance. The night is what we live for.

I am a nightclub comic. Many of the people I work with I've never seen during the yellow hours. Occasionally I'll be asked to do a show during the daytime. Day shows always seem wrong: empty of heart, a money grab. Even strip clubs are open for the lunch crowd. But never comedy clubs.

I love the sound of rain as it pings off the roof of a car on a dark street. I love staring out the window of a beat-up cab with busted shocks and underinflated tires as it zips me across Central Park at 3:00 a.m. The night is when the big cities or small, drab towns all come alive in the shadow of the moon and stars. I come alive in those shadows.

From age twenty to thirty, I mostly woke up after the strike of noon, dying for the night to take a bow. Growing up, I remember hearing my father saying, "I can't sit in that rush hour traffic anymore. I have to find a better way." He never did find that better way. Most taxi drivers will tell you they would rather drive at night when there is less traffic, but they don't because they are afraid of being robbed or slain. Murderers, thieves, prostitutes, drunks, dopers, short-order cooks, people trying to forget their jobs by burning through their paychecks, people cleaning bank safes and office buildings, runaways, broken hearts looking for an answer, new lovers hopeful they can finally stop looking—these are a few types that comics share the night with.

The night is when romance gets its charge. Is there such a thing as romance during the day? Lovers like to hide in the corners of dimly lit booths. Can Dylan Thomas be fully understood before it gets dark?

The night is what many love songs are written about. After a harsh breakup, put on Sinatra's album *Frank Sinatra Sings for Only the Lonely* at 1:00 a.m. Good luck trying to make it to daybreak.

During my school years, they never suggested any type of night work. Comics don't punch clocks, we punch lines. I'm in a profession that allows you to tell your loved ones you have no idea when you will be home, but you promise to kiss them on your return. It's a profession that allows you to booze with the opposite sex while you're working. But the night plays tricks. It can get you thinking "This is the one" when you already have the one. It can lead you to never go home and plant that kiss you promised. It's rare, but occasionally two hearts do meet on a barstool, but rarely without a sad story attached.

I'm in a profession that if you have something of a poet's soul, and if you don't mind not sleeping with the one you love, and if you don't mind rarely having a home-cooked meal, and if you don't mind working every holiday while the rest of the world is off, and if you don't need to own sunglasses unless you're on drugs, and if you don't mind traveling alone in towns you have never been to and will probably never go back to, and if you don't mind having the stars and moon as your umbrella, and if you don't mind being lonely much of the time, and if you think you can be funny in a room of complete strangers under bright, hot lights, then the night is where you belong.

And that's where you might find me.

"There Goes the Neighborhood"

I remember the time I was kidnapped and they sent a piece of my finger to my father. He said he wanted more proof.
—Rodney Dangerfield

My angel was comedian Rodney Dangerfield, one of the last of the wave of great Jewish comedians. I have never seen anyone more suited for his or her chosen profession than Rodney was for his.

My parents celebrated their thirteenth wedding anniversary by going to a nightclub and taking me with them. I was twelve years old. The opening act was Rodney Dangerfield. Before that evening, I had never seen a comedian perform live. I remember Rodney busting through the curtain and rapid-firing his one-liners for almost forty minutes. He spent most of the time complaining about his horrible sex life and his nagging wife. Remember, I was twelve. I had no idea what this man was talking about. But I do now.

What I did know was that he was by far the funniest human being I had ever seen, and to this day, he still holds that title for me. When I looked over at my parents, I realized I had never seen them laugh this hard or seem this happy about anything. While watching Rodney perform, I understood

I was witnessing something extraordinary. Thanks to Rodney Dangerfield, that night I decided to become a comedian.

I'm still one some fifty years later. Sometimes life speaks so loud it just can't be ignored. I didn't know it then, but I already possessed all the qualifications to become a comic. I hated my parents, hated many of my relatives, and definitely hated most of the kids at the school I went to. I was a twelve-year-old deadpan sad sack. With this realization, my life now took on meaning.

After doing stand-up for just a couple of years, one night in the flesh, my angel came walking into Catch A Rising Star, the legendary New York comedy club. He was there to try out new jokes for Johnny Carson. I went in to watch his five minutes. It was hilarious. He was still the funniest person alive. He had it all: the looks, the voice, the sad face, the best one-liners ever, and of course, the greatest tagline in history, "I don't get no respect." Haven't many of us felt that at one time? That even the people closest to us don't care.

Rodney was truly an everyman, and he knew how to touch a nerve. He was the John Steinbeck of punch lines. Over the years, I got to know Rodney pretty well. The first money I ever made as a writer was $25 when I sold Rodney a joke that he used on *The Tonight Show*.

One night in the early 1980s, Jerry Seinfeld, comedian Steve Mittleman, and I were in Los Angeles hanging out. Jerry said Rodney was opening in Las Vegas the following night, so the next morning, we jumped into Jerry's tiny Fiat, and like Jews of old, we made the trek across the desert to see the Moses of comedy, Rodney Dangerfield.

At this point, none of us knew Rodney. When we arrived in Las Vegas, we realized we had one big problem. None of us had any money for food, tickets, or a hotel for the night. We were all dead broke. We went to the maître d' stand, and when he asked for our tickets, we told him we were comics and friends of Rodney from New York. He asked our names and then told us to wait while he checked backstage.

About ten minutes later, he escorted us to a booth, brought us a few drinks, and said Rodney wanted to see us after the show. We had no money to tip the guy. None of us knew Rodney at all. We'd lied. But wouldn't you lie if you thought you might be able to get in to see Moses?

The show was amazing, and after, we went backstage to Rodney's dressing room. When he told us he didn't remember us, we told him we met him at Catch a Rising Star. It was a half-truth. We'd been at the club in New York one night and he came in to do a set. When he walked by us, we all said, "Hey, Rodney!" Still sweaty from his Vegas show, he looked at us and asked where we were staying. We told him we were driving back because we didn't have money for a hotel. With that, he almost lost it. "You kids come to Vegas with no money for food, the show, or a hotel. What, are you out of your fucking minds?" Then, "Come with me. I'll take you to dinner."

First stop was the deli, where he told us to wait outside for a minute. When he came back out, we went to the Chinese restaurant. About ten minutes later, a Jewish waiter from the deli brought Rodney a giant bowl of matzo ball soup. Rodney loved matzo ball soup before his Chinese food. He told us he had an extra room at the hotel that he wasn't using and offered it to us for the night. He made us promise we would not make any long-distance calls and stick him with the bill.

Maybe seven or so years later, he called me up and asked me to be on his HBO *Young Comedians Special*. His specials at the time were huge events. He was making comics famous. I turned him down because I worked clean, and everyone else on the show was working dirty. I didn't want to do it. He flipped out, got terribly angry, and read me the riot act. He told me how he'd made the careers of Sam Kinison and Andrew Dice Clay and how I was blowing a big opportunity. It's possible he was right. I'll never know.

Eventually Rodney forgave me, and we continued our friendship. There were so many great nights I got to hang with him. I say nights because I never saw him during the day.

On October 4, 2004, I received a call from Rodney's wife, Joan. She told me that Rodney was dying and if I wanted to say goodbye, now was the time. As quick as I could, I got over to the UCLA hospital. There my angel was resting, while his final call home was coming in. He had earned his wings and was getting ready to return his funny soul. His job here was to make millions of people laugh, and that job, which he did perfectly, was complete.

After a few minutes of thanking him for everything he had done for me, I took his hand, gently rubbed it, and did the Hebrew prayer Shema Yisrael.[67] He was in a coma, so I'm not sure if he knew I was there. But because it was Rodney, somehow it seemed like a funny coma. He was still making me laugh. The next day, my angel flew home to get some respect.

The Road

The road is long
With many a winding turn
That leads us to who knows where.
—Bobby Scott and Bob Russell, "He Ain't Heavy, He's My Brother"

Phone calls long distance
To tell you how you've been
You forget about the losses, you'll exaggerate the wins.
—Danny O'Keefe, "The Road"

---

67 *"Shema Yisrael"* ("Hear, O Israel") are the first two words of a section of the Torah that is the centerpiece of the morning and evening prayer services, encapsulating the monotheistic essence of Judaism: "Hear, O Israel: God is our Lord, God is one." The Shema is also the last thing said before going to sleep, and if you can, you're supposed to say it right before you die. The question many people ask is, how does one know when one is going to die? One way is for a man to tell his wife that he finds her sister smarter and more attractive than she is. Then he should say the *Shema* as quickly as he can, because his time on this planet is up.

With all its ups and downs, I still love the road. When my work came to a screeching halt from the pandemic and there were no more shows, I felt like a drunk in a bar who just heard the clanging of the last call triangle and still needed a few more.

I was flying high doing my gigs. There were some great ones, allowing me to stay in the finest hotels and circle the skies in private jets, and there were some not so great ones, which involved circling my room in a Motel 6; eating dinner off a thirty-year-old faded flowered Melmac plate; hopping in a cab at 6:00 a.m., alone on a thunderous rainy morning in Mobile, Alabama, to do a local radio show; or taking the 2:00 a.m. mail train out of Philadelphia back to my three-hundred-square-foot New York studio apartment. I didn't care—a gig is a gig. It's a simple life. If you get out a new joke and it works, it's a great night. If not, the road is long and lonesome. That was my life.

For forty-plus years, I've been a working road comic. I've been almost everywhere at least twice. My dream was to do it until I couldn't do it anymore. Had the pandemic made that a reality? Maybe. Even after the pandemic, would I have to step aside for the younger people coming up? Maybe.

Working comedians hardly ever quit. Mel Brooks said, "If you're on the merry-go-round, don't jump off till it stops." Redd Foxx, Zero Mostel, Dick Shawn, and Harry Einstein all died either during or right after their shows. Al Kelly was in the audience watching a Friars Club show when he had a heart attack. He died on his way to the hospital.

The great George Burns, who lived to be one hundred, was once asked about retirement. He replied, "Retirement at sixty-five is ridiculous. When I was sixty-five, I still had pimples."

Comedy, like any job, can keep you young and vital if you enjoy your work. For many of us, that may have now dried up. So how do we all stay sane? How do we not get depressed? How do we not eat ourselves out of our clothes?

At the beginning of the pandemic, I was making jokes about it. Then after two months, I noticed I was starting to get serious. (The only thing worse than a serious comedian is an upbeat funeral director.) I started asking myself the big questions: Will I die from this? Will my kids have a future? Will my wife be OK? You know, those late-night questions that have no answers.

Then the student was ready, and the teacher appeared. I read that there were two new books on Yogi Berra. Yogi was a Hall of Fame catcher who played eighteen seasons with the Yankees. I wondered what the great *reb* Yogi[68] would have to say about all of this.

Yogi was famous for his Yogi-isms. Here's a few:

"When you come to a fork in the road, take it." I think he meant just keep going. Don't stand still or go back. Moving forward shows you believe in the future.

"I usually take a two-hour nap from one to four." When you're not working, it's easy to forget what time or what day it is. It's easy to get depressed. A friend told me he knows when it's Shabbas because that's the only day of the week he wears pants.

"The future ain't what it used to be." *Reb* Yogi is saying that we may have to find other ways to grow and be happy. That what we thought our life was going to be may not be what it is anymore.

"You can observe a lot by watching." Here he's saying it's good to take the focus off yourself and try to focus on others. Watch and learn how they get through this.

"The towels are so thick, I could hardly close my suitcase." Travel light and don't overpack your brain with scary nonsense. Otherwise you may not be able to close it down at night.

And finally, my favorite, "It ain't over till it's over." Truer words were never spoken. Thanks, *reb* Yogi. Now everybody, play ball. We are all still in the game.

---

68 *Reb* is a traditional Jewish title or form of address, corresponding to "sir," for a man who is not a rabbi (used preceding the forename or surname). An example is "I never met *reb* Kolitz." In sixth grade, many times preceding my forename or surname was "Hey, jackass," when my teacher wanted me to stop talking in class.

Caesars to Cedars

Mann tracht, un Gott lacht. (Man plans, and God laughs.)
—Yiddish proverb

I'm all right now, but last week I was in rough shape.
—Rodney Dangerfield

I had just performed fourteen shows on the Las Vegas Strip. In an expensive suit, shiny shoes, and with polished teeth, I busted them up. On Monday, I drove back to Los Angeles. Then life did what life does. It spun my world in a different direction. Shabbat afternoon, my *machatunim* (in-law) Roz came for lunch. She told me how good I looked and how the few pounds I put on were perfect. Little did I know that this was the kiss of death.

Around midnight I awoke with a familiar stomach pain. This pain is like a bad relative. As much as you try to forget it or them, you can't. In the past, it was a bowel blockage. I was hoping that this time it was not. In constant contact with my internist, I tried to wait it out. But that afternoon, I was in so much pain I had to go to the emergency room. My wife drove me to Cedars-Sinai, but because of COVID I went in alone.

After a CAT scan it was confirmed that I had a small bowel blockage. This was my fourth blockage in thirty years. With my first one, I needed emergency surgery. I remember the surgeon telling me that if he did not operate, I would be dead in eleven hours. Hello! This time, it took seven hours just to get me into a room. While I was lying in the hallway, a nurse with a clipboard asked me that, if necessary, did I want to be resuscitated? I told her to ask my wife. She said I had to answer this question on my own. I wanted to explain to her that I'm a Jewish husband and am not allowed to answer questions, but I mumbled "Yes." I called my wife and started crying. She also started crying when she realized how little life insurance I had. The little jokes we tell ourselves to cope with fear.

No beautiful suit and shiny shoes now. Instead, I was now draped in a Cedars-Sinai hospital gown, the kind that shows everyone your flipside. These gowns make your butt feel like there is an open window somewhere. After a rough five days, with no surgery but lots of intervention, my colon popped back. I was ready to go home.

But here goes life again. Four o'clock in the morning, a few hours before my release, my atrial fibrillation (A-fib) kicked in. Instead of my going home, a nurse rushed me up to the cardiac floor. A-fib is when your heart goes out of sinus rhythm. Mine was galloping at 160 beats a minute. It felt like an electric eggbeater running inside my chest. They quickly gave me a drug to slow down my heart. My cardiologist was on the phone, talking me down off the wall.

Again, life takes another turn. It was now 8:00 a.m. and my heart was very much still running like an Alaskan salmon heading upstream. I asked my wife, who'd been allowed to spend the night, to hand me my tefillin[69] bag. She did, and I placed the tefillin on my head and left arm. I did a few of my truncated prayers. I also thanked God for all He has given me and taken from me. I even thanked Him for what I was going through because I knew that if I was willing to look, there was a great lesson there somewhere. Then I rattled off important names for Him to keep safe. I always feel better when I remind God about the people I love.

Fifteen minutes after putting on my tefillin, I was out of A-fib. Was it the drug they were giving me, or was it something else? I told my wife that we'd just been handed a miracle. She was happy and stopped Xeroxing my insurance policy. In my mind, from the beginning until the end of this episode, there was a constant series of miracles. If not, then I was just lucky, and just lucky is something I can't accept.

---

69 Tefillin, or phylacteries, is a set of small black leather boxes with long straps containing scrolls of parchment inscribed with verses from the Torah. Tefillin are worn by observant adult Jews during weekday morning prayers. Jews are careful never to put these on in public because it looks like they are wrapping so they can shoot up heroin.

Now I need to get back into my expensive suit, without an opening in the back, and make people laugh. Or I could leave an opening in the back and see how that goes.

Portrait of a Young Comedian

Laughter is an instant vacation. —Milton Berle

What a kid I got. I told him about the birds and the bees, and he told me about the butcher and my wife. —Rodney Dangerfield

Imagine you tell people what you are going to do for a living, and they look at you like you have gone freaking berserk. Imagine a job where, your first time ever doing it, there are anywhere from one to two hundred strangers watching and scrutinizing your every move. Then imagine you are standing on a raised platform, speaking into a microphone under blazing hot lights while you are doing it. To top it off, you are all by yourself on that stage.

Imagine that every word you utter and every face you make, you created on your own. If it does not work, you shoulder all the blame. Imagine you know that you need to fix almost all of it, but the problem is you have no idea how to fix it.

Imagine that your parents and their friends are sitting in the audience and it is by far the worst show they have ever seen in their entire lives. When you look into the audience, you can see their blank, expressionless faces staring right at you. Imagine your parents overhear the people at the next table say, "This guy is the absolute worst."

That was my life, night after night, for my first five years as a comic. Can you imagine the nerve it took for me not to quit after not one but hundreds of nights like that in a row? Imagine the chutzpah that, when people asked me how it was going, I'd mutter back, "Pretty good."

Guess what? I wouldn't trade those days for anything, and neither would any of the friends whom I started with. We came up through the ranks in what was called the "showcase clubs." On any given night, there were twenty of us vying to go on. There wasn't any other way to put it except that I never felt so alive.

Some of us had to take odd jobs to pay the landlord. Seinfeld was working at a hamburger joint and selling light bulbs. Paul Reiser, star and creator of *Mad About You*, worked for his family. Larry Miller was a bartender, Gilbert Gottfried sold candy, George Wallace did advertising, Richard Belzer was the club MC, and Elayne Boosler showed people to their tables. Hanging around on any given night were the likes of Andy Kaufman, Richard Lewis, Robert Wuhl, Carol Leifer, Sandra Bernhard, and Larry David.

On Sunday mornings, down on my hands and knees, I cleaned toilets, windows, and mirrors in the restaurant that I performed in the night before. I was also a short-order cook on Monday nights and would sneak free meals to my comic friends.

The comedy stage floors were filled with swimming pools of sweat from the brows of comics on nights that things did not go as planned. To become a stand-up comedian, you must be able to take a beating. You must be able to handle failure. In boxing, the beating is on the outside. In stand-up comedy, it is deep within the heart where the comic and only the comic can feel the hurt. It is palpable to say the least.

Some of the comics you did not mind following onstage. Guys like Seinfeld, Reiser, Larry Miller, or Carol Leifer, when they handed you the baton, the audience was usually in good shape. When Larry David finished his set, the audience was often upset or bewildered. It was not uncommon for Larry, after just three minutes onstage, to put the microphone back in the stand, put his hands in his green army jacket pockets, and say, "Good night. I've had enough."

Many nights we would sit and watch each other perform. We all knew each other's material almost as well as we knew our own. We were all miners—mining for comedy material and, more importantly, mining for our comedy voice. We were trying to find out who and what we were when we were on stage. Unless you found your true voice, you did not break out of the pack. When someone did find a great new bit, it gave us all hope.

Without my comedian friends to talk with and without their support, it would have been much more difficult. It might have been just another dream that floated out of my mouth and then out the car window. We were all struggling together—a herd of elephants plowing through a dense jungle, knocking down one tree at a time—and at the same time, we were all growing creatively and having the time of our lives. We loved what we were doing, and we loved being with each other. We were blessed.

Around 3:00 a.m., after the clubs locked their doors, for many of us the night was still young. It was either a pizza and poker, fishing for love, or the Green Kitchen for coffee and freshly baked blueberry muffins the size of a person's head. Besides us, the diner was filled with cabbies, truckers, hookers, and insomniacs. Here we would discuss what we did onstage that night and try to help fix up whatever "bit" the person was struggling with. Most of the time we were of no help, but we sure had fun trying. If you're the type of person who likes to give comedians great gifts, give them an idea that they can make work on stage. Even if they get Alzheimer's and forget their own family, there's a very good chance that they will still remember that bit.

The amazing thing about stand-up comedy is that everyone begins at the same place. There is no head start. There is no family advantage. Daddy and Mommy cannot get you into this college. In fact, to become a good comedian, coming from less is more. This is one business in which no matter how long you wait, help is not on the way. You are pretty much on your own to figure out funny.

To me, that is a great thing. To not be dependent on anyone was the best gift there was. Night after night going back to wherever it was I was staying to try to figure out this insane puzzle was amazing. If you did grab hold of stand-up and got good at it, it was yours to keep. Nobody could take it from you. Your house and all your possessions could burn to the ground. After the smoke clears, you would still have your comedy chops. I own what I am. I earned every nook and cranny of it. The world offered few better feelings than that.

My funny bone is a gift from God. It is a huge responsibility. It needs to be nurtured every day, not unlike my community and my friends. I am thankful for my comedic gift and my friends and family. If I make the best possible use of these gifts and all that I have been given and if I keep working hard, polishing all these things, I guess that is my gift back to me, my gift to you, and my thank-you to God. Be well.

ACKNOWLEDGMENTS

....

I would like to acknowledge the word "acknowledgments." As a word, "acknowledgments" is longer than any other word in the entire book. With that out of the way, here we go.

To God, thank you. You know what you did.

To my parents, who are such a big part of this book that they are on the cover with me. If I'm lucky, we will meet again one day.

To my wife, Nancy, and kids, Jacob, Eli, Noah, Anna, and Chloe, and my grandson, Ben. Without you all, I'd be very lonesome.

To my terrific literary agent, Murray Weiss, who did a mitzvah by helping an old white Jewish man get his book published.

To Rabbi Joe Schames, who every time I had a question about Judaism or wives was always there to answer it.

To Rabbi Abraham Lieberman for his never-ending support since I typed the first word of this book.

To Bernie Ferrera and Steve Mittleman, who read almost everything in the book before anyone else.

To Bill and Bob for the clarity.

To Jerry Seinfeld, who has been a great friend forever and without hesitation gave me the foreword to this book, and one afternoon gave me a car.

Maz Siam who, without fail, is always there.

To Kylie Lobell for her keen eye and suggestions, most of which I used.

To everyone at Apollo Publishers: Julia Abramoff, who championed the book before ever meeting me; my editor, Adam O'Brien, so helpful, so kind, and so smart; Alex Merrill; Larry Dorfman; my publicist, Frances Gordon; and designer Rain Saukas.

To Judy Gruen, a confidence builder and a terrific writer.

To David Suissa, my friend and the editor of the Los Angeles *Jewish Journal*, who has always been so supportive of my work.

PRAISE FOR
MARK SCHIFF
AND *WHY NOT?*

....

"Mark Schiff is one of the funniest, the brightest, the best stage comics I have ever seen."

—JERRY SEINFELD, comedian, actor, and creator of *Seinfeld,* author
of *Is This Anything?* and *SeinLanguage*

"Starting out in stand-up comedy with Mark Schiff was a blast, and the humor he brought to the stage back then is now between the pages of this book, plus the wisdom you get when you add time."

—BILL MAHER, comedian, actor, and host of *Real Time with Bill Maher*

"Mark's book is funny, philosophical, and gentle.* And it makes sense because so is Mark.
*Not gentile, gentle."

—COLIN QUINN, comedian and actor, *Saturday Night Live* and *Tough Crowd with Colin Quinn*

"Mark Schiff knows how to tell a story and Mark Schiff knows how to write a book. I hope this is also an audiobook because nothing lulls me off to sleep more than Mark Schiff reading hilarious stories."

—KEVIN NEALON, comedian and actor, *Saturday Night Live* and *Weeds*

"We've known for a long time that Mark Schiff is funny. Now we know that he's also thoughtful, empathic, and a great Jew. *Why Not?* is an insightful look at the human condition. Poignant, bravely self-examining, and psychologically acute. Also funny."

—JONATHAN KELLERMAN, *New York Times* best-selling author of the
Alex Delaware series

"Mark Schiff is one of the funniest comedians I know. We came up together in the New York comedy club scene and he is endlessly entertaining and creative. This book will make you laugh, make you cry, and make you glad you bought it."

—CAROL LEIFER, comedian, writer, and producer

"Mark and I started in comedy together at the exact same time, and year after year he's just gotten better and funnier, which irritates me to no end. And as you'll see in this funny and uplifting book, he's a great writer too. I'm just so annoyed. But you will love this book."

—PAUL REISER, comedian, actor, and creator of *Mad About You*

"I've always loved Schiff's comedy and really love who he is as a person, especially his kindness. . . . His wonderful book of essays . . . makes you laugh, think, and cry a little, that's actually something we should all do every day. Reading it made me miss him and appreciate him. I'm calling him right now. Get this book."

—LOUIE ANDERSON, comedian and actor, *Baskets*

"The word 'genius' is overused, so I won't use it here. But Mark Schiff's unique and honest insights on parenthood, childhood, husbandhood, and pet ownerhood are hilarious without being mean-spirited and sentimental without being mawkish."

—JEFF ASTROF, writer, showrunner, and producer, *The New Adventures of Old Christine, Veronica's Closet,* and *Trial & Error*

"Heart, comedy, soul, insight—a treasure chest of wonderful moments await all who open these pages."

—DAVID SACKS, writer and producer, *The Simpsons, 3rd Rock from the Sun,* and *Murphy Brown*

"Is there nothing better than a book that is funny and sensitive? That's what Mark Schiff has created: a book that'll make you laugh and warm your heart."

—STEVE BLUESTEIN, comedian and cofounder of the Groundlings comedy troupe and school

"Mark Schiff is a great comic, a one-of-a-kind singular voice in comedy. Everyone in our generation of the stand-up world can rattle off Mark's best bits. This book perfectly captures and showcases his ghoulish, childish, Jewish, foolish, and hilarious style. The book reads fast and funny. It's just like Mark. Once you've read it and loved it, it'll be very hard to get it out of your house."

  —MIKE BINDER, director and writer, *The Mind of the Married Man, Reign Over Me,* and *The Comedy Store*

"If laughter is the best medicine, then Mark Schiff is a doctor. As a stand-up comedian, Mark has been dispensing laughter for decades. In his new book, *Why Not?*, instead of going to a comedy club, you get to take his wit, wisdom, and lots of laughs home with you. The best part is there is no two-drink minimum."

  —MICHAEL PLATT, producer and writer, *Grace and Frankie* and *Weeds*

"Add 'outstanding author' to Mark Schiff's previous credits of hilarious stand-up and quality notary public!"

  —JON HAYMAN, writer and producer, *Seinfeld, Curb Your Enthusiasm,* and *The Chris Rock Show*

"Mark Schiff writes irresistibly about friendship, family, faith, and the business of being funny, sprinkling his stories with wisdom and killer laugh lines. Oh, and he's also a genius and handsome to boot. There, Mark, I said it."

  —JUDY GRUEN, author of *The Skeptic and the Rabbi*

"Schiff may be known as a stand-up comic, but he's also a stand-up guy who really knows how to tell stories."

  —DAVID SUISSA, editor-in-chief of the *Jewish Journal*

"Mark Schiff's comedy always seemed effortless to me. We met at The Improv in the '80s and his act is always funny, but nobody gets hurt, just like a pro bank robber. That he's from the Bronx makes that fact all the more amazing. The stories in his book *Why Not?* are also very funny, yet show his deep humanity, and they're a joy to read."

  —MARK BRAZILL, writer and producer, *In Living Color, 3rd Rock from the Sun,* and *That '70s Show*

"Mark Schiff's stories of childhood and beyond make us feel as if they are happening to us in real time. The interweaving of wonder, confusion, rebelliousness, angst, strangeness, and humor speak to something deep within all of us. Unpretentious, insightful, and bristling with humanity, Schiff takes us on an unpredictable rollercoaster, tempered with resilience and compassion."

—BOB NICKMAN, writer and producer, *Freaks and Geeks*, *Mad About You,* and *The Drew Carey Show*

"Mark and I spent a lot of time together in our formative years in New York. He was always funny. Always kind. Always Jewish."

—RITA RUDNER, comedian, writer, and TV personality

"I loved reading this book. Schiff gives us a funny and inspiring look at his life. Part memoir, part Judaism guide, and part self-help book. Plus, most importantly, Seinfeld wrote the foreword."

—WAYNE FEDERMAN, comedian and author of *The History of Stand-Up*

"Mark Schiff is one of those legendary comedians we all looked up to, and now that he's grown old and decrepit we can finally look down to him. But he's still hilarious as always. He is a stellar comedian who's consistently at the top of his game, as you can see when he's on stage and in his writing. The best part of reading this book is that you get all of Mark's comedic genius, and you don't have to stare at his stupid face."

—ELON GOLD, comedian and actor, *Stacked* and *Chosen and Taken*

"Mark's humor combines a keen sense of observation with the wisdom he's gained while making his way from one end of life to the other. He's a really good guy. Read this wonderful collection and you'll agree."

—ALAN ZWEIBEL, comedian, original *Saturday Night Live* writer, and author of *The Other Schulman*

Here I am at seven years old. This was my first time on stage and the first of many nonpaying gigs. My routine about being just a few years out of diapers was killer.

Why is this night different than all other nights? This is the night when I was twelve and my parents took me to see Rodney Dangerfield, the night I had the epiphany that I wanted to become a comedian. It was also the night my father gave me a few sips of his scotch and I tried to pick up the old lady behind me.

Every New Year's Day for almost thirty years, Jerry Seinfeld, Michael Hampton-Cain, Larry Miller, Paul Reiser, and I all got together for brunch at the River Café in Brooklyn. This one year Steve Mittleman (bottom right) came along. It wasn't uncommon for one of us to do a spit take from laughing so hard.

Being on *The Tonight Show Starring Johnny Carson* and sitting next to Johnny on the panel as a comedian was the equivalent of climbing Mount Everest. Johnny could not have been nicer to me.

Me, Judd Apatow, and Mike Binder. Both Judd and Mike have gone on to become terrific movie directors. Judd put me in his movie *Funny People*, and Mike put me in his movie *Blankman*.

Here I am in 1991 with Milton Berle, the first inductee into the Just For Laughs International Comedy Hall of Fame, at the Montreal International Comedy Festival. He gave me a Cuban cigar and a pep talk before my show.

In 1991 I went with three other comedians to Kuwait with the USO to entertain the troops. The good feelings from that trip are still with me more than thirty years later.

My wife, Nancy, and I went to see Jackie Mason do his one-man show in Beverly Hills. After the show, we took Jackie out to a diner for something to eat. While waiting for his food he went from table to table, entertaining the customers.

In the studio with Jeff Bennett, June Foray, Candi Milo, and Brad Garrett, where we were recording *2 Stupid Dogs*. I played Little Dog, and Brad played Big Dog.

We bumped into Bob Saget at a play in the Westwood neighborhood of Los Angeles. Bob was truly one of the funniest and nicest guys you could ever meet.

I wrote a play called *The Comic*. Before my play, Larry Miller was in one of Neil Simon's plays and brought Mr. Simon down to see mine. Mr. Simon not only liked the play, he gave me pointers on how to improve it. It was another of the greatest nights of my life.

Jerry Seinfeld and I went up to see Rodney Dangerfield at his apartment on the Upper East Side of Manhattan. Rodney was famous for wearing bathrobes when he wasn't working, and I once saw him crossing Wilshire Boulevard in Beverly Hills midafternoon in his bathrobe. I bet Jerry a dollar Rodney would answer the door in his bathrobe. Jerry said that was impossible. Guess who won a dollar.

My friend Nigel, George Carlin, and me. Comedy Central's "100 Greatest Standups of All Time" has George Carlin as number two, second only to Richard Pryor. Not too shabby, me hanging with a fellow Bronx boy.

Jay Leno, me, Larry Miller, Paul Reiser, Jim Brogan, and Jerry Seinfeld at Larry's wedding. You can't seat five comedians in the same row at a wedding and expect them to be civil.